W9-CJW-522

'Why *Buffy Matters* negotiates big ideas about literature, television, culture, values, and language with verve and commitment - it's the best *Buffy* book so far. When it comes to *Buffy* studies, Wilcox is the Slayer.'

Michael Adams, author of *Slayer Slang*

'If there's anyone who doubts *Buffy* matters, Wilcox's accessible, well-written, and carefully argued book is for them. For the rest of us who know *Buffy* matters, Wilcox provides a generous and richly textured reading of the series sure to provoke discussion and expand our appreciation of its achievement. *Why Buffy Matters* is a first-rate work of criticism.'

James B. South, editor of *Buffy the Vampire Slayer and Philosophy: Fear and Trembling in Sunnydale*

'*Why Buffy Matters* assembles in one volume the astonishingly perceptive critical commentary of the Mother of Buffy Studies. Like the amazing series it delineates, it brings the funny and brings the tears – or am I the only one deeply moved by interpretive brilliance? This book confirms Rhonda Wilcox as the chosen one among television scholars, the one with the intellectual strength and hermeneutic skill to do battle with one of the most complex popular culture texts of our time.'

David Lavery, Co-editor of *Slayage: The Online International Journal of Buffy Studies*

'Rhonda Wilcox's *Why Buffy Matters* explains how *Buffy the Vampire Slayer* changed television forever. As I pored through this brilliant book, I finally understood why I burst into tears during the series premiere. *Why Buffy Matters* elicited an identical reaction: it was so good I cried. This book is something I can hand to people who can't fathom my devotion to "just a TV show" – and to others who have always realized that *Buffy* is a work of art. If that's not artful in itself, I don't know what is. Congratulations, Rhonda Wilcox – and thank you. You are totally effulgent.'

Nancy Holder, Co-author, *Buffy the Vampire Slayer: The Watcher's Guide*, Vols. 1 and 2

For Richard, who read everything first

Why Buffy Matters

The Art of
Buffy the Vampire Slayer

Rhonda Wilcox

I.B. TAURIS

LONDON · NEW YORK

Reprinted in 2010 by I.B.Tauris & Co Ltd
6 Salem Road, London W2 4BU
175 Fifth Avenue, New York NY 10010
www.ibtauris.com

In the United States of America and in Canada distributed by
Palgrave Macmillan, a division of St Martin's Press
175 Fifth Avenue, New York NY 10010

First published by I.B.Tauris & Co Ltd in 2005, Reprinted 2006, 2010
Copyright © Rhonda Wilcox, 2005

The right of Rhonda Wilcox to be identified as the author of this work has been
asserted by the author in accordance with the Copyright, Designs and Patents Act
1988.

All rights reserved. Except for brief quotations in a review, this book, or any part
thereof, may not be reproduced, stored in or introduced into a retrieval system, or
transmitted, in any form or by any means, electronic, mechanical, photocopying,
recording or otherwise, without the prior written permission of the publisher.

ISBN 978 1 84511 029 1

A full CIP record for this book is available from the British Library
A full CIP record for this book is available from the Library of Congress

Library of Congress catalog card: available

Typeset in Quadraat by Steve Tribe, Andover

Contents

Acknowledgments

It will not be possible for me to name everyone who has helped me make this book a reality—there have been so many kind people along the way. It really is true that among Buffy scholar fans and fan scholars, there is a Scooby philosophy of dealing with the world. But I want to mention at least some of the people who have helped.

I could never say enough about David Lavery. Everyone who knows him knows his generosity and energy and critical acuity. He has also always talked me up to everyone—including me, when necessary. Thanks always, David.

Thanks to Philippa Brewster and Tatiana Adamopoulos of I.B.Tauris for really paying attention and caring about this project. And thanks to Mary Alice Money for doing the substitute lecturing that got Philippa interested in my work in the first place (and to David for, of course, talking me up to Philippa). Thanks, too, to Steve Tribe for his thoughtful copy editing.

Thanks to David, Mary Alice, Michael Adams, Nancy Holder, Sue Turnbull, Tanya Krzywinska, Jana Riess, and James South for agreeing to read the book before publication. I am blessed to have such readers (though of course the remaining problems in the text are mine).

I am grateful to the unfailing friendship (professional and personal) of Gordon College's former English Department Chair Gloria Henderson and for the support of the new administration at Gordon College, including President Larry Weill, Dean of the Faculty Robert Vaughan, and Humanities Chair Richard Baskin. I appreciate the many Gordon faculty members who have encouraged me over the years.

Thanks to the extraordinary people who make up the editorial board of *Slayage: The Online International Journal of Buffy Studies*, for, as James South has noted in Nikki Stafford's *Once Bitten*, keeping the level of Buffy Studies scholarship high and for giving a home to some of my work (and thanks, by the way, to Nikki for helping to explain *Buffy* academics). These people are true scholars: Editor David Lavery and board members Stacey Abbott, Michael Adams, Gerry Bloustien, Lynne Edwards, Greg Erickson, Roz Kaveney, Don Keller, Tanya Krzywinska, Beth Rambo, Jana Riess, James South, and Sue Turnbull.

Thanks to Carol O'Sullivan, Claire Thomson, Catherine Fuller, and Scott Mackenzie for the wonderful honor of being the opening keynote speaker for the first academic conference on *Buffy*, at the University of East Anglia. It was an experience I will never forget. Thanks to Roz Kaveney for befriending me and Mary Alice in London. Thanks to Dawn Heinecken (and Tom Byers and Dennis and Susan Hall) and Lynne Edwards for involving me (and thus more *Buffy*) in the intellectual life of University of Louisville and Ursinus College, as well. Thanks to Gerry Bloustien and all the folks at the University of South Australia for making what seemed impossible happen—for bringing me to Australia to speak on *Buffy*. Thanks to Angela Ndalianis and the crew at the University of Melbourne for giving me further Australian opportunities. And thanks to all the wonderful people in that wonderful country for making us feel so welcome, but particularly to Katy Stevens, Sue Turnbull, and Trisha Pender. Thanks to Janet McCabe and Kim Akass for inviting me to Trinity College, and for setting up the long-distance question and answer session between Dublin and Decatur, Georgia, when I got sidetracked by my close encounter with the eighteen-wheeler truck. And I am grateful to John Lowther, Robert Cheatham, and all the folks at Eyedrum for inviting me to lecture there more than once.

Thanks to the long encouragement of all the folks of the Popular Culture Association in the South and of the Buffyology list—and especially to Jen Godwin for starting the list and Derik Badman for continuing it. Thanks even more to Derik for that most invaluable of Buffyology tools, the Academic Buffy Bibliography. And thanks to every single person who attended the Slayage Conference of 2004. What a joy you all were. Now if only next time I can hear more of the papers.

Thanks to the even longer encouragement of all my wonderful family and friends. My mother and father—June Lee Tugman Wilcox and Zeb Marshall Wilcox—and my sister and brother—Marsha Lee Wilcox and Patrick Wilcox—and all the rest of the family have always cheered me on. Thanks also to my son Jefferson Gess, whose occasional insights have more than once found their way into my work. And thanks to my inexpressibly wonderful husband Richard Gess, with whom I have laughed and cried at *Buffy*, and on whose talents as a writer and reader I have always relied. There are many reasons this book is dedicated to him. For all my family and friends in the end, their patience was one of their greatest gifts.

Above all, I want to thank Joss Whedon and all the creative company of the series for making *Buffy the Vampire Slayer* part of this, our magic world.

Introduction

This Our Magic World

It's wonderful to get lost in a story, isn't it?

> Andrew, "Storyteller" (7.16)

I know this bloke—well, not so much a bloke ... as demon—but still, bookish—all tuned into the nastier corners of this our magic world.

> Spike, "The Weight of the World" (5.12)

The evil is this way?

> Giles, "The Freshman" (4.1)

It's always real.

> Buffy, "Lessons" (7.1)

Every time I start one of these essays, I feel like I'm leaping off a cliff into deep water. Those who know *Buffy* understand what the deep water is—the depths of the text of the series itself. Like any great story, *Buffy* is something you can get lost in; like any great story, it is both magic and ultimately real. One power who is tuned into both the nastier corners and the laughter of this our magic world is Joss Whedon, the creator of *Buffy the Vampire Slayer*; but he does not work alone. That fact—television as creation by committee—is one of the reasons some people doubt that television can be art. I want to try to talk about those reasons, those doubts, because in the coming chapters I want to show that *Buffy* is art, and art of the highest order.

Who hasn't sucked a book from time to time, huh?

Nicholas Brendon

During a panel discussion at the Academy of Television Arts and Sciences, Nicholas Brendon, Buffy's Xander, referred to the scene in which Alyson Hannigan's Willow became Dark Willow by visibly pulling the words of dark magic books into her body: she is covered in words, she becomes a witch of words—a ripe image in a series so rich in language. But witches, ghosts, spells—what kind of stuff is that for a story? Still, for some reason people keep studying Shakespeare—*Macbeth, Hamlet, A Midsummer Night's Dream*. Spontaneous combustion, mysterious doppelgangers, long-lost relatives—how believable are they? Yet people keep reading Dickens— *Bleak House, A Tale of Two Cities, Nicholas Nickleby*. Buffy suffers from prejudice related both to its medium, television, and its genre, fantasy. There are many fine defenses of fantasy, one of my favorites being Ursula K. Le Guin's "Why Are Americans Afraid of Dragons?" (and she notes it's not just Americans).[1] She reminds us that "Fantasy is true, of course. It isn't factual, but it's true" (40)—and that certainly can be said of Buffy. And as for the medium—as a teacher of literature, I see Buffy as part of a long cultural stream. Whedon and Co. are quite conscious of their use of sources from television, film, and literature: they have sucked a few books. Though I recognize and wish to speak of the special nature of television, I see far more similarities than differences between Buffy and earlier fictions.

The similarities include their early reception. A fictional form which is popular is often not respected for quite some time. Ben Jonson had to battle for serious consideration of Elizabethan drama—not only his own, but that of his contemporary the actor/author Shakespeare. Non-dramatic poetry was considered the higher art form in that period. Similarly, when Dickens published his novels in serialized "shilling numbers," they were widely enjoyed but condescended to. The historian Thomas Carlyle, Dickens's friend, considered most novels worthless but magnanimously told an acquaintance that Dickens was worth a penny. Yet now we consider the nineteenth century the great age of the novel. And consider how very many bad Elizabethan plays were not passed down to us; and there must have been even more bad Victorian novels. The form of art most suited to an age will produce both its best work and its most work—so, by statistical likelihood, many bad works will be produced in that form. This is as true for nineteenth-century novels as for prime-time television. And even great work is not always immediately appreciated. There is a series of books called *The Critical Heritage* (e.g. *Dickens: The Critical Heritage*). These volumes collect contemporary critical responses to significant authors. The pundits who automatically dismiss works of television would probably have been among those who dismissed Dickens in his time ("He has risen like a rocket, and will come down like the stick") or, a bit earlier, Wordsworth ("This will never do").[2] Percy Shelley wrote the anonymous preface to his wife Mary Shelley's anonymously published 1818 *Frankenstein*, trying to argue that the book would not have the same ill effects as most novel-reading (Shelley 5): parents in that day and age wanted to keep their children away from novel-reading the way parents today want to keep their children from too much time with the television.

It seems that the more one knows about the history of literature, the less reason one would have for excluding television from serious consideration. It is another form of drama—authors write teleplays, after all—and a direct descendant from Elizabethan theater. (Whedon held readings of Shakespeare on weekends for *Buffy* cast members and writers in his home.) It also shares qualities of the serialized novel: novels would often come out over the course of a year and a half in weekly or monthly installments. Of course the academy moves slowly: in the nineteenth century, Harvard University did not allow American literature to be taught in its hallowed halls, so it should not perhaps surprise us that television has not been embraced more quickly in more places.

It is also true that—logically or not—there is a tacit hierarchy amongst fictional art forms. In the past few decades, film studies departments have made great advances in universities, but most professors would acknowledge that film is considered by many to be a less prestigious study than traditional drama and novels. Television would be considered lower still. There are very, very few departments of television studies such as one finds at Syracuse University. Television studies have usually been made part of communications departments and have generally been given a sociological rather than an aesthetic slant. In 1989 I published an indignant little essay complaining of this state of affairs ("TV and the Curriculum");[3] more recently, Sue Turnbull published a marvelously thorough exploration of the problem as it relates to *Buffy* in particular ("'Not Just Another *Buffy* Paper': Towards an Aesthetics of Television").

In fact, despite its lower status, there is a great deal more scholarship written about television than most normal people realize. Normal or not, I know: I wrote the chapter on television for the *Greenwood Guide to American Popular Culture* (a short history of television followed by a bibliographical essay). I am not going to go into a survey here; please, if you're interested, go look at the chapter (which is already out of date in the flood of new work). Or look at Horace Newcomb's *Encyclopedia of Television*; or David Biancull's *Teleliteracy*; or any of David Lavery's collections of essays on excellent television shows—*Twin Peaks, The X-Files, The Sopranos,* or, of course, the one we edited on *Buffy*. Slowly, more and more of this work does discuss TV from an aesthetic point of view, though not a great deal of it expresses admiration. And in this regard, of course, the study of television is very different from the study of literature. Who would think twice about a *Hamlet* scholar pointing out the felicities of that work? And yet, in 1765, the great scholar Samuel Johnson complained of *Hamlet* that "the catastrophe is not very happily produced; the exchange of weapons is rather an expedient of necessity than a stroke of art"—eighteenth-century nit-picking (148). Not that there's anything wrong with Dr. Johnson's expressing a negative opinion about Shakespeare; it's just that we would do well to remind ourselves that literary opinion is a flexible thing. The canon is not carved in stone. Still, while *Hamlet* scholars may praise away, as far as *Buffy* scholars—well, many people seem to think we had better come to bury, not to praise her. Of course, if you bury Buffy, she's likely to climb right back out of the ground.

Truth in advertising here: this book praises *Buffy*. At length. That is its purpose. And one of the things I want to say in this introduction is that I know I am very fortunate to be allowed to do so. There are already quite a number of works of solid *Buffy* scholarship out: take a look at the bibliography at the end of this book; or better yet, take a look at Derik Badman's *Academic Buffy Bibliography*. (My bibliography is guided by the Modern Language Association criterion of listing only what is cited in this book; his includes much more.) And, of course, there is *Slayage*, the online journal I coedit with David Lavery, a refereed quarterly in its fifth year, having produced seventeen issues to date. There are also many, many people writing interesting commentary on websites and in online discussion groups; I cite some of them here, though I certainly have not read them all. I am lucky indeed to be allowed to put my work in a book and send it out into the world. I know of several collections still looking for publishers; some publishing companies fear that interest will die now that the series has ended. I think that highly unlikely. People are still talking about Shakespeare and Dickens, and about two of my other favorites, Molière and Baudelaire, which—I recently realized—find familial connections in *Buffy*, too—odd though it may seem to think of the two combined. Yes,

Molière + Baudelaire = Buffy. The 2004 Slayage Conference on Memorial Day Weekend in Nashville, Tennessee, was the largest scholarly conference (as opposed to convention) on a single television show ever held. It was convened a year after the series ended. Over 180 papers were presented; there were 395 registered attendees (and a few extra students). There were scholars from television and film studies, literature, history, religion, philosophy, sociology, classics, women's studies, communications, even math, among other disciplines. The papers were cogent; the discussions were lively. People from several different countries, several different continents, attended (see David Lavery's chart on *Slayage: The Online International Journal of Buffy Studies*). Those who were able to attend (in terms of finances and scheduling) represented a much larger number who wished they could come. And here's a thought: not to mention millions of other intelligent viewers, perhaps the fact that thousands of academics have a passion for the show could be considered evidence of its worth.

Our crew sang, too.

Alyson Hannigan

So what are all of us excited about? Why do we care? Well, I hope the rest of this book will help to explain. But first I want to say a few things that are not explicitly addressed later in the book. In the first paragraph of this introduction I mentioned that Joss Whedon does not work alone. Part of the occasional snobbery of aesthetic evaluation has to do with the idea of the control of the creator, the single mind unifying the work of art. Films are of course made by increasing numbers of people (have you stayed in the theater to watch the credits roll lately?),[4] and film scholars have dealt with this issue by proposing the *auteur* theory—the idea that one person, generally the director in film, is in artistic control. (Of course this may or may not be ultimately the case, depending on the film.) More recently, critics have made the same argument for a number of television producers (*The Producer's Medium*, as Robert Alley and Horace Newcomb called it), such as Steven Bochco or David Kelley.

I would like to propose a slight variation to this way of viewing the work—a model which I suspect most serious *Buffy* admirers will find fairly easy to accept. For years now, when I have thought of the art of a television series, I have thought of the master builder of a cathedral and his workers: a cathedral is a creation which is certainly accepted as art, but which was worked on by many differing people over many years (far more than the seven seasons of Buffy). Buffy itself—reading about it, listening to DVD commentaries by those associated with the show—has taught me to envision the interaction in a much livelier and less one-way top-down fashion. It seems to me that among the many skills necessary for an artist of television, this very special medium, is the ability to work dynamically with a cast and crew of high quality. How else can fine work be done so fast and for so long? Part of Joss Whedon's genius is his ability to bring out the best in those he works with. I would posit this as a necessity for a great television artist. It struck me only recently that one of the great themes of the show—the importance of community, trust, friendship—is found not only in the episodes but also in their creation. The cast and crew of Buffy were extraordinary, and Joss Whedon set the tone for their collaboration. Nancy Holder, in her speech at the Slayage Conference, said that while she and Chris Golden were working on the Watcher's Guides and visiting the Buffy set, every single crew member they talked to spoke of how fortunate he or she felt to be involved in the work on Buffy. Joss Whedon in effect created a school of writers (cf. a school of painters) who grew more and more sharply skillful with Whedon's support—people like Marti Noxon, who helmed the show in its last two years; Jane Espenson, who also wrote for Gilmore Girls; David Fury, who now writes for Lost, and Steven DeKnight, Tracey Forbes, Doug Petrie, Rebecca Rand Kirshner, and more. This is assuredly not the case in every company of television writers.

Not just writers, but the cast and the rest of the crew were highly talented professionals involved in active collaboration. There were two highly skilled long-term Directors of Photography, Michael Gershman and Raymond Stella. There were thoughtful directors like David Solomon. There was the "heavily textured" (quoting actor James Marsters) production design of the versatile and money-saving Carey Meyer, who could turn one set into fifteen (and created hundreds over the years), but who also would go so far, for example, as to photocopy the tiles from UCLA buildings in order to give UC-Sunnydale the right look. Then there were Emmy-winning make-up artists Todd McIntosh and John Vulich, about whose work guest star John Ritter said "this is as blue ribbon as you can get in film-making." There is the astonishing symphonic scoring of the Emmy-winning Christophe Beck (now working in movies), the composer of the Buffy-Angel theme, the Buffy-Riley theme, the score for "Hush," for "The Zeppo," for "Restless" (see the extras on the CD for "Once More, with Feeling"). "Every episode we treat as a movie," he once said. And there is the thematically significant work of costume designer Cynthia Bergstrom, who worked in symbiosis with actor Sarah Michelle Gellar. And of course I have not even mentioned the cast: that none of these gifted people was ever nominated for an Emmy for work on Buffy seems to me only explicable in terms of prejudice against genre television. They managed to straddle genres with ease, moving from tears to laughter to song and dance.

Again, however, it is not just the talent of each individual that matters here, but the synergy invoked by the central figure—Joss Whedon. And one can imagine it growing—the more good people were working well, the more good people would want to join in. The Academy of Television Arts and Sciences Panel Discussion with Joss Whedon, Marti Noxon, Ray Stella, Carey Meyer, Nicholas Brendon, Alyson Hannigan, James Marsters (Spike), and Michelle Trachtenberg (Dawn), makes clear that the energy flowed more than one way. "The energy that's on a set, a lot of it comes from the DP," Whedon stated, for example. Discussing the musical episode "Once More, with Feeling," he gave a specific illustration of the collaboration. Michelle Trachtenberg noted, "Our writers are really listening to us"; they considered the actors' specific strengths. And Joss Whedon added, "I wrote not just to their talents but to the sets. I wrote Nicky [Brendon] and Emma's [Caulfield's] song as a kind of thirties pastiche because of the look of that set, being so deco—and sort of also the way her costumes had been the year before." Similarly, Bergstrom notes that she costumed Robia LaMorte's Jenny Calendar as she did because she knew that Jenny was to be a gypsy (Golden and Holder 275). And this creative feeling runs, as Holder noted, throughout the entire crew (even though they called the show "Buffy the Weekend Killer" because of the extra work involved). In the panel discussion Joss Whedon said, "You can tell when the dolly grip ["Wayne," James Marsters added] is excited about a camera move because it's part of the story—he's not punching a clock, he's telling a story." When they were working on "Once More, with Feeling," Alyson Hannigan said, "Our crew sang, too." And Whedon stated, "I have people with whom I trust my artistic life." Clearly, these were the Scoobies of television production. The success of communal effort so important as a theme in the stories was just as important in the real life of the series' creation behind the scenes.

I cannot give my readers the benefit of access behind the scenes for the series. This book is just the reaction of a woman sitting in front of a television screen (though I've had the help of many kind folk sitting on the same side of the screen as I do; there are Scooby critics, too). Nonetheless, I have commented at certain places in the book on the work of the cast and crew as I have observed it or have been able to learn of it from secondary sources.

I hope someday someone will be able to explore their contributions more specifically. For here, at least, and with the recognition of Joss Whedon as the creator and catalyst and air traffic controller, I do want to acknowledge the nature of their collaboration as a cause of the art that is *Buffy*.

> Don't get linear on me now, man.
>
> Xander, "Restless" (4.22)

There are, of course, other elements specific to the nature of television art. Both film and television combine the complexity of sound and specifically charted sight, and I discuss these in the pages to come. Television is also temporally unique as an art. Charles Dickens (on whom I wrote my doctoral dissertation, and whom Joss Whedon names as a favorite writer—and who does indeed get mentioned a few times in the chapters of this book) was seen as having an extraordinarily close relationship with his audience; he gave public readings and wrote directly to his readers in magazines he edited; and, as noted, he published novels in weekly serial installments. *Great Expectations*, like *Buffy*, came out once a week. But even his characters did not have as long a relationship with their audience as a long-running series such as *Buffy*—and more significantly, a long-running series with a rare respect for the integrity of the characters. The characters have continuity, but are not static: as Michelle Trachtenberg said in the ATAS panel, "The whole life thing? Characters need to progress." If *Great Expectations* is a Bildungsroman (a novel of growth), so is *Buffy*. And as Marti Noxon explained, "The emotional reality of the show is what we strive for every week"; emotional realism has been Whedon's watchword from the start. I see films as comparable to short stories and television as comparable to novels: both are art. But novels and television provide more opportunity for the growth of character.

The use of time is more similar for the serial novelist and the television creator than most people realize, too. (I hope someday to write about the specific similarities of Whedon and Dickens, not just in terms of creative process, but also in terms of language (see Chapter 8), narrative, social themes, symbolism, and fantasy elements.) Dickens wrote with a long arc in mind, but sometimes followed where characters led; Sam Weller bounded into *The Pickwick Papers* in much the same lively fashion (and at about the same narrative point) as Spike bounded into *Buffy*. Dickens set up foreshadowing which he then sometimes reworked; for instance, early in *Great Expectations* Pip envisions Miss Havisham hanged, but by the end of the story Dickens had decided to burn her. At least she got to live long enough for redemption, when apparently she had been slated for an ignominious death; so, too, Spike. Whedon notes (in the "Surprise" DVD interview), "We try and leave things open for characters … We tend not to tell everything about a character till we need to because it leaves openings like this," this being the connection of Jenny Calendar to the gypsy clan which had cursed Angel. (Dickens left things open, too—thus we will never know the resolution to The Mystery of Edwin Drood, since he died without having written it out.) Part of what is necessary for television art is the ability to balance the long narrative plan with the ability to respond to sudden opportunities or stresses, whether they be internal (e.g. wanting more of Emma Caulfield's Anya) or external (the fact that Seth Green, Oz, was moving on to movies). Dickens had to react, too; he made changes sometimes based on the complaints of readers; and, in fact, his career expanded when the graphic artist with whom he was to have created The Pickwick Papers died, and Dickens then made the words more central to the project than the pictures. So the ability to flex with the changes is as important to the serial artist as the long view.

In the commentary for the pilot, "Welcome to the Hellmouth," Joss Whedon mockingly notes, "By the way I did notice in that last scene that Cordelia says that she's always wanted to live in LA, and the fact is she did move to LA four seasons later for the spinoff, so as you can see this is all one big, brilliant master plan and nothing happens by chance." Fans talk of retcon—retroactive continuity (see Kaveney 2004, 82)—giving information that explains an earlier event, especially seeming plot contradictions or lacunae. With some elements, as Jane Espenson says, "The only way to make it happen is after the fact" ("Writing," 107); the text is indeed unified afterward, not by plan. But with other elements it is not so clear: Espenson adds, "In Doppelgängland, [Willow] notices that her vampire self is 'kind of gay.' When we started plotting the Tara arc in Season Four, Joss said, 'Were we planning this back then?' And even he didn't know for sure" ("Writing," 107). Then there are elements of foreshadowing which are clearly intentional before the fact. In the ATAS panel discussion, in speaking of the painful death of Tara by very non-magical gunshot wound, Whedon stated that in both the fourth and fifteenth episodes of the sixth season (and he knew the numbers of the episodes) there were references to the danger of guns, foreshadowing Tara's demise. (In the last episode of the fifth season when Buffy calls Willow her "big gun," Willow replies, "No—I was never a gun.") Whether or not the elements are planned beforehand or tuned afterwards, they are made to work under the guiding touch of "perfectionist" Whedon. Both in terms of the long narrative arc and the subtle details of interconnection, no one has ever taken fuller advantage of the medium of television than third-generation television writer Joss Whedon and his creative company.

> Dawn: Maybe that's your power—seeing, knowing.
> Xander: Maybe it is. Maybe I should get a cape.
>
> "Potential" (7.12)

No fans are more thoughtful than Buffy fans. Traditionally, film scholars evaluate the television-watching experience as being of a lesser order. They typically assume interruption and distractions of various sorts. This is not the viewing experience of the serious Buffy fan (or the serious X-Files fan, or the serious Twin Peaks fan, etc.). Many Buffy viewers—or readers, as I like to call them (see Chapter 2 on Fiske and Hartley)—took their telephones off the hook during first-run episodes. Some watched with a group of like-minded friends. As for me, I watched with my husband and son (until the sixth season, at which point my teenage son moved to a television in a different room). People also, of course, are now building VHS and DVD libraries. And people who did not see Buffy when it was first broadcast are getting caught up in it through the DVDs (this happened recently to an administrator at my college). We can—and do—re-view as we can re-read. Whedon and Co. are artists of the age of the television library.

And I, frankly, want to be sure they are part of the canon. The original title of this book was The Art of Buffy the Vampire Slayer: The Canonization of Television. Some modern critics are uncomfortable with the idea of a canon because of its hierarchical and class implications. John Fiske, in Television Culture, rejoices in television's "'semiotic democracy,' its opening up of its discursive practice to the viewer" (239). But I have the feeling that there will be a canon whether we like it or not. Even more so than with books, the continuity of television depends on a large machinery of commerce to sustain it: i.e., I need someone to keep making the DVDs (not to mention the DVD players). Do you remember the movement, for music, from LPs and tapes to CDs? Do you remember waiting for certain artists to come out on CD? I want Buffy always to be reproduced in whatever is the technology of the time, so that people in the future can experience it as well. No lost quartos for us (well, other than that first pilot). I think the series will probably last in any case, and there are already other works of criticism to support it; but if I can do anything to help, I will.

And as for the semiotic democracy—well, for those shows which are reproduced, the democracy will still exist. I have called myself one woman in front of a television screen. In this book I have the great good fortune to tell you what I see there. But I would certainly never imply that it is the only thing to be seen. Part of my great good fortune has been that, as I have written more and more about Buffy over the years, more and more people have told me their thoughts. It is, after all, a show that provokes thought. There is a second Slayage Conference planned for 2006, and it will be a wonderful opportunity for further conversation, in the best sense of the word.

> To read makes our speaking English good.
>
> Xander, "I Robot, You Jane" (1.8)

Every one of the chapters in this book was written for an audience intent on the pleasures of understanding Buffy. I hope the form of the chapters has been clarified because of the fact that they were originally meant to be read aloud. The lectures were delivered in five different countries (the USA, Canada, England, Australia, and Ireland) over a lucky seven years (1998–2004). The structure of my book grew, in a sense, like the series—a combination of long overview and following what pulled me. And perhaps this is as good a place as any to note that I am no more a purist about critical theory than Buffy is purist about genre. I first started writing about broad patterns that I saw in the series: the story of the hero's journey, the ubiquity and gradually accrued meaning of the naming symbolism. It seems to me that television, as I have described it above, has special potential for long-term development of such patterns, and I certainly wanted to discuss them. But it also seems to me that any work worthy of the term art must invite close scrutiny; a reader will want to be able to dwell in the details. I am not going to try to define art (have you got a definition in your pocket?). But I will venture this: to be most likely to endure as art, a television series should both take advantage of its possibilities for long-term construction and produce individually powerful episodes. Hence the two sections of this book: Panorama and Tight Focus, six chapters on broad patterns and six on individual episodes. The Tight Focus section demonstrates the variety in Buffy as well; the chapters are on Love and Loss; Laughter; Fear; Poetry; Death; and Song.

I must say that while it was easy to choose four of the six episodes, it became extremely difficult to pick the final two. I knew that I would write on "Restless," "Hush," "The Body," and "Once More, with Feeling," in part because of their emotional and thematic significance, but also because of their formal experimentation, particularly unusual within the confines of weekly broadcast television. "Restless" is made completely of dreams; much of "Hush" is silent; "The Body," the episode of Buffy's mother's death, has no non-diegetic sound; and "Once More, with Feeling" is a musical. But I struggled over whether or not to write about "Becoming," parts one and two, or the two-parter "Surprise"/"Innocence"—until I learned that Joss Whedon's favorite episode was "Innocence"; then I had my answer. Most difficult of all was the decision of what to write on for Laughter, because the choices were so numerous. My first thought was to write about "Pangs"—but then I realized that three of my six episodes would be from Season Four, a season I had never thought of as my favorite. (Whedon says on the DVD Fourth Season Overview that while the season does not have the strongest narrative arc, it includes many of the series' best episodes.) Though I did not choose to pick an episode from each season, I did want to have a fair chronological spread, so I wanted a third-season episode. I also already had "The Zeppo" nibbling around the back of my mind. But how could I write about comedy and not include an Espensode, an episode by Jane Espenson? She joined the series in the third season, and I seriously thought about using "Band Candy." In addition, I gave long consideration to making all the episodes Whedon-written (except for Marti Noxon's section of "Surprise"/"Innocence"), and I considered "Doppelgängland" for quite a long time, the more so because it was on Whedon's list of top ten favorites. But in the end, I wrote about "The Zeppo" because it insisted that I do so.

I only wish I could have written about Dan Vebber's other stunningly good episode, "Lovers Walk" (the script apparently does not carry an apostrophe, by the way—making for a short, sad, declarative sentence for a title). In fact, the only way I could come to terms with my choices was to console myself with the thought that I might be able to write about other episodes later. And, in my own small way, I have had external pressures affecting some of my decisions, too. It's probably just as well: once you start writing about individual episodes, it is very hard to stop. (Like wanting one more potato chip—or maybe a Cheeto. With an expiration date that's a long time from now.) And the complex fecundity of text driving this response is, I think, one sign of lasting art. With an expiration date that's a long time from now.

If you are open-minded enough to have taken up this book, I hope you will read the succeeding chapters and find it easier to believe that television can be art—and that you will then begin (if you have not already done so) to watch *Buffy*. (I hope you'll read some more Dickens, too.) The first chapter was written with a broad audience in mind, and it will make the easiest entry point for those less familiar with the series. I do not include episode summaries, which can be found in many other volumes. Roz Kaveney and Jana Riess provide excellent season-by-season summaries, and Kaveney's and the three *Watcher's Guides*, by Nancy Holder, Chris Golden, and Paul Ruditis, are among those with individual episode summaries. Those who know the series well can pick and choose the chapter order—and, assuming that some readers will do so, I have reiterated certain points for the sake of clarity. Even for those familiar with the series, it will work best to read Chapters 2–6 in order; the discussion of light imagery which begins in Chapter 2 concludes in Chapter 6, for example.

My own text is limited. There is much, much more to say about *Buffy*, in many ways. My commentary is, by choice, not entirely discursive. I will also note that, while this introduction is in some ways a defense, the rest of the book is a celebration. One of the ways I have chosen to show that *Buffy* is art is to write with the assumption that it is art. That is, in fact, the way in which we usually treat great literature—and *Buffy* can easily bear such treatment. Sue Turnbull reminds us of the Greek term *ekphrasis*: as she notes, Lesley Stern and George Kouvaris translated it in 1999 "as a desire to transform the lived experience of a work of art into a description couched in words" (n. 13).[5] Every one of these chapters is intended to share some part of the lived experience of *Buffy*.

Why does *Buffy* matter? It matters because it shows that television *can* be art, and deserves to be so studied. It is a work of literature, of language (you'll find me quoting a lot); it is a work of visual art (I will try to convey some of the composition, the framing, and the color); it is a work of music and sound (I'll try sometimes to describe the pitch of an actor's voice). It is a work of television. The depth of the characters, the truth of the stories, the profundity of the themes, and their precise incarnation in language, sound, and image—all of these matter. Last and first of all, *Buffy* matters for the same reason that all art matters—because it shows us the best of what it means to be human. The characters do so within the show, and the makers do so with the show. Joss Whedon and his creative company are artists, and *Buffy* is art.

Let me tell you why.

Part I

Panorama

Chapter 1

There Will Never Be A "Very Special" Buffy

Symbol and Language[1]

Buffy: I told one lie. I had one drink.

Giles: Yes, and you were very nearly devoured by a giant demon snake. The words "let that be a lesson" seem a tad redundant.

     "Reptile Boy" (2.5)

I have often said, "There will never be a 'Very Special Episode' of *Buffy*."

     Joss Whedon[2]

From the start, it was different. In the comment above—made in 1997, the year the show began—Joss Whedon, the creator of Buffy the Vampire Slayer, repudiates those television series which aim for redeeming social value by focusing episodes on unmediated presentations of social topics such as AIDS or alcoholism: sending Hallmark cards of virtue. Whedon specifically mentions *Beverly Hills 90210*, but one could add the names of many series—*The Wonder Years, Party of Five, Seventh Heaven*—to the list of those which over the years have advertised those "very special" episodes. Whedon expected more mental action from his audience. The opening seasons set the template. In *Buffy*'s world, the problems teenagers face become literal monsters. Internet predators are demons; drink-doctoring frat boys have sold their souls for success in the business world; a girl who has sex with even the nicest-seeming male discovers that he afterwards becomes a monster. From the earliest episodes, it was apparent to attentive viewers that *Buffy* operated on a symbolic level. Furthermore, some of the symbols began to extend. For example, underlying the various threats is a repeated one: the horror of becoming a vampire often correlates with the dread of becoming an adult. Yet even in the face of all these monstrosities, the context of dialogue and interaction makes the characters believable.

In fact, *Buffy*'s dialogue establishes a second level of significance directly related to the symbolic social monsters. Language is always a matter of delight in *Buffy*; and the larger language patterns are themselves symbolic. The striking differentiation of the teen language in *Buffy* has often been commented on. The language of the teens starkly contrasts with that of the adults. This linguistic separateness emphasizes the lack of communication between the generations, as does the series' use of the symbolism of monsters to represent social problems. The teen attitude towards parents' inability to deal with real-world horrors is suggested through Buffy's concerned but naive mother, who throughout two seasons never truly sees the monsters or knows her daughter is the Slayer. The symbolism recreates the need to bridge generational division which is suggested by the language patterns. Viewers must understand both the language and the symbolism to see the reality of teen life. Life and language are not so simple as problem-of-the-week TV would suggest, and *Buffy* acknowledges that fact.

The situation and relationships in *Buffy* are on the surface mundane. As the series starts, sixteen-year-old Buffy Summers, a high school sophomore, has moved from LA to the small California town of Sunnydale with her divorced mother, after having been expelled from her earlier high school. Her looks and conversation at first win her an entrée with high school social queen Cordelia Chase. However, she refuses Cordelia's advice to avoid Willow Rosenberg and Xander Harris, who are stigmatized as, respectively, a brain and a geek. Buffy's refusal to scorn the two—in itself a bit of heroism in the teen social world—combined with the discovery of her past expulsion leads to her being consigned to "loser" status.

The other side of Buffy's life, however, roots her even more firmly in loser territory. As soon as she enters the school library, librarian Rupert Giles informs her that he knows she is the Slayer: Into every generation a single girl is born—the one chosen to fight the vampires, the demons, the powers of darkness. Giles has moved from a job as curator of a British museum ("or the British Museum") to be Sunnydale High's librarian expressly in order to be Buffy's Watcher—her adult advisor and trainer. While Buffy has exercised social heroism, she has absolutely no desire to be a superhero. "A Watcher," says Giles, "prepares [the Slayer] ..." "Prepares me for what?" asks Buffy. "For getting kicked out of school? For losing all my friends? For having to spend all my time fighting for my life and never getting to tell anyone because I might endanger them? Go ahead—prepare me" ("Welcome to the Hellmouth," 1.1). Buffy Summers' life is considerably more difficult than Clark Kent's.

Her romantic life is even more problematic. Charming but hapless Xander falls for Buffy literally from the moment he crashes his skateboard at first sight of her outside school. Since Willow has been romantically fixed on Xander since their childhood, this is an inconvenience only made worse by the fact that Buffy's affections lie elsewhere. Angel, a dark, handsome, mysterious stranger occasionally appears to warn Buffy of threats from the vampire world. He cites his being older as the reason he is resisting a relationship, but when, inevitably, they kiss, he "sprouts fangs" (McDonald 20). In the Buffy variation on vampire lore,[3] vampires have the memories and personalities of humans, but the human soul has been replaced by a demon. The single exception—the single trustworthy vampire to be found as we enter the world of Buffy—is Angel, who was cursed by gypsies after he killed one of their teenagers, and who himself appears much younger than the standard first-season vampire in Buffy. Rather than stake him, the gypsies decided to expel the demon and restore Angel's human soul so that he would feel the pain of the knowledge of his misdeeds. The gypsies want him to exist only to suffer, and indeed, Angel, who no longer feeds off humans, is a tormented creature who is as much an outsider of the vampire community as Buffy is an outcast in the high school world. The fact that these two fall in love with each other only makes their lives more difficult. As Giles says, "A vampire in love with a slayer. It's rather poetic, really—in a maudlin sort of way" ("Out of Mind, Out of Sight," 1.11).

It might come as a surprise to some that when the magazine George published its September 1998 list of "20 Most Fascinating Women in Politics," Sarah Michelle Gellar's Buffy was the second in the list (right after Elizabeth Dole, but with a much bigger picture). *George* contrasts Buffy's healthy strength with the teenage girls discussed in Mary Pipher's *Reviving Ophelia*, and notes "... what she's really taking on is the regular assortment of challenges that threaten to suck the lifeblood out of teenage girls, like a suffocating high school hierarchy and a sexual double standard" (Stoller 113). Kathleen Tracy's 1998 guide to the series includes, with every episode synopsis, a brief description of the "Real Horror" to which the plot correlates. In *Our Vampires, Ourselves*, Nina Auerbach provides a larger symbolic context when she notes that "every age embraces the vampire it needs" (145)—or, one might add, the slayer it needs. And while Auerbach's use of the term "age" refers to cultural period, her statement could be extended to apply to a stage of life—in this case, adolescence. Instead of a patriarchal Van Helsing, *Buffy* provides a short, slight, teenage girl. It is nothing new for the science fiction and fantasy category of television series to symbolically represent teen difficulties: Harvey Greenberg's essay "In Search of Spock" explains how in the 1960s *Star Trek* represented teens' alienation in the famous half-Vulcan character. *Buffy* is especially successful at that symbolic representation.

The first episode, "Welcome to the Hellmouth," establishes the series' mapping of the high school social minefield and the series' satirical stance. The show starts with a role reversal: a series of shots of the darkened high school explore the building after hours, and we are then shown two teens breaking in—a pretty, stammering, demure little blonde named Darla following a teenage boy who clearly hopes to "take advantage" of her. When she gets his assurance that they really are alone, her face changes to the demonic feeding visage of the undead. It is the little pleat-skirted cutie who will eat the boy alive. Their images descend from the frame, leaving only a school trash can in the distance of the shot. This is the teaser.

After the credits and theme song, enter Buffy—in nightmares, dreaming of the demons she has to fight. (It was her fighting of vampires at her old school that resulted in her expulsion.) She is awakened by her mom to tackle instead the difficulties of her first day at a new school. The seemingly un-Shakespearean Cordelia[4] warns her, "You want to fit in here, the first rule is know your losers. Once you can identify them all by sight they're a lot easier to avoid." At this stage, Xander and Willow have another friend, Jesse, a slightly taller, geekier version of Xander who internalizes the high school code. At the local teen hangout, the Bronze, Jesse is humiliated by Cordelia's rejection. Chatting with her girlfriends, she later classes him among "children" and says he's like a "puppy dog—you just want to put him to sleep." In fact, Jesse is put into the sleep of death when he is taken by the vampires. When the vampire Jesse shows up at the Bronze, he is immediately able to make Cordelia dance with him; dismayingly, he embraces the change. Confronted by his old friend, Jesse says, "I feel good, Xander; I feel strong" and later, again speaking of himself, adds, "Jesse was an excruciating loser who couldn't get a date."

Harvey Greenberg, in his psychoanalytic discussion of teens and Spock, suggests that Spock's half-alien body reflects the physical changes adolescents sense taking place in themselves. The physical changes in this series' vampires' faces, along with their greater bodily strength, might be said to perform the same function (not to mention the fact that they stay up late). In the first season, the series focuses on confronting adulthood through confronting distinctly older vampires. "The Old Ones," both Giles and the vampire Master call them—and both their physical traits and their language (of which, more later) suggest adulthood. And as Brian Aldiss says, aside from its sexual qualities, the typical vampire's most notable characteristic is that "It is ancient" (x). Of course, vampire feeding has long been paralleled to sexual activity,[5] a rite of passage to adulthood which none of the teen protagonists of Buffy have undergone (in the first season, at least). When Jesse becomes a vampire, his sexual maturation is clearly suggested. But it is his rejection of "loser" status that really damns Jesse—his willingness to do whatever it takes to be accepted in high school, whether it is embracing vampirism or losing his virginity. At the moment he makes his declaration—"I'm a new man!"—he is destroyed, staked, turned to dust, the stake held in the unwilling hand of his best friend Xander ("Welcome to the Hellmouth").

It is a distinct element of the heroism of Buffy's teen protagonists that they will not go to any lengths to avoid "loser" status. Buffy, Willow, and Xander endure regular mockery, but pursue what they see as right. Buffy and Xander, both of whom are considered irresponsible by adults, take responsibility for their friends time and again. Auerbach notes that early, pre-Stoker, nineteenth-century incarnations of vampires seemed to stress, in their relationships with chosen humans, the intimacy of friendship (14). In Buffy, the most notable bond of friendship is among the teenage vampire-fighters.[6] "Jesse's my responsibility," says Buffy, and, as they skip school to go looking for him, Xander says, "Jesse's my bud, OK? If I can help him out, that's what I gotta do. It's that or chem class" ("Welcome to the Hellmouth"). For her part, Willow declares, "I'm not anxious to go into a dark place full of monsters—but I do want to help. I need to." The result of this heroism is not praise, but the painfully realistic irritation of those whom it inconveniences. When Buffy's mom gets a call from the principal about her skipping class, the mother grounds the Slayer just as she is about to go out to face the demons. "Mom, this is really, really important," Buffy pleads. And mother answers, "I know—if you don't go out it'll be the end of the world." In fact, it may be exactly that; according to Giles the Watcher, hundreds of vampires are making a concerted attempt to release the vampire Master, open the mouth of hell, and end the world as we know it—unless the reluctant Slayer saves the day. As the mom says, "Everything is life or death when you're a sixteen-year-old girl."

Buffy does succeed in her life and death struggle; though she, Willow, and Xander can't save Jesse, they do save the world; they do make it possible for life to go on. And so Xander says, the morning after the vampire battle has been witnessed by a nightclub full of teens, "One thing's for sure; nothing's ever gonna be the same." Perhaps the most important moment of the first episode, and one of the most important in the series, comes in the sunshine of the next morning at Sunnydale High, when absolutely nothing has changed. Almost all the adults and the vast majority of teens have managed to deny what they saw. "The dead rose," says Xander; "we should've at least had an assembly." But, led by Cordelia, the students have decided it was "rival gangs." Giles, the Watcher, one of those rare adults who really sees what is going on, explains: "People have a tendency to rationalize what they can and forget what they can't." And of course his words apply to the social problems of the real world just as emphatically as they do to monsters.

Even the socially heroic are sometimes vulnerable to peer pressure. The first-season episode "The Pack" (1.6) is ostensibly about Masai stories of possession by animal spirits—in this case, unusually vicious hyenas imported to the local zoo. But the humans the laughing hyenas possess are a clique of mocking high school students who take Xander into their fold. The episode opens with the four students teasing Buffy for having been kicked out of her earlier school. When they shift to weaker prey, the timid young man ironically named Lance, Xander pursues them into the off-limits hyena house to protect Lance, and so happens to be present when the possession takes place. In many episodes, Xander's lines are often jokes; but in this episode, after he is possessed, for the first time his jokes pass over into cruelty. Buffy can't believe that Xander would act this way, and so she consults Giles about possible supernatural explanations. "Xander's taken to teasing the less fortunate?" asks Giles. "Uh huh," says Buffy. "And there's a noticeable change in both clothing and demeanor?" "Yes!" "And—well—otherwise all his spare time is spent lounging about with imbeciles?" Buffy says, "It's bad, isn't it?" and Giles replies, "Devastating. He's turned into a sixteen-year-old boy. Of course you'll have to kill him."

Since this is the world of Buffy, it is not merely hormones at work, but possession. The result is different only in degree, however, not in kind. Xander finds it impossible to study; is cruelly rude to the adoring Willow; and lustfully leaps on Buffy. The latter activity is rather fortunate than not, since, while Buffy subdues Xander, he is separated from the pack for long enough to miss their attack on kindly Principal Flutie. In some schools, a teacher or administrator may be stabbed or shot by students. In Buffy's school, the students eat him. In the end, with the help of Giles and Willow, Buffy is able to return Xander to himself—and the instant after he comes to himself, he saves Willow from the knife-wielding, animal-worshipping bad-guy zookeeper who arranged the possession. But the upshot of the whole episode is that Xander is left deeply embarrassed by his own animalistic/adolescent behavior. "Shoot me, stuff me, mount me," he says to Giles, the only other male regular in the first season.

Some episodes of Buffy deal with more specific external threats. In "I Robot, You Jane" (1.8) shy, sweet Willow is drawn into the clutches of an internet predator. When Buffy notices that Willow, an outstanding student, is missing classes, she is concerned to find that her friend is skipping school to chat online with the mysterious Malcolm. Willow, who is attractive but far from glamorous and even farther from popular, is indignant at Buffy's concern over her online relationship. "Why does everything have to be about looks?" she wonders. And Buffy replies, "Not everything, but some stuff is. What if you guys get really intense and then you find out he has a hairy back?" From worrying about the fact that Willow has not met Malcolm, Buffy and Xander soon move to worrying that she will meet him. As Xander says, "Sure he can say he's a high school student ... I can ... say I'm an elderly Dutchwoman. Get me? And who's to say I'm not if I'm in the Elderly Dutch Chat Room?" As Buffy observes in alarm, "This guy could be anybody. He could be weird, or crazy, or *old* ..." The series implicitly calls attention to generational conflict and the horror of facing adults/adulthood as well as the particular horror of the internet predator. As viewers would have known since the beginning of the episode, Malcolm is downright ancient: he is in fact the demon Moloch, the corrupter. Once again, the friends put themselves on the line, and this time it is Willow who is saved—from one of the diabolical corrupters who are indeed out there on the internet.

In the second-season episode "Reptile Boy," Cordelia, who is only gradually and unwillingly drawn into the circle of friends with knowledge of the supernatural (read: adult) world, puts herself and Buffy in jeopardy when they go to a college fraternity party. One of the frat boys has decided he wants the good-looking Buffy to come, and to Cordelia's irritation her invitation is conditional on her bringing Buffy along. Buffy and Angel have been fighting over his reluctance to enter into a relationship with her; as he says, "This isn't some fairy tale. When I kiss you, you don't wake up from a deep sleep and live happily ever after." "No," says Buffy to her vampire, "When I kiss you I want to die," the death/sex metaphor echoing through the scene. As a result of their argument and Giles's insistently overworking her, Buffy decides—to the dismay of Xander and Willow—to lie to Giles and attend the party with Cordelia. Buffy and Cordelia end up easy prey at the party: "God, I love high school girls," says one of the frat boys. Each of the girls accepts a drink which turns out to be drugged, and each ends up out cold in an upstairs bedroom.

But the fraternity's humiliations are not limited to the females. One of the most interesting elements in the episode is the display of damage done to outsider males—in the shape of Xander, who crashes the party because he is worried about Buffy. (They repeatedly just miss seeing each other.) In a truly painful scene, the party crasher is forced—under the guise of his being treated as a pledge (an element of the story which suggests issues of its own)—to dress up in a blonde wig, half-slip, and giant stuffed bra, and made to dance in the center of a hooting crowd. After he is paddled and kicked out of the building, Xander mutters, "One day I'll have money—prestige—power—and on that day they'll still have more." Indeed, this is an unusually powerful fraternity—in large part because its members have sold themselves to the service of a snake-shaped, unpleasantly phallic white demon.[7] The leader chants, "We have no wealth, no possession except that which you give us. We have no place in the world—and no power—except that which you give us." A Marxist would find a broad field to plow in this segment. If the patriarchal power structure has not been made clear enough, when the frat boys prepare to sacrifice Buffy and Cordelia to their demon lord, the leader tells Buffy that "no woman speaks to him." (One can hardly wonder why.) However, Buffy—with the help of Willow and the three outsider males Xander, Angel, and Giles—is able to win. Once again, friendship defeats the monster. But the moral about fraternities could hardly be clearer if Camille Paglia had preached it. As Buffy says, "I told one lie. I had one drink." And Giles replies, "Yes, and you were very nearly devoured by a giant demon snake. The words 'let that be a lesson' are a tad redundant."

For any viewers who might not have caught on to the overall pattern yet, the second-season two-parter "Surprise"/"Innocence" (2.13, 2.14) makes the social symbolism eloquently clear. In the second season, Buffy's confrontation of the shift from adolescence to adulthood focuses on sexuality. Like the first episode, "Surprise" begins with Buffy having nightmares, this time before she wakes up on her seventeenth birthday. In one of the nightmare images, her mother asks, "Do you really think you're ready, Buffy?" and drops and breaks a cup and saucer. Buffy's dreams are sometimes prophetic, and later in her waking hours this cup-dropping scene is played out in the context of her asking permission to get her driver's license, but the question of her readiness also relates to her having sex with Angel (see Chapter 7). The nightmare image most important to Buffy is the vision of Angel being killed by Drusilla, a vampire he sired (and with whom he has in his demonic past had a relationship which is in effect incestuous; Appelo 25). In her alarm, she goes to Angel's apartment, where he reminds her that not all her dreams come true, and they passionately embrace, parting with difficulty.

At school, Buffy discusses the situation with Willow. (One might contrast this behavior with the failure to talk to each other of "most women in vampire movies"; Auerbach 57.) Willow notes that Angel is "cool" because "he would never push," and asks what Buffy wants to do. Buffy replies, "Want isn't always the right thing to do. But what if I never feel this way again?" This very believable teenage concern leads her to accept Willow's advice to "seize the day"; as Buffy says, "Once you get past a certain point, the seizing is sort of inevitable." Later in the day, when they face yet another encounter with a demon threatening Armageddon and Buffy worries that they can't know how long either of them will survive, Angel reminds her, "Nobody can. That's just the deal." But when they are actually attacked and barely escape, making their way to Angel's nearby apartment, they do— after one last "maybe we shouldn't" from Angel—go to bed together. The episode ends with Angel rushing from the sleeping Buffy out into the alley in the pouring rain, pain apparent on his face.

The symbolic implications of having Buffy's first sexual encounter be with a vampire of course emphasize the dangers of sexual encounters, especially with an adult. Angel claims to be around 240; he appears to be about twenty-four, as compared to Buffy's seventeen years. In terms of the plot, the serious problem with their encounter is that the gypsy curse which restored Angel's soul did so for the sake of his unremitting pain. When he finds a moment's true happiness, his soul is once again exiled and the demon takes its place. Angel becomes Angelus, who now notes, "the pain is gone," and—immediately after making love with Buffy— seizes and feeds off a hooker. Afterwards, heated by feeding on the woman's blood, he lifts his head and blows steam through his pursed lips in a gesture that suggests a post-coital smoke. (The gesture is clarified when, later in the episode, Angelus smokes a real cigarette with the same motion. Angel does not smoke.)

Buffy is left frantic with concern because Angel is missing; she is the girl waiting for a call after a sexual encounter, as another conversation with Willow makes clear. When she does finally find Angelus, he tells her, "You have a lot to learn about men, kiddo—but I guess you proved that last night." "I'll call you," he says, as he walks out on the weeping Buffy. Even then, Buffy cannot understand why her boyfriend would act that way. Angel originally introduced himself as "a friend" ("Welcome to the Hellmouth") and has repeatedly acted as one in a series which often focuses on friendship. But Buffy gradually discovers that having sex with her has literally turned Angel into a devil (who writes in blood over a dead body he knows she'll find, "Was it good for you, too?") Understanding now that he is not the man she thought he was, Buffy is able to endure his sneers in a later scene when he says, "You know what the worst part was? Pretending I loved you. If I'da known how easily you'd give it up, I wouldn't even have bothered." They fight ferociously and she wins. When she threatens him with a stake, he gloats that she is unable to kill him, and he is right. But Buffy being Our Heroine, she manages to draw on some inner reserve of strength and give him a good hard Slayer kick in the balls.

One of the rare moments during the first two seasons when Buffy's mom seems to be almost aware of what is going on comes in this episode. The morning after Buffy has had sex for the first time, her mom asks if something is wrong and says "you just look ...," trailing off, shaking her head. Adults in general and Buffy's mom in particular consistently misinterpret what is happening in the teens' world. Encounters with vampires, demons, and assorted other monsters get translated into more palatable problems: attacks by gangs on PCP, a gas leak, even an out-of-control scavenger hunt. This need for translation is emphasized throughout the series by the linguistic patterns of the different groups. Teen language is so clearly marked as separate in *Buffy* that *Entertainment Weekly* gave it the special name "Slayerspeak" (Howard; cf. Wyman). The bridge of symbolism needed between literal monsters and social problems is recapitulated by the bridge needed between teen and adult language in *Buffy*.

The fact that many of the cross-generational conversations are between Buffy and Giles, the British librarian, accentuates the separation. As Buffy says to him in the first episode, "You're like a textbook with arms." When Giles considers asking computer-whiz Willow for help in a crisis, for instance, he says, "I've been researching this Harvest affair. It seems to be some sort of pre-ordained massacre. Rivers of blood—hell on earth—quite charmless. I'm a bit fuzzy, however. It may be that you can wrest some information from that dread machine." At the students' blank looks, he translates, "I want you to go on the net" ("Welcome to the Hellmouth"). Buffy voices a common response when she says in another episode, "I think I speak for everyone here when I say, 'Huh?'" ("Out of Mind, Out of Sight").

Interestingly enough, most of the first-season vampires are placed on the side of the adults linguistically. The Master emits comments such as, "Tonight I shall walk the earth and the stars themselves will hide" ("Welcome to the Hellmouth") and "Here endeth the lesson" ("Never Kill a Boy on the First Date," 1.5); other vampires make similarly pompous, quasi-religious remarks: "And like a plague of boils the race of man covered the earth. But on the third day will come the Harvest ..." ("Welcome to the Hellmouth"). In the episode "Nightmares" (1.10) there is a cut from Buffy's nightmare of the vampire Master's hand around her neck to her awakening to find her mother's hand in approximately the same spot, shaking her awake. The symbolic identification of the two adult characters is disturbing: vampire and mother, both, it seems, moving Buffy towards some sort of awakening. Later in that episode, the Master says, "We are defined by the things we fear"; both vampirism and adulthood seem to be frightening experiences in *Buffy*. There could hardly be a nastier incarnation of the patriarchy than the ancient, ugly vampire Master. The Master compares his vampire group to a "family" which is "work[ing] together for the common good" in an ugly parallel to a standard adult line ("Angel," 1.7). As Nicola Nixon points out in her discussion of the 1987 films *Near Dark* and *The Lost Boys*, vampire groups can sometimes be seen as "dysfunctional families" (120). Buffy's mother's desire for her to work hard and fit in is curiously echoed in the Master's chastisement of his disciples, which sounds alternately like the reaction of a disappointed father or a coldly dissatisfied CEO. While the darkly beautiful Angel (who speaks neither marked slang nor overly erudite archaisms) suggests the dangerously attractive sexual aspect of adulthood, the Master is associated with work and family. As Buffy moves closer to adulthood in later seasons, the vampire opponents are not just adults, but distorted reflections of herself—vampires such as the young-appearing leather-clad Spike[8] or Sunday, the cool college vamp, who speak in contemporary slang. But in the first season almost all of the vampires and the adults are clearly tied together linguistically, among other ways.

Occasionally the teens will display their ability to speak the foreign language of adulthood. In "The Pack," for instance, Buffy speaks with Principal Flutie about the little pig mascot he has bought for the school's team. To placate the principal, she shifts from "He's so cute" to "He's a fine mascot and will engender school spirit." Similarly, Giles displays the ability to use teen language. When Buffy proves him wrong about the supernatural element in Xander's behavior, he promises to go to his volumes of paranormal lore and "Look stuff up" ("The Pack"). (Of course, it must be noted that he is merely quoting an earlier line of Buffy's, rather than creating teenspeak himself.) Even the Master vampire occasionally displays consciousness of the other language, though he does so with scornful intent—as when he remarks preparatory to temporarily killing Buffy, "Oh good—the feeble banter portion of the fight" ("Prophecy Girl," 1.12).

More often than not, however, the difference is accentuated. And the difference is not simply that adults use big words and know more, but rather that teens know different things. When Buffy says, "My spider sense is tingling," she has to apologize to Giles: "Pop culture reference—sorry" ("I Robot, You Jane"). When she complains in another episode that Giles is refusing for once to consider a supernatural explanation, she says, "I can't believe that you of all people would Scully me," ("The Pack") assuming knowledge of The X-Files television character famous for stretching rational explanations to cover unusual events. When Xander asks, "Does anyone else feel like they've been Kaiser Sozhed?" he counts on knowledge of the popular film The Usual Suspects, in which one of the characters assumes multiple false identities ("The Puppet Show," 1.9). And Cordelia translates Shakespeare by declaring that Shylock uses a "Twinkie defense," referring to recent and popularly discussed jurisprudence ("Out of Mind, Out of Sight").

Furthermore, the students show their willingness to work outside the rules by their comfort in re-casting the language. Barbara Bell has commented on this change of word form and function regarding the series *My So-Called Life*. Sometimes the changes come in word order, as when Buffy says, "We so don't have time" ("Welcome to the Hellmouth"). Sometimes they come in word form, as when another character refers to "Willow kissage" ("Innocence") or when Willow and Buffy admire a boy for his "Owenosity" ("Never Kill a Boy on the First Date") or when Buffy asks, "What's the sitch [situation]?" ("Welcome to the Hellmouth"). Parts of speech may be varied, with an adverb becoming an adjective: "You're acting a little overly, aren't you?" ("Never Kill a Boy on the First Date"). Or an adjective may become a noun: "Love makes you do the wacky" ("Some Assembly Required," 2.2).[9] Sometimes the words are metaphorical or metonymic substitutions, as in "You're that amped about hell? Go there" ("Prophecy Girl"), wherein amped = excited, from audio amplification; or "I'll talk to you later, when you've visited Decaf Land" ("The Dark Age," 2.8). Students who are willing to operate outside the high school code are certainly not afraid of coloring outside the lines of language. Their use of the language is, in fact, daring. In the third-season opener, with Buffy missing, Willow points out that "The Slayer always says a pun or a witty play on words, and I think it throws off the vampires" and Xander responds, "I've always been amazed with how Buffy fights, but in a way I feel like we took her punning for granted" ("Anne," 3.1). And the use of language is highly conscious, to the point of adding to series continuity. When Buffy finally conquers her nemesis the Master, her last word to his disintegrating corpse recalls the social stigma she, Willow, and Xander have endured: "Loser," she calls him ("Prophecy Girl").

In sum, the use of language in *Buffy* reinforces the theme of adult ignorance—and the grace and wit of the language embody one element of the heroism of the teen characters. One might recall E. M. Forster's definition of the purpose of art—that human creation of order in a chaotic world—to understand the power of the ludic elements of *Buffy*'s symbolism and language. Buffy confronts the vampires of adulthood not only with weapons, but also with words of her own. It is part of the grace and wit of the *series* that the courage of these adolescents in fighting social problems is translated into symbolism—a mediation of meaning which parallels the mediation of the teen language. Through both symbolism and language, in *Buffy*, the mediation is the message.

Chapter 2

Pain as Bright as Steel

Mythic Striving
and Light as Pain[1]

Dare I hint at that worse time when, strung together in great black space, there was a flaming necklace, or ring, of which *I* was one of the beads! And when my only prayer was to be taken off from the rest, and when it was such inexplicable agony and misery to be part of the dreadful thing?

> Esther Summerson, in *Bleak House* (Dickens 370)

Where there's life there's hope.
Every day's a gift.
Wishes can come true.
Whistle while you work
So hard all day
To be like other girls—
To fit in, in this glittering world.

> Buffy Summers, in "Once More, with Feeling" (Whedon, 6.7)

In the world of television, there has probably never been a greater work of language than *Buffy the Vampire Slayer*. Whether we consider its style, as do such writers as Karen Eileen Overbey and Lahney Preston-Matto, or its narrative structures, as do such writers as Roz Kaveney and Elisabeth Krimmer and Shilpa Raval, its power, delicacy, and richness are apparent. Less attention has been given to the visual elements of the series, though on occasion writers such as J. P. Williams and Dave West have discussed the subject. But as Camille Bacon-Smith has pointed out in her essay "The Color of the Dark," television creators like Joss Whedon "can depend on a meshing of the visual and verbal to create both a narrative message and a metaphoric one ..." (xii). Light imagery is a particularly important example of the connection of the visual and the verbal in *Buffy*. Karen Sayer, in her analysis of the use of space in *Buffy*, argues that "light always contrasts with dark, mapping out the territories of good vs. evil ..." (104). While in many cases this has been true, I would argue that we can follow the presentation of light imagery much farther as the show becomes more complicated morally, especially if we expand beyond consideration of the setting to the larger narrative and its thematic implications. As many of us have noted, Joseph Campbell's hero monomyth can be seen to operate in *Buffy*;[2] and I would point out that it functions with the accompaniment of pervasive light imagery. The characters of Spike and Buffy—one from the morally dark and one from the light side—both illustrate the monomyth; and, among a variety of suggestive characters, these two pre-eminently illustrate the shadowed significance of light as pain.

At the outset, a caveat: I am not attempting an allegorical interpretation here—I am not trying to argue that a given image equates to a single absolute meaning. Instead, I am invoking a much more open symbolism. Fiske and Hartley, many years ago, used the term *reading* television; and I use the term *reader* for any viewer who actively engages with the text.[3] It has been generally acknowledged that each television viewer brings to a series a different set of life experiences, thus enabling a different reader-response: Bring Your Own Subtext, as Joss Whedon says (Golden, Bissette, and Sniegoski 172). It is also true, however, that any single reader may have multiple responses to the same material, a complex of responses which are not necessarily consistent in a straightforward fashion. When you buy at the *Buffy* store, meanings do not come just one to a customer. There are variations over time and within the context of any given moment of such a rich text. This is particularly true of light imagery, which is so pervasive, and which is applicable to so many different themes. However, I hope to identify some recognizable patterns.

Light in the Dark

It will come as a surprise to no one that, in a series with a large population of vampires, light can be seen as equivalent to pain. The quotation in the title of this essay comes from a conversation between Buffy's Watcher Giles

and his former friend the chaos-worshipping sorcerer Ethan Rayne, who is
telling him of a mysterious threat (which we later learn to be founded in the
Initiative, that bastion of scientific rationality), a threat which is troubling
the creatures of darkness—though they will not specify their fears: as Ethan
says to Giles, "Oh, you know demons—it's all exaggeration and blank
verse. 'Pain as bright as steel,' things like that" ("A New Man," 4.12). The
steel, or sword, of the quote connects the idea of light with weaponry, and
of course sunlight is one of the methods for killing a vampire. The standard
symbolic implications of light equating to good and dark equating to evil
are present here, though one might note the connection of brightness and
pain with the sterile rationality of the Initiative and its gleaming white labs;
and one might note the indulgent, half-humorous tone of Ethan's remark
as he goes on to identify himself and Giles with the night. Countless
vampires in *Buffy* are dispatched by light or even the threat of light, as is
the brutal Vessel Luke in the "The Harvest" (1.2).

But for two vampires, the patterns of light imagery are especially
significant. When Buffy must kill her beloved, the ensouled vampire Angel,
she delivers that pain with steel, and sends him into a swirling vortex of
light: yes, Angel moves into the light, but it is the light of hell, and its
reflected shimmer flickers across Buffy's face as she delivers the killing
blow. This light does not signal the uncomplicated triumph of virtue,[4] but
the shared and reflected pain of a complicated moral decision, in effect
almost a wedding of ethical destiny, with the woman operating the sword
of moral choice: his soul has been returned to him, but Buffy must kill
him nonetheless to save the world—and thus his atonement begins again
("Becoming" Part 2, 2.22).

Later, after Angel is returned from hell, he is tormented by the memory
of past victims and, impelled by a force called the First Evil, he tries to kill
himself by staying outside for the sunrise. In this episode ("Amends,"
3.10), advertised as a "*Buffy* Christmas show," his act seems clearly to fit
the description of the sin of despair of the mercy of God. Saying "It's not
the demon in me that needs killing, Buffy, it's the man," he asks her, "Am
I a thing worth saving, huh? Am I a righteous man?" And, in the robe of
Jesus which she often wears, Buffy answers, "I know everything that you
did because you did it to me": "Inasmuch as ye have done it unto one of
the least of these, ... ye have done it unto me" (Matthew 25:40). Despite
his despair, he is saved from the vampire's fate of burning in a localized
hell. Since he cannot withstand the sunlight of pure virtue, he is instead
given the cold white light of snow, a California miracle foreshadowing

his spiritual redemption. When he moves to Los Angeles and his own series, he drives a convertible—and a character in the series asks what Angel's choice of vehicle tells us about the vampire. Clearly, aside from the opportunity for good headshots of actor David Boreanaz, the convertible in the dark provides a wistful representation of the vampire's desire for the moral light.

But which vampire dares to move in the light most often? As almost any *Buffy* reader would know, it is not the heroic Angel, but the marvelously irritating Spike. Spike arrived in the second season with a demonic crash into the cartoon sun on the sign for Buffy's town of California light (Sunnydale), and has never lost his intolerance for cartoon goodness. But as Michele Boyette explains, he has been transformed from villainy in part by his role as comic anti-hero. I would add that many of the comic moments come from his encounters with sunlight—as when in "Lovers Walk" (3.8) he drunkenly spies on and sneers at Angel, saying "I'll show you who's the cool guy," only to pass out and wake up far from cool, flaming in the morning sun until he douses himself with water in vampire slapstick. After the Initiative implants in his head the chip that prevents him from harming humans, Spike takes to roaming the daylight under a blanket (first seen in the Thanksgiving episode, "Pangs," 4.8). These comic forays into daylight normally constitute some approach to Buffy, and they proliferate after Spike realizes in the fifth season that he has fallen in love with the Slayer. Hence when Buffy's Initiative soldier boyfriend Riley finds Spike in her bedroom sniffing her clothing and tosses the vampire outside, Spike calls for his "Blanket! Blanket!" ("Shadow," 5.8). Or when in "Tabula Rasa" (6.8) the Scoobies meet at Giles's magic shop, Spike is smoking from the sun under a ludicrous flap-eared cap which he had donned atop a protective three-piece suit in an instance of what Giles terms "sartorial humor." These excursions into the light have become so frequent as to seem almost unremarkable. When he cannot reach his desired goal through the darkness of the sewers, this vampire will dare the daylight.

And when we finally learn about his past, we can see the roots of his later desires. In the fifth-season episode "Fool for Love" (5.7), Buffy asks Spike to teach her how he killed two earlier Slayers. In recalling this part of his past, he also recalls (for himself and for us, not for her) his mortal existence in 1880 as an ineffectual young man writing lovesick poetry. William (later known as William the Bloody) is, when we first hear him, alone at a party, mulling over words for a poem: "Luminous"; "irradiant"; "gleaming"—he is searching for words that mean light, and he finally settles on the most unusual: "effulgent." Mocked by the other partygoers and rejected by the woman he loves, he rushes out into the darkness, which offers him weird light in the form of the psychic, mad vampire Drusilla: "I see what you want—something glowing and glistening—something *effulgent*," she says. With this word, apparently born of a telepathic connection, William's initial rejection turns to vehement acceptance of Drusilla's approach: "Oh, God, yes." William longs for the light.

And a long strange trip it will be before he reaches it. While a number of us have noted that Buffy's story follows Campbell's monomyth (of which, more later), more recently some of us have seen the patterns in a strange form in Spike's story as well. The basic pattern is separation—initiation—return (Campbell 30): in Spike's case, separation from humanity and a form of return to it. More specific elements of the pattern include the call to adventure; the refusal of the call and subsequent acceptance; supernatural aid; resisting a figure of sexual temptation; triumphal marriage; crossing the threshold into another world—often the underworld; numerous trials; the return; and the hero's dispensing boons—not necessarily in that order (Campbell 36, 109, and *passim*). The scene in which Drusilla turns Spike encapsulates several of the elements—the call to adventure, his refusal then acceptance, and her supernatural aid in enabling him to cross the threshold into the vampiric world of dark immortality.[5] Interestingly, in order to cross the threshold into the dark world, the initiate gives in to the sexual temptation. A case can be made, on the other hand, for seeing another call to adventure, in a different direction, in Spike's fifth-season dream-recognition of his love for Buffy, which he also initially rejects: "Oh god, no. Please no" ("Out of My Mind," 5.4). Once he enters the world of the Scoobies—certainly an other-world for him—his real trials begin, most notably as he willingly suffers torment by the hell-god Glory for the sake of Buffy and her sister Dawn (in "Intervention," 5.18), and again when he risks himself for them in "Blood Ties" (5.13), "Spiral" (5.20), and "The Gift" (5.22), when he is flung from the sacrificial tower and, bloody and weeping, witnesses Buffy's death.

In the sixth season, after Buffy's return from death, Buffy and Spike have become for each other both the monomyth's temptation figure and, potentially, the partner in the triumphal marriage.[6] In Chapter 5, I discuss the Buffy/Spike relationship at length, particularly focusing on them as shadow figures for each other. Buffy and Spike first have sex with each other in the ninth episode of the sixth season, "Smashed," the title of which indicates the violent physicality of the encounter. Buffy flings

Spike through the door of the building in which they have intercourse, smashing through more than one kind of threshold. Repeatedly during the sixth season (and indeed before then), Spike tells Buffy she is drawn to darkness. But late in the season, in "Normal Again" (6.17), still trying to help her after innumerable rejections, he says, "You're not drawn to the dark like I thought. You're addicted to the misery ... Stop with the bloody hero trip for a sec and we'd all be the better for it." While Spike accuses her of addiction to misery, she has told him that he is "in love with pain" ("Smashed")—and they are both right to argue that pain for its own sake is not profitable. But Buffy is not going to "stop with the bloody hero trip," and that trip into the light entails pain, as Spike is coming to know, more and more thoroughly. In the scene in "Normal Again," in her bedroom to bring her his message to "live, already," he steps far enough into the light that he recoils as if from a blow.

But of course he must travel farther before he can return. After Buffy has broken off their affair and her friend Xander has left his ex-demon girlfriend Anya at the altar, the unhappy Spike and Anya have sex "for solace," as Anya later describes it ("Grave," 6.22). When Xander, in a jealous fury, comes to stake their sometime ally Spike, Buffy rushes to save him ("Entropy," 6.18), but not to stay with him. After Buffy's sister Dawn tells him, in the next episode ("Seeing Red," 6.19), that he has hurt Buffy, he feels compelled to apologize, and enters not only her house but her bathroom uninvited, in foreshadowing of his attempt at uninvited sexual entry. (Nota Bene: A vampire cannot enter uninvited.) He wants to believe that if they have sex again, she will recognize within herself not just the "feelings" she admits to in this scene, but also real love.

Buffy and Spike's sexual encounters have been repeatedly depicted in a violent fashion, but the difference in emotion here is made clear by a simple but effective device. In "Smashed," they break down walls both metaphoric and physical to the accompaniment of vocalized music which is almost poignant in tone.[7] There is no music in the cold light of the bathroom scene of "Seeing Red"—we hear only the sounds of the attack. And no visual darkness in *Buffy* has approached the grimness of this brightly lit scene. Hurt by an earlier encounter with a vampire, and apparently hoping that Spike will restrain himself, Buffy struggles and pleads, throwing him off physically just at the last moment. Only afterwards does Spike seem to recognize that he has attempted to rape her.

This episode is the turning point in Spike's journey, because in it he finally recognizes his own wrongdoing, truly sees his own darkness. As

Barbara Hardy says in her discussion of the conversion pattern in Dickens, the character "is converted by seeing and understanding his defect and its origins" (39). Spike's attack on Buffy represents his attacks on all his earlier victims: the horror is brought home. We are not allowed to distance the evil he has caused. Once again, Buffy could say to her vampire lover, "I know everything you did because you did it to me"; once again, in a very different way, Buffy takes the pain for us all. Thus the difficulty of forgiveness—so easily recommended as a moral choice—is made very real in this series. After the attempted rape, Buffy's reaction is shown mainly through language, in her painful conversation with her friend Xander, but Spike's is shown in visual representations of his thoughts, flashbacks of his memories of Buffy's struggle, and the discordant music suggests that the memories horrify him. "What have I done? Why *didn't* I do it? Oh— what has she done to me?" And, ringing changes on his speech to Buffy in "The Gift," he says, "I may be a monster, and I can't be a man—I'm nothing."[8] Spike has reached his moment of existential despair. He has only been able to glimpse this recognition of his own wrongdoing because he has entered into a relationship with Buffy. Good or evil must be seen in terms of relationship with others, not absolutes of action. For Spike, Buffy is no longer just an object, just vampire food, or a Slayer to conquer, or even just a sexual object.

The transformational nature of this event (the reaction to the attempted rape) is further signified by his leaving behind his coat. Any *Buffy* reader knows that Spike's black leather coat is his signature of self—"It's Spike! And he's wearing the coat!" ("Intervention"). In "Fool for Love," we learn that he took it from the body of the second Slayer that he killed, so the coat suggests, among other things, power, death, and gender-crossing (a subject for another day). Now, in "Seeing Red," he is so emotionally overwrought that after the attempted rape he leaves behind both the coat and his earlier self. Spike drives off alone into the darkness, crushing underfoot a cigarette, part of a long-running motif of cigarettes symbolizing sexuality, and he promises to return.

In the last three episodes of Season Six, Spike engages in a very overt form of the hero quest, as he travels to a far land (apparently Africa) and even enters the underworld, represented by a dark cave inhabited by a powerful demon. Though Spike has left behind his coat, he still has with him his second-most notable signature possession, his lighter (see, e.g. "Gone," 6.11): and he uses this small light as he enters the place of trials which will bring him to a greater light in the end, just as the fire of his sexual connection to Buffy leads him to the illumination of empathy.

Spike's goal is presented ambiguously. Does he want to get rid of the chip so that he can revenge himself on Buffy for softening him, or does he want to regain his human soul so that he has a chance at her love? Or does he plan to get rid of the chip but subconsciously wish for the return of his soul? Spike's use of the term "bitch" to refer to Buffy indicates anger— perhaps an anger he has assumed in order to blame the victim and avoid the regret he earlier expressed over his actions, but anger nonetheless—as opposed to his usual use of terms such as "pet," "love," or "Goldilocks." His phrasing of his request to the demon is expressed with such precise ambiguity that it performs two functions: (1) it allows audience members to be surprised when the angry Spike receives a soul, and (2) it suggests Freudian slippage, as he says "Bitch is gonna see a change" ("Villains," 6.20), and "it'll get me what I need to take care of the Slayer," "Give her what's coming to her," and "make me what I was so that Buffy can get what she deserves" ("Grave"). Each of these remarks can, of course, be taken in either a negative or positive fashion, while his repeated use of the word "bitch" suggests conscious antagonism. And though the demon's use of the term "restoration" could refer to restoring Spike to chip-free condition, nonetheless for attentive Buffy readers the use of the term recalls the soul-restoring spell which reverted Angelus to Angel at the end of Season Two. Altogether, the ambiguity of language suggests Spike's ambivalence and the likelihood of at least a subconscious desire for his soul.[9] The result recalls countless tales in which a person making a wish is surprised by the granting of only too right a reward.

Whether the reader believes Spike chose to undergo horrendous trials from a conscious or subconscious desire for a soul, certainly it is significant that he is given the soul as a result of his own agency (as opposed to Angelus, who had his soul forced upon him). However, I admit that I was at first troubled by the fact that Spike's monomythic labors take a relatively short time and take place out of the context of relationship with other characters—such relationship being the only place, it would seem, where moral growth could occur. But, as my then fourteen-year-old son Jeff Gess pointed out when I voiced this complaint, Spike had already been going through his trials and growth in relationship for years. Thus, Spike's physical trials in the cave are just a synecdochic expression of what he has endured in the past. The trials in the cave with the threshold guardian more overtly and visually display the monomyth pattern that can also be seen in a subtler fashion in the long-term narrative of the series.[10]

For both the brief physical journey and the long spiritual one, the culminating image is the last of the season. And it very directly represents the pain of light, the pain of illumination: the demon touches him, and Spike's eyes and heart are infused with light as he screams, receiving his reborn soul. The image is led into by the sound of the prayer of St Francis of Assisi fading out with sung words referring to Jesus, who also emerged from his cave-tomb: "It is in dying we are born to eternal life." The burning light in Spike's eyes is an image that is fulfilled when, at the end of Season Seven, Spike's entire body becomes a weapon of light as he sacrifices himself to close the Hellmouth (see Chapter 6).[11]

It is worth noting that, of the seven seasons of Buffy, four close with images of the group (which is thematically important for the series); two close with an image of Buffy alone (second and fourth season). The sixth is the only example of closing a season with the image of another character. While the choice allowed the season to close with what would have been a surprising moment for many viewers, it also indicates the significance of this character in particular and the motif of the spiritual journey in general.

Pain in the Light

While Spike struggles in the cave of his rebirth, Buffy struggles in the "Grave" of the episode's title, where the grief-maddened Willow has magically placed Buffy and Dawn. It is not difficult to see the monomyth pattern for the hero Buffy. Buffy refuses her call to slay, and then accepts it; she faces trial after trial, crosses over to death, and then returns. In fact, there are smaller and larger versions of the monomyth pattern throughout Buffy. As Campbell says, "Within the soul, within the body social, there must be—if we are to experience long survival—a continuous 'recurrence of birth' (palingenesia) to nullify the unremitting circumstances of death" (16).[12]

The monomyth, found many times in the many mythic narratives of the world, can also be found many times in the one narrative of Buffy. Buffy experiences her first rebirth at the end of the first season, when she is killed by the Master and returns (and as Campbell notes, "the hero may have to be brought back ... by assistance from without," 207). In Fighting the Forces, I noted that at the end of the second and beginning of the third season, Buffy again follows the monomyth pattern as she "travel[s] to a strange land (in this case, Los Angeles), fights monsters, and return[s] home changed" (6); and part of the journey is a confrontation with the underworld, a harrowing of hell, as Z. J. Playdon puts it (131). As the series continues, the larger arc of the larger journey is exposed, as Buffy sacrifices her life to save the world in general and her sister in particular, and is dead and buried for 147 days (the figure is of Spike's providing), a sort of anti-Persephone who disappears over the summer months ("After Life," 6.3).

When she reappears, she illustrates yet another of the varying elements of the monomyth identified by Campbell: "The return and reintegration within society, which ... the hero ... may find the most difficult requirement of all" (36). If the hero "has won through, like the Buddha, to the profound repose of complete enlightenment, there is danger the bliss of this experience may annihilate all recollection of, interest in, or hope for the sorrows of the world" (36). Many fans have complained about the grimness of Season Six, with its stories of addiction, attempted rape, broken weddings, and—worst of all—Social Services employees and fast food jobs, but I would argue, like Laurel Bowman, that the series is simply reflecting the difficult return element of the monomyth. Furthermore, in terms of narrative balance, the reaction to the hero's death should weigh heavily. Whedon and Co. have carried us to the point where we can feel the cost of death and moral sacrifice.[13] It should not be too easy for Buffy to return from that plunge from the tower; death should not be cheaply cheated. If, in real life, someone has to deal with death, major illness, or other life trauma, then that person should be allowed to be less than sunny. Or to put it another way, a year of mourning seems appropriate.

Like Spike's struggle in the cave, then, Buffy's struggle in the grave of the sixth-season finale is a brief metaphoric expression of an experience which has extended for months. In the first hour of Season Six, Buffy's hand, in close-up, bursts through the ground from her grave—a hand reaching into the darkness. In the last hour of the season, her hand reaches up from the grave into the light. Season Six constitutes the "difficult return" portion of the monomyth; and Season Seven constitutes the portion wherein the hero dispenses boons to the people (see Chapter 6).

Thus, over the course of many years, the monomyth has been reworked again and again in the series, with increasing complexity. As Playdon points out, redemption is open to all in the Buffyverse; and she instances Angel's resurrection (131). I have discussed Spike's transformation at length both in this chapter and elsewhere. It could be argued that Faith has taken this trip as well. And Willow undergoes a similar sea change as a result (in part) of her journey to that far-off, alien world called England. Buffy herself has lived and died and lived through many changing versions of the monomyth.

Similarly, the imagery of light has refracted over the course of the years as well. The light imagery associated with Spike's spiritual journey is a relatively straightforward connection of light with good: Spike finds moving into the light painful because, after all, Spike is a vampire. Buffy, on the other hand, is introduced to us from the start as the hero who "fight[s] ... the forces of darkness" (voiceover, "Welcome to the Hellmouth," 1.1). But Buffy's moral nature and the moral universe of the show have become more complex, just as the reworkings of the monomyth have become more complex. Light has become pain for Buffy, as well.

The epigraphs to this chapter indicate this complexity—and the continuing literary heritage of this imagery of the monomyth, from Charles Dickens to Joss Whedon, who names Dickens as his favorite novelist. Esther Summerson and Buffy Summers: their surnames indicate their mythic connection. But these two Persephones, unlike the Greek original, *choose* to go into the dark place: Esther risks disease to save others, and Buffy risks dangers of another sort. Esther descends into illness, blindness, and delirium, and returns physically marked; Buffy comes back marked morally and emotionally. Each—Esther the illegitimate, and Buffy the odd hero—has fought to be a normal girl. And each realizes the shining pain involved in the cost of return and connection: One of the great themes of Dickens's *Bleak House* is our interconnection, and one of the great themes of *Buffy* is the virtue of community (Playdon; Rose; Wilcox, "Who"). Through the pain of light, the authors of each imagaically recognize both the desire and difficulty of such goals.

In "After Life," Spike and the audience learn from Buffy just how difficult her return from death has been: Extricating herself from a group hug in the Magic Box, having thanked the friends who, led by Willow, have returned her to this world, she slips into the alley to find Spike sitting in the shade, and they conversationally note the thematically appropriate fact that he is "not on fire," though it is "daylight." The camera calls attention to the border between light and dark as he walks to the edge of the shadow and stops, and Buffy tells him he may remain. When he offers to talk with her about the hell everyone believes she must have suffered, she tells him:

> I was happy. Wherever I was, I was happy—at peace. I knew that everyone I cared about was all right. I *knew* it. Time didn't mean anything. Nothing had form, but I was still me, you know? And I was warm and I was loved—and I was finished, complete. I don't understand theology or dimensions—any of it, really. But I think I was in heaven. And now I'm not. I was torn out of there—pulled

out—by my friends. Everything here is hard and bright and violent. Everything I feel—everything I touch—this is hell.

Clearly, as Buffy describes Campbell's "difficult return" from the world beyond, she associates the brightness of this world with violence: "hard and bright and violent," "pain as bright as steel." It is the brilliance of the light of pain she has flung herself through in "The Gift" in order to do her appointed task, "the work I have to do," to save lives and to cross over (and as she falls, cruciform, her face in the light shows both pain and ecstasy). In "After Life," she crosses over the border of light and dark which Spike has marked, and she must painfully force herself into the light.

In the Buffyverse, the pain of light is not associated solely with the "difficult return," but with crossing in either direction. At times of a major step in the story, at a point of what might be called cognitive dissonance, repeatedly there is a visual image associating strong light with pain and with a border or threshold. Up and down the stairwell of Buffy's house (a locale for many significant moments) are hung four prints of slightly varying threshold images, pictures of arches through which greater or lesser darkness can be seen. Campbell, of course, emphasizes the threshold that, in varying forms, the hero must pass by means of bravery or wisdom. He refers, for example, to the Pawnee "sun door, through which souls pass back and forth from time to eternity ... burned in the fire of life" (42). In a story of vampires, the threshold is naturally highlighted: the vampire's invited entry can be symbolically equated with sexual entry and/or the entry of evil, or darkness, or the id. (The stairwell threshold pictures appear clearly for the first time in the second season's "Innocence," 2.14, as Buffy confronts her mother after her sexual initiation with Angel.)[14] But also through these openings can come light, illumination (and even sexualized love). Three episodes written and directed by Joss Whedon (with Michael Gershman as Director of Photography) which strikingly illustrate the light-threshold motif are "Graduation Day," which closes Season Three; "The Body" (5.16) from mid-Season Five; and "Restless," which closes Season Four.

In "Graduation Day" Part 2 (3.22), the external threat Buffy faces is the ascension to full demonic status by Sunnydale's mayor, who, after a hundred years, has given new meaning to the word incumbent. Mayor Wilkins will morph into a giant snake, Mr. Patriarchal Phallus of 1999.[15] The more emotionally significant threat, however, is the other Slayer, Faith. Buffy is as replete with foils as Hamlet, and a number of us have written about Faith as a shadow figure for Buffy. In their struggle, Buffy stabs Faith with a knife given to Faith by the mayor (I need a little neon "phallic symbol" sign), but as Faith lies in a coma, Buffy reconciles with her dark side in a dream, in one of the most beautifully shot and scored scenes in the series. Faith, near death, is a figure on the threshold of another world, a threshold represented by the window out of which she gazes, and which covers her face with an unusually bright light. Buffy says, "There's something I'm supposed to be doing," and Faith, her face filled with light, answers, "Oh, yeah, miles to go ...."[16] And when Buffy complains of hearing "riddles" (as, of course, the hero often must), Faith, still bathed in light, replies "It's my head—lotta new stuff": she has absorbed new truth. We see, fading in and out, first an image of Faith lying in her hospital bed, and then, moments later in Buffy's hands, the bloody knife with which she stabbed Faith. While the images shift, Faith quietly says, "Scar tissue. It fades. It all fades [and here the knife fades in and out]. Want to know the deal? Human weakness. It never goes away." The scars, the pain, can be lived through; and if one accepts one's human weakness—one's dark side—one will be ready to face the test. This is the illumination that Faith brings from the other side; and whether or not the Faith of Buffy's dream is a real woman or a projection of Buffy's own mind, Buffy is now ready to face the mayor, to let Angel go, and to graduate—in short, to pass another stage in her testing and growth.

"The Body" is one of the most acclaimed episodes of the series. In it, Buffy discovers the body of her mother and at first struggles fruitlessly to revive her. With no music, the visual images and diegetic non-musical sounds of the episode are highlighted. The episode is saturated with threshold images, of which I will discuss only a few. Just after a paramedic says that her mother is dead (and through most of his scene, the top of his head is out of camera range, his mouth thus emphasized as he delivers the dreadful announcement), Buffy stands in the light of her open front door, watching the paramedics leave for another emergency. Earlier in the scene Buffy, refusing to believe her mother's death, had flashed back to a memory of a Christmas dinner, and the dinner scene is cozy and dark. Now she is in the process of accepting the death. The camera moves with her as she walks through the living room and into a back hall. As she approaches the brightness of a window in the hall, the window's wind chimes ring; she falls to her knees on the floor and vomits. The light of this dreadful knowledge is at first too painful to bear; and the beauty which still resides in the world, suggested by the sound of the chimes, is intolerable. But Buffy lifts herself from her knees again (as she always does) and opens herself up to that light: she opens the back door and receives illumination. In one of the most memorable images of the series, the light fills her face to the point that the image is overexposed. She hears the sound of children playing and, it seems, the sound of an ocean wave: she hears, as Wordsworth puts it in the Immortality Ode, "the children sport upon the shore /And hear[s] the mighty waters rolling evermore." Her mother's death leads Buffy to look across the shore, across the threshold of her own back door to the other side, and she in that moment sees life and death forever interwoven. Her later voluntary sacrifice of her own life is enlarged by this moment of painful vision.

The episode "Restless" takes place earlier than "The Body," having aired at the end of the fourth season. However, a case could be made that "Restless" is an adumbration of much of the future course of Buffy.[17] For example, when Xander looks up the stairs from his basement to hear the sounds of his parents fighting and he says, "That's not the way out," he foreshadows his choice to leave Anya at the altar in Season Six; or when Giles refers to the "blood of the lamb," a reference to Christ, when speaking of Buffy, he foreshadows her world-saving self-sacrifice in "The Gift." (And of course Jesus says, "I am the light," John 8:12.) The four major segments of the teleplay consist of dreams by the four core Scoobies— with Willow's first and Buffy's last (Willow, like Faith, is a Buffy foil). The dreams represent the psychic cost the four have borne—most recently in their fight against the Initiative; but in fact, throughout their time together, the time of the series (for instance, Willow recalls her early high school days, even being shown wearing a jumper that looks like the one she wore in the first episode). However, "Restless" displays not only the past but also the future.

As Willow's dream begins, she and Tara are alone in Tara's dorm room. While Willow writes a Sapphic ode on Tara's back, Tara murmurs, "I think it's strange—I mean I think we should worry—that we haven't found her name yet—Miss Kitty." The two young women talk further, and Willow says, "I don't want to leave here." Apparently there is something threatening outside; as she pulls back the drapes, she says, "It's so bright—and there's something out there." We see the harsh brightness of a desert; and we catch a glimpse of something, which we later learn is the First Slayer. Immediately after, we see the kitten stalking towards us as the music heavily strikes with a suggestion of thunderous footfalls (heavy kitty). In this dream and in the dream in "Graduation Day," it seems a cat suggests the Slayer herself. Of the cat in the earlier dream, Faith says, "it's a she. And aren't these things supposed to take care of themselves?" (Keller identifies the cat with Faith, 167.) Here in "Restless" we realize that we have not found her name yet; no one yet knows Buffy's true nature (see Chapter 3). As the image of Tara says later in Buffy's own dream, "You think you know what you are—what's to come. You haven't even begun." In fact, as their dreams suggest, all three of the younger Scoobies are searching for themselves, still searching, even now. And Willow emblematizes the beginning of that search when she pulls aside the dark red curtain of the womb-like room to reveal another threshold of light, the window which opens onto the desert. Campbell includes the desert among "the regions of the unknown [which] are free fields for the projection of unconscious content" (79), and which represent that other world in which the hero must quest (58; see Chapter 10). Each of the younger Scoobies ventures into the desert in these dreams. Before her venture, Buffy is told by the Tara-image to "be back before Dawn." Aside from being an allusion to sister Dawn's arrival next season, the reference also indicates that Buffy must search through "unconscious content," the night world of the mind "before Dawn," to find her true self. Though she fights the forces of darkness, she must somehow reconcile with the shadows in herself (see Chapters 5 and 6). The Scoobies face death in dreams while searching for understanding; each must be prepared to suffer (and facing death also signifies facing one's deeper self). In the end, though she has denied her ability to do so, Buffy, struggling in the desert, simply chooses to awaken. Once again, the bright light coming through the dangerous threshold has visually represented spiritual illumination. "Graduation Day" marks a rite of passage to maturity; "The Body" initiates into the true knowledge of death; and "Restless" marks the search for self.

The implications of light imagery in Buffy could be explained much farther, of course. For instance, Buffy protects Dawn—whose name does not mean simply light, but more truly that lightening edge between the night and day—the border between dark and light; Buffy, as many of us have noted, is a border-crosser—as befits a hero of the monomyth. For another instance of light imagery, while Buffy is inhabited by the First Slayer in "Primeval" (4.21), her eyes lighten in a way reminiscent of a vampire's; on the other hand, Willow's blacken when she does dark magic, though with Tara she draws circles of light ("Who Are You?" 4.16). One might, following Z. J. Playdon, discuss Apollo versus Artemis, yin versus yang— the archetypal male light versus female darkness (see Campbell 152 n.87)— and the fashion in which Buffy plays with those patterns. The possibilities are invitingly various. But for now, I hope I have shown something of the richness of this text: narrative, wording, and visual imagery all unite in the *Buffy* version, or rather versions, of the monomyth. No series plays games better than *Buffy*; but at its heart is an incandescent heroism. In all the ways available to television art, *Buffy* shows us the enlightenment necessary for sacrifice, and the sacrifice necessary for enlightenment.

Chapter 3

I Think
I Can Name
Myself

Naming and Identity
in *Buffy the Vampire Slayer*[1]

I sort of happened on *Buffy the Vampire Slayer*. Actually, it was—I believe Rhonda the Immortal Waitress was really the first incarnation of it.

> Joss Whedon, on the *Biography* episode "*Buffy the Vampire Slayer*"

Like Hawthorne, Dickens, Dostoevsky, and many other great authors, Joss Whedon and his company of writers use names very consciously to advance meaning in *Buffy the Vampire Slayer*. Sometimes the names suggest meaning through sound effects and social context, as in the case of Ebenezer Scrooge or Wesley Wyndam-Pryce. Sometimes the names are directly allusive, as in the case of *Buffy*'s Cordelia—who recalls the problematically straightforward daughter in Shakespeare's *King Lear*. Very often, the names are symbolic, as in the case of Faith—Hawthorne's or Whedon's—both of whom tread an ambiguous pathway into darkness. In the very long text of *Buffy*, 144 one-hour episodes (minus commercials), there are also intratextual patterns of names that are worth investigating.[2] How many versions of William are there? Finally, and perhaps most interestingly, the series thematically investigates the act of naming as it is integrated into the storyline for certain characters. The semantics of naming presents, in philosophy, a very different face from the discussion of naming in literature or cultural studies; but there is a common feature in both: the question of essentialism. The characters who explore the nature of naming in Buffy confront that same question. In particular, Buffy, role model for independence, opposes essentialism with the idea of existential self-determination through the symbolism of naming.

Faith; Will; Adam; Eve; Angel; Grace Newman. Is this Pilgrim's Progress? Jack O'Toole; Dick Wilkins; Spike. Is this Debbie Does Dallas? Goodman, Brown; Cassandra; Cordelia. Is this World Lit I? Buffy is, of course, a rich text with many intertextual allusions; not infrequently those allusions come in the form of characters' names—some well known, some less so. The name of one of Buffy's two best friends, Xander Harris, ironically alludes to Alexander the Great: Xander, whose name of course is a curtailed form of the name of the great warrior, announces in the first regular episode of Buffy, "I laugh in the face of danger—then I hide until it goes away" ("The Witch," 1.3).

The irony is not simple, however. True, despite his later absorption of military knowledge, Xander is no great general; but as the series progresses, his bravery is displayed again and again. Another case of a name which seems a simplistic irony but is revealed to be more is that of Cordelia. In the first season, Cordelia is presented as a vain, self-centered cheerleader, so for her to be named after the faithful, loving daughter of King Lear seems little more than a joke. (She is campus royalty: her license plate announces her as Queen C.) As the series proceeds, however, Cordelia too is shown to be brave in the face of evil; and, as Mary Alice Money discusses and many fans realize, the tart-tongued cheerleader is one of the series' major truth-tellers (103). As she memorably remarks, "Tact is just not saying true stuff" ("Killed by Death," 2.18). And in her unwillingness to sweeten the truth that she tells to her loved ones, she very directly echoes Shakespeare's Cordelia—and, like that earlier Cordelia, is not always appreciated for it. Mary Alice Money also makes the connection between Riley Finn and Huck Finn, both of whom "light out for the territories" (107). A minor naming allusion comes in "Out of My Mind" (5.4), wherein we are introduced to Agents Goodman and Brown—amusing for anyone familiar with one of Hawthorne's most famous short stories, "Young Goodman Brown"; and they are associated with Riley Finn, who, like Hawthorne's main character, has trouble with moral ambiguity. The seventh season's Cassie, who predicts true future but is not believed, of course refers to classical mythology's Cassandra. Not only literature but religion provides a naming source: the fourth-season villain Adam, a Frankensteinian combination of human, demon, and machine bits, is a new creature blasphemously given the Judeo-Christian name for the first human—a hubristic connection Mary Shelley also made when she called her similarly doomed monster a "New Adam." (And of Buffy's Adam, more later.) It is worth noting that Buffy succeeds in her struggle against both Adam and Eve—the name of a character whose form the First Evil takes in Season Seven (see Chapter 6). Other Buffy critics have suggested that Adam's creator, Maggie Walsh— aka "the evil bitch monster of death," aka "Mommy"—may in her maternal dominance of a largely male military-industrial group (the Initiative) be meant to echo British Prime Minister Margaret Thatcher. Drawing from history, religion, literature, and politics, the names heighten viewers' appreciation of the characters' natures.

In addition to the well-known sources of allusion, there are more obscure connections that provide a different sort of pleasure. Steven Moore suggests that Buffy's surname alludes to eccentric vampire scholar Montague Summers. Kip Manley points out that Robin Wood, a seventh-season character who is the latest Sunnydale High principal and also that rarest of creatures, the child of a Slayer, is named after a film scholar for whom Joss Whedon has expressed admiration. Given that Principal Wood's character is at first ambiguous (good or evil?), one might argue that knowledge of the source of his name might have given an early clue to his nature (which does turn out to be good, despite an unfortunate predilection for attempting to murder Spike)—a special level of information for particularly knowledgeable and devoted viewers.[3] However, the less generally known allusions do not always have such a direct correspondence to meaning: as Nancy Holder notes, the Polgara demon mentioned in "The I in Team" (4.13) was writer David Fury's tribute to a Buffy fan who frequently posted online (Watcher's Guide 2, 228), who presumably named herself after David Eddings' 1997 Polgara the Sorceress. It seems unlikely that a direct fan-demon equivalence was intended. In other words, knowing the name source in this case does not reveal the nature of the entity. The more obscure allusions, therefore, may perhaps most often provide the pleasure of recognition for devoted viewers, while not denying to others information of major significance for the delineation of a character.

Probably much more important in terms of their resonance for the text are the more broadly symbolic names of many characters. Faith,

Will, Angel, Spike, Dawn, Tara—rarely since *Pilgrim's Progress* have so many names in a text demanded to be taken as *charactonyms*, to use the term from onomastics—as trait names, more than simple nomenclature. *Pilgrim's Progress*, of course, is allegory, while *Buffy* uses a much more open symbolism. (Please insert standard disclaimer on polysemy here.) Each of the names and characters could be explored at much greater length, but for now I will only briefly comment on some. Faith, of course, is a literary allusion as well as a symbol: one of the most famous examples of symbolic nomenclature comes in the previously mentioned "Young Goodman Brown," another narrative which contemplates the supernatural: Young Goodman Brown's young wife Faith finds her way to the side of demons and witches in the dark forest—or at least so it seems to him. At the end of the story, readers are unsure of whether or not Faith is genuinely fallen. For *Buffy*'s Faith, the doubt resides not only within viewers but also within the character: for a considerable time in the series, Faith doubts her own goodness—or believes that she is evil. She eventually finds faith in herself and a willingness to atone for wrongdoing. *Buffy* makes frequent use of foils and shadow characters; Faith is a shadow and foil for Buffy, as is Buffy's best friend Willow, often called Will. Faith and Will: if these characters were set up along a continuum of control, then Faith, with her sometimes criminal lack of control, would be on the far left and Buffy in the center. Will, with a dangerous desire for control repeated and emphasized over the years, would be on the far right—as in the episode "Something Blue" (4.9), in which Willow enacts a spell to have her "Will done." In the last episode of the series, Willow fears the lack of control needed for a world-changing spell, but finds enough trust in herself to carry it out.

Faith and Buffy both have a guardian in Angel, the ensouled vampire who sponsors Faith's redemption, who loves Buffy and wishes to atone for his past sins. While Will wants control in her relationships, Angel is forced to exert control over himself: if he ever experiences a single moment of true happiness, then by the terms of a gypsy curse, he loses his soul—as he learned when he made love with Buffy in the second season. Given his name, it is only too appropriate that the controlled Angel character can thus be identified with the superego, in opposition to the violent, sexually wild character of Spike, Buffy's other vampire lover—the id character with the phallic name (more on Spike later). The name of Buffy's sister, too, fits into the symbolic category. Since Buffy fights the forces of darkness, it is not surprising that the sister she gives her life to protect is named for light: Dawn—not just light, but more truly the borderline between night and day, a liminal place with which Buffy as a character more and more clearly comes to associate. And their friend Tara Maclay just as surely connects through her name and her nature to the power of the earth (which of course *Tara* means) and the limitations of the clay of human flesh: Tara, who comes from the country and weighs a little closer to American average than Hollywood standard, and who sometimes mothers Dawn when Buffy can't—Tara can be seen as something of an earth mother. Of course Willow, the tree, is rooted in Tara, the earth—and uprooted when Tara is lost. She is perhaps the most closely connected to nature of any of the Scoobies. And this beloved character emphasizes the fragility of the physical when she is shot and killed.

Symbolic names, charactonyms, are occasionally used to notable effect for minor characters as well. The kindly demon Clem is named for mercy, clemency. He is one of the first non-vampiric demons to become humanized for Buffy. In the humorous episode "The Zeppo" (3.13), Xander is taunted with his lack of macho status and searches for Cool. He shows up in a flashy borrowed car which all and sundry recognize as "a penis metaphor." Xander's antagonist in the episode flaunts a Bowie-knife-sized blade and sports the ridiculously appropriate name of Jack O'Toole. The name's obvious phallic reference (both surname and given name) is part of the episode's unusually self-conscious and delicately self-mocking format, in which the secondary plot is yet one more apocalypse engaged in by the other characters, while the primary plot involves Xander's gaining self-confidence. It is, not coincidentally, the episode in which Xander has sex for the first time, but the episode's climax (you should pardon the expression) is his final face-off with Jack O'Toole. As Xander says in "Beer Bad" (4.5), "Nothing can defeat the penis!"—but here Xander does, strictly by means of self-control, defeat Jack O'Toole.

A very different tone pervades the episode titled "I Only Have Eyes for You" (2.19). It takes place shortly after Buffy and Angel have made love and Angel, experiencing that one moment of true happiness, has lost his soul and reverted to the powerfully evil vampire Angelus. The plot involves a parallel to the Buffy-Angel situation: the ghosts of two doomed lovers from the 1950s—a student and a high school teacher—are possessing people in order to relive the night on which the teacher broke off the affair with the student and he shot her, then himself. Buffy, who feels she has in effect killed Angel, identifies with the high school student James: "James destroyed the one person he loved in a moment of blind passion, and that's not something you forgive. No matter why he did what he did." Cordelia:

"Okay—overidentify much." When Buffy and Angel are possessed, it is James who possesses her and the older lover, the teacher, who possesses Angel (Buffy's older lover). James/Buffy is unable to kill the vampire body, so the teacher inhabiting it is able to stay long enough to express a forgiveness which helps both James and Buffy. The teacher is named Grace Newman—her surname suggesting the rebirth (New man) that comes with forgiveness, and her given name directly expressing her function of granting spiritual grace.[4] As Buffy's mentor Giles says, "To forgive is an act of compassion ... It's not done because people deserve it; it's done because they need it."

A more recent example of a significant name for a minor character comes in the seventh season, which has as its Big Bad the First, or the First Evil (cf. Original Sin). One of the Potential Slayers whose dead form is repeatedly taken by the First Evil is named Eve. A first reaction might suggest that it is reactionary to have the First Evil identified with the character named Eve—who, in Judeo-Christian tradition, initiated the Fall of Man when she fell to the temptation of the serpent. However, it should be noted that in the *Buffy* story the First Evil *falsely* takes the place of the true Eve, just as one might say women have been falsely represented, wronged by the more recent (in the millennial scheme of things) patriarchal story of Eve. The use of the name occurs in a context overtly challenging certain religious attitudes towards women by having them espoused by the First Evil's right-hand man, Caleb—the handsome preacher who secretly attacks choir girls and always advises young women to accept the fact that they are naturally depraved—a view the series clearly represents as repugnant despite the superficial attractiveness of its proponent (see Chapter 6).

Individual names, then, often emphasize meaning in the *Buffy* text. Over the course of the series' seven years, however, many close readers of the series have noted a pattern involving multiple names: Spike's name as recorded in the archives of the Watchers' Council is William the Bloody; his name as a human was William; Buffy's best female friend is called Will; Angel's name as a human was Liam (See *Angel*, "The Prodigal" 1.15). Three major characters, then, all share forms of the name William. Many have also noted parallels between Spike/William and Will: as Madeleine St. Romaine says, "They are both trying to reinvent themselves as no longer geeky, sensitive outcasts"; and she asks, "So is Spike Willow's double or her shadow or the embodiment of her desire for Buffy?" This parallel does not, however, apply to the never-geeky Angel/Liam—though of course he too desires Buffy. The *Buffyverse Onomasticon* (a site devoted to *Buffy* names) notes that William means "a willing protector"; this meaning, though it is not general knowledge, could be said to apply at some points in the plot to Spike, Angel, and Willow. It can hardly, however, be said to apply to the recurring character of Willy the Snitch, the operator of the bar variously called Willy's Place and The Alibi Room; Willy is, in multiple senses, a diminished form of William. The notable episode "Lie to Me" (2.7) contains another significant William—Billy Fordham, aka "Ford," Buffy's old friend from LA, her fifth-grade crush, and a human who is willing to give her to the vampires in order to be released from terminal illness by being made a vampire himself.[5]

"Lie to Me" is an early declaration of Buffy's rejection of simple black and white morality (see Tanya Krzywinska on Manichaeanism in *Fighting the Forces*): the title refers to the closing scene, in which Buffy, having just staked Billy Fordham, asks Giles to lie to her about the world. His lie is "It's terribly simple: the good guys are always stalwart and true, and the bad guys are easily distinguished by their pointy horns or black hats." This passage—a well-known one for *Buffy* readers—applies not only to Billy Fordham, but also to the overall William-Will-Liam-Willy naming pattern. I would argue that one effect of the pattern is to remind viewers, on some level, of the connections between the bad guys and the good guys—and the fact that any of us could cross that line.[6] Billy Fordham, as the episode makes clear, is not a simple black-hat bad guy. Willy the Snitch will happily turn Buffy over to a Slayer-hating Spike ("What's My Line?" Part 2, 2.10) but also sincerely wish her a merry Christmas ("Amends," 3.10). And Spike himself, Angel, and Willow are perhaps the most notable examples in the Buffyverse of characters who are capable of memorable good or vicious evil. The name William is perhaps above all, in this culture, a *commonplace* name, as ordinary a name as Sam, or Joe: so the series seems to suggest that any ordinary person has within the power of good or evil.

This implication is consistent with the last element of naming I wish to focus on in the Buffyverse, and the one to which I refer in the title of this chapter. Philosophers who discuss the semantics of naming debate the virtues of ostension (i.e., naming as equivalent to pointing) vs. description (e.g. Bolton, esp. 150–1) or the usefulness of so-called rigid designators. Underlying much of the debate, however, is the question of essentialism, posed perhaps most notably by Saul Kripke in *Naming and Necessity*. Writers such as Cynthia J. Bolton and D. S. Shwayder, on the other hand, resist entering what Shwayder calls "the *cul-de-sac* of essences" (452). To grossly oversimplify: is naming based on essence or relation? Essence or existence? If one may take a long mental stride—or to use the language of the Buffyverse, step into another dimension—the question of essentialism in relation to naming appears in cultural studies and literature as well. From Rumpelstiltskin to Ursula Le Guin, knowing someone's true name can give power over that someone (see especially the *Earthsea* trilogy), whether dwarf or sorcerer, dragon or human. The implication is that, in folk tale or fantasy, one magically connects with the true being through the true name. As Le Guin says in *The Language of the Night*, "to know the name of ... a character is to know ... the person" (46; and on naming in Le Guin, see John Algeo). Le Guin is also, however, the author of the well-known story "She Unnames Them," in which a female frees a world of beings by releasing them from their names.

Le Guin's main character from "She Unnames Them" can be seen as a sort of anti-Adam. Those familiar with Judeo-Christian scriptures will recall that Adam, as the first human steward of the world, was given the job of naming all the creatures. And here we reconnect with the *Buffy* story. Of all the many-meaningful episodes of *Buffy*, perhaps the most richly resonant is the finale of the fourth season, the almost all-dream episode "Restless" (4.22). In Chapter 10, I compare its technique to that of T. S. Eliot in *The Waste Land* because of, among other things, its hyper-allusiveness; and I also note that it serves, among other things, as a predictor for many elements of the series yet to come. (In fact, the episode closes with the statement to Buffy, "You think you know what you are—what's to come—you haven't even begun.") Each of the four acts of the teleplay comprises a dream by one of the four main characters. In Buffy's dream, in one section she sees her current all-American hero boyfriend Riley. Riley (identified as a dress-up cowboy in Willow's earlier dream) is Joe Normal grad student to the world, but secretly an officer in the demon-fighting experimental, governmental, scientific-military unit called the Initiative. In Buffy's dream, Riley appears with a monstrous creation of the Initiative—Adam, the Frankensteinian monster described earlier; but Adam here, for the only time, appears in completely human face. Riley tells Buffy, "We're drawing up a plan for world domination" and Buffy asks, "World domination—is that a good?" Riley replies, "Baby, we're the government—it's what we do." In the background we see a blurry, dark image that we later learn is the First Slayer—very separate from Riley and Adam's world; also part of the scene is a gun close to Riley's hand. He says, "Buffy, we've got important work to do. [The gun image is shown here.] Lot of filing, giving things names." Buffy turns to Adam and asks him, "What was yours?" He replies, "Before Adam? Not a man among us can remember."

Buffy has asked him for the name he bore before he was changed by the Initiative, the military-industrial complex, and he is unable to recall it. This inability can of course be interpreted as a loss of human identity. But it can also suggest the inability to recall what the world was like before the current forces in power controlled it—before the military-industrial, patriarchal way was pervasive. "Before Adam" means, among other things, before the first person of the Judeo-Christian world—before that world was categorized, filed, named by Adam. Z. J. Playdon connects Buffy to pre-biblical, female-centered mythology (Inanna, Ereshkigal) that most are unfamiliar with—or, in Adam's words, "not a man among us can remember." In this scene Buffy turns from Riley and Adam's filing and naming as inadequate: when an intercom alarm warns, "The demons have escaped," Riley cogently responds by saying, "We better make a fort," and Adam adds, "I'll get some pillows." Clearly Buffy in her dream is indicating that their method of dealing with the world is unsuccessful. And the demons they plan to fight may be within: just before the intercom announcement that demons have escaped, an interchange between Adam and Buffy has suggested that they may be demonic—something that Buffy subconsciously, in her dream, fears at this point and learns three years later to be partly true ("Get It Done," 7.15; and see Chapter 6). The Riley way of dealing with the world—filing, naming by the Man (or the first Man, Adam)—does not really work either for the world at large ("world domination") or for the individual. Buffy, as she tells the men, has weapons of her own; and she turns to go on her own quest for self into her dream of the desert, from which she chooses to awaken.

Not only the last dream in "Restless" but also the first dream, Willow's, focuses on naming and the nature of self. Chapters 2 and 10 both discuss this scene of the two lovers, Willow and Tara, alone in Tara's red-curtained, womb-like room. Willow's dream starts with Tara's saying, "I think it's strange—I mean I think we should worry—that we haven't found her name yet." As Jes Battis points out, when Willow replies "Miss Kitty?" she provides one possible referent, the cat—but Battis argues that the course of the dream suggests that Willow herself is seeking her name. I also believe that Willow is seeking herself—and furthermore suggest that the reference to the cat may indicate the Slayer as well (who is figured as a cat in the dream from "Graduation Day," Part 2, 3.22). Thus I would argue that this opening dream implies that both Buffy and Willow (and, for that matter, Xander) are searching for their identities. Buffy's dream later in the episode suggests that true identity is not to be found in established forms, in names bestowed by others. Or to put it another way, the Adamic attempt to trap an essence denies the existential freedom of growth.

A seventh-season episode titled "Selfless" (7.5) explores the idea of naming and self through the character of Anya. "Selfless" is Anya's origins episode. Faithful watchers of *Buffy* have first seen Anya appear in Season Three as a vengeance demon who then becomes trapped in the incarnation of a teenager and in later episodes goes to the prom with Xander. Like Willow's lover Tara, Xander's lover Anya becomes part of the Scooby gang, remaining connected even after she is left at the altar by Xander. The fifth-season episode "Triangle" (5.11) reveals that Anya began her thousand-year career as a demon after using a magic spell to turn Olaf, her unfaithful beloved, into a giant troll. Now in "Selfless" we see the pre-vengeance Anya: a naïve young woman who wants to selflessly give away her excess bunnies (yes, bunnies) to the other townsfolk—not for money but for "good will" and a "sense of accomplishment"—an idea that provokes laughter in Olaf and an attitude that results in the townsfolk saying "perhaps you should take your furs and your literal interpretations to the other side of the river."

Anya's friend the vengeance demon Halfrek, or Hallie, says in a sixth-season episode that she prefers the term "justice demon." It is a joke about politically correct terminology, but the righteous pre-demonic Anya gives a glimpse of the reason the two might actually feel this way. Even after being made a demon, Anya seems to retain some assumptions that suggest a naïve reliance on naïve virtue. To Hallie in 1905, speaking of the coming Russian Revolution, Anya says (a bit redundantly), "The workers will overthrow absolutism and lead the proletariat to a victorious communist revolution resulting in socioeconomic paradise on earth. It's common sense, really." (Viewers' knowledge of Anya's later embrace of capitalism as well as historical knowledge of the results of communism cast this remark into irony.) Her career as a vengeance demon begins when Olaf is unfaithful to her and lies about it. "What did he do?" asks the demon D'Hoffryn. "A bar matron," answers Anya.

In this early existence, we see, as in a foreign film, the words on screen and learn that her original name is A-U-D. Had one not seen the writing, merely hearing the word as the actress pronounces it might lead one to think her name is O-D-D, fittingly enough for the character. But it is worth remembering that her oddity started in innocence and good will (distorted by a choice to control). In the first act, Olaf, in AD 880, repeatedly uses her name, and we cut from his saying, "Fear not, sweet Aud. You will always be my beautiful girl," to a shot of the Anya of 2002 washing blood from her hands and looking at her bloody face in a mirror. She has finally killed again as a vengeance demon. We hear a voice from the upcoming scene before the visual cut is made; as Anya looks in the mirror, Spike's voice says, "I don't trust what I see anymore."[7] The episode continues to move back and forth from the past to the present, and we see the first meeting between Anya, or Aud, and the leader of the vengeance demons (lord of Arashmahar), D'Hoffryn:

Anya:	I am Aud.
D'Hoffryn:	Are you? I'm afraid you don't see your true self. You are Anyanka. I'm a patron of a family of sorts. We're vengeance demons. … I get the feeling that your talents are not fully appreciated here, Anyanka. We'd like you to join us.
Anya:	Why do you keep calling me that? My name is Aud.
D'Hoffryn:	Perhaps. But Anyanka is who you are.

Aud takes the name he gives her; later in the episode she declares, "Vengeance is what I am." When she kills again at the start of the episode—a house full of cruel frat boys—Hallie declares, "Anyanka is back to her old self again."

In the intervening time she had tried on another self, again indicated by a choice of name: Anya chooses to be Mrs. Xander Harris. I still remember being briefly confused the first time I heard someone ask a young woman if she had come to college to get her MRS degree. One should not oversimplify the relationship between Xander and Anya, but in the "Selfless" episode that MRS aspect is emphasized—most notably through a flashback to the time of the famous sixth-season musical episode "Once More, with Feeling" (6.7). This musical scene in "Selfless" is interpolated into a fight scene between Buffy and Anya; because Anya has begun to kill again, Buffy has reluctantly come to kill her. It should be remembered that the device in "Once More, with Feeling" is that the characters are magically forced to sing their true feelings—in effect, they are given song soliloquies. Now in "Selfless" Anya sings about identifying herself with the role of Xander's wife. She starts by singing his name: "Mr. Xander Harris—that's what he is to the world outside. That's the name he carries with pride. I'm just lately Anya—not very much to the world I know. All these years with nothing to show." "Who am I?" she asks, and answers, "I'm the missus—I'll be his missus—Mrs. Anya Christina Emanuella Jenkins Harris"—or, as she says later in the song, "Mrs. Anya lameass made-up maiden name Harris." The made-up names of this ex-demon are in part flagrantly religious—Christina, from Christ, and Emanuella, God with us, another name for Christ; but forgiveness is not Anya's middle name. Also, of course, even more obviously, Anya is taking the not-at-all-unusual female path of identifying herself through the name of her man. In her June Cleaverish dress, for the climax of the song she sings "Here comes the bride"—bursting through the outer doors to the balcony to appear clothed in her wedding gown. Then she claims the role over and over: "I'll be his missus—I will be his missus—I will be—" and in the middle of the sentence and in the middle of the high note, we cut to the sight of Anya, silent, head fallen forward, a sword pinning her through the heart.

Anya has, of course, repeatedly suffered a sword through the heart, whether from Olaf or Xander. Identifying herself with either of them has not worked. Neither has her role as a vengeance demon; in fact, the parallel between marriage and prostitution that some sociologists and activists point out is made through the role of D'Hoffryn, who has seemed to be something of a father figure. The "patron" of the vengeance demons (who has also invited Willow to join the group) is polite, perceptive, and patriarchal. He is also, in effect, a pimp: when he returns during the fight scene, he tells Anya, "I've got plenty of girls. There will always be vengeance demons." He says this immediately after having killed Hallie because of Anya's wish to break away from vengeance. The kindly, courteous male in charge is willing to terrorize in order to keep his "girls" in line. And Anya's choice to change is framed by her naming. When Willow and D'Hoffryn earlier in the episode discuss Anya's future, Will refers to her as Anya while D'Hoffryn persistently refers to her as Anyanka. In the final fight scene (and one might note that *Buffy* makes it a practice to avoid oversimplifying even its villains), D'Hoffryn says, "I'm not sure if anyone's bothered to find out what Anyanka herself really wants." Xander interrupts, "Her name is Anya." D'Hoffryn replies, "Actually—funny historical sidebar—her original name was"—and Anya says, "*I want to take it back.*" In the continuing context of the scene, it becomes clear that Anya selflessly wants to take back the vengeance wish that killed all the young men—even though she knows that the price is the life and soul of a vengeance demon, presumably her own. But the "it" in "I want to take it back," given the structure of the lines, could also refer to taking back her original name, reclaiming her original self. When Xander tries to help, she says, "I'm not even sure there's a me to help." *Buffy*'s executive producer Marti Noxon has said that one possible interpretation of Buffy's self-sacrificing fifth-season death to save the world is that it is also suicide; and here, a parallel can be made with Anya's willingness to sacrifice herself to save a dozen young men—selfless, and/or suicidal. But once again the young woman is required by the series to go on living, required to find or create her own name. The name Anya, the name she continues to go by, is a variant she herself chose, and which she now inhabits/incarnates. She does not create herself out of whole cloth, but neither does she succumb to the urge to lose herself in Xander and marriage, or D'Hoffryn and his stable of girls (or—to see the demonic relationship as parallel to something which the series often endorses—in her job). As the semanticists might say, she will establish the descriptors. She ends the episode by choosing to walk away alone.

Buffy does not suggest, however, that such a struggle is limited to women. One of the most notable examples of naming and the reclamation of self in the series is the memorable character Spike. I have elsewhere discussed Spike's unusual placement in the series' moral cartography. While Anya is an ex-demon and Angel is a vampire who has been given a soul, Spike, until the last episode of the sixth season, is a soulless vampire who, though he starts out gleefully evil, nonetheless ends up doing good. Angel, as an ensouled vampire, capable of good, is an important part of the Buffyverse's complication of morality, but the necessity for possession of a soul suggests an essentialist definition of good. Spike carries the question, and his quest, into existential territory: even before he has a soul, he chooses repeatedly to act for the good. And he finally gains a soul through his own choice, through his own action (see Chapters 2 and 5). There is still far more to be said on the subject, and I certainly cannot say it all here. For now I wish to concentrate on the correlation of Spike's anti-essentialist nature and his naming patterns.

We first meet Spike in an early second-season episode, "School Hard" (2.3). Throughout the episode, others repeatedly ask his name. "Who are you?" asks high school hellion Sheila. "Who do you want me to be?" Spike responds. From the beginning, his predilection for role-playing and performance is hinted at by his naming patterns. Spike, as many observers have noted, performs himself. In this, his first episode, we already learn that he has more than one name. He wears not only the "unorthodox" name Spike, but also, as Giles reports, is "known as William the Bloody. Earned his nickname by torturing his victims with railroad spikes." When Buffy asks Spike the question of the episode—"Who are you?"—he answers, "You find out Saturday." "What happens on Saturday?" she replies. "I kill you." For her, he claims no name but death. The fifth season's Big Bad, Glory, is introduced as a being who cannot be named—a hell god who does not relate on a human level. In the second season, Buffy and her cadre of supporters will not allow Spike to claim the status of nameless power, of course, and he is forced into a more and more complex, more and more human relationship with her and them.

In the well-known and widely admired fifth-season episode "Fool for Love"—and the title does refer to Spike—we finally see the human version of Spike (5.7). We learn that, in 1880, alive, he was a sentimental poet who lived with his mother and was rejected by a haughty woman. We also learn that the moniker of William the Bloody was bestowed before his death: As a party-going acquaintance says, "They call him William the Bloody because of his bloody awful poetry." Another partygoer replies within earshot of William, "I'd rather have a railroad spike through my head than listen to that awful stuff." The common social cruelty is such that some may find it satisfying to contemplate the presumably predictive nature of the partygoer's complaint: as we soon learn, this is the night that William becomes a vampire. And later in the episode, still in 1880, he has already taken on not only new, rougher clothes and a new, rougher accent, but also a new name. Literally strangled by his sire's sire Angelus, he chokes out, "It's Spike now. You'd do well to remember it, mate." Spike is the name of his own choosing: it is phallic, it is violent, and it is clearly embedded in response to the mockery of the shy young poet. When Buffy, after she and Spike have engaged in a torrid affair in the sixth season, breaks off their sexual relationship, she calls him William—an implicit recognition of his humanity, even before he has regained his soul. In spite of the importance of their relationship to him, however, when he does regain his soul— and it is his soul, William's soul—Spike still returns to the name he has himself chosen. And perhaps this is as good a place as any to note that Joss Whedon was born with the ordinary-guy name of Joe, and chose legally to rename himself Joss (Havens 17)—an interesting parallel to William/ Spike. After a passage through months of madness, Spike also reclaims his signature black leather coat. Both the name and the coat are part of his performance of himself, and here, performance represents choice. Spike is not only an anti-hero, but an anti-essentialist. And the complexity of his self-representation—through clothing and name—reflects the complexity of his self-creation. Spike's regaining his soul and his sanity does not mean a simple return to the name or the state of William—a state of innocence, but not necessarily a state of grace. Spike is a work in progress.

It is, perhaps, not surprising, then, that in the sixth-season blueprint episode "Tabula Rasa" (6.8), in which all the main characters suffer magic-induced amnesia, Spike and Buffy are the only ones who do not operate under their usual names. I will pause for a moment to note that the term "blueprint episode" derives from a discussion of the Buffyology list: we have noted that there are a variety of episodes which serve as predictors of future episodes, blueprints for events to come—and, in a sense, representations in small of relationships and patterns which stretch through the series. I have noted before that "Restless" is such an episode; one might also argue for "Fear, Itself" (4.4); and certainly "Tabula Rasa" fits the category. "Monsters are real. Do we know this?" asks Buffy. In their amnesia, they rediscover their situation and explore their natures. Through driver's licenses, a necklace, Magic Box store documents, and college id's, most of them discover their names. Buffy and Spike's exploration of self, however, is highlighted by the fact that, unlike the others, they do not discover their given names. Spike has arrived at the shop wearing a three-piece suit that recalls the one he wore in "Restless" in Xander's dream, in which Rupert Giles announced that Spike was like a son to him; and here in "Tabula Rasa" the characters decide that they are father and son. Giles is also an appropriate father figure for Spike in his naming patterns: the younger, wilder Rupert was called Ripper—as opposed to the tweed-clad Rupert—a mirror reversal of the William–Spike progression.

Spike in the opening of the episode is disguising himself to avoid a gambling debt—and thus, when they awaken literally and metaphorically in the dark, his unrecognized disguise emphasizes the way he has incorporated role-playing into his nature. He discovers in the suit a tag that declares it was "made with care for Randy." In one sense the name is ludicrously inappropriate, because of its mildness; but of course the word "randy" has another implication, and Spike complains to his supposed father Giles, "Why didn't you just call me Horny Giles or Desperate For A Shag Giles?" Given the fact that the episode after "Tabula Rasa" is "Smashed" (6.9), in which Buffy and Spike first have sex, the name seems more than appropriate. One might argue that the name Randy reiterates the sexual implications of the name Spike—without the violence of the latter. Spike's three-piece suit leads the others to see him as mild-mannered—as Buffy says, no one in the group looks all "hatchety murdery"—though later in the episode another fact we and he discover is that he is brave enough to risk his life alongside Buffy, even not knowing of his vampire strength; and he is the one she calls on to do so.

In the middle of the episode, when attacking vampires demand to be given "Spike," Spike-as-Randy suggests, and the other characters accept, that the vampires are demanding to be given wooden stakes. (The episode, written by Rebecca Rand Kirshner, is a wonderful example of the series' writers' ability to combine the humorous with the serious.) Thus the name Spike, as well as being phallic and generally violent, is here identified with Buffy's weapon of choice. Furthermore, Spike's black leather coat is a trophy he has taken from the second Slayer he killed. Thus, like his name, it can be seen not only as a sign of violence and power, but also of his associating himself with, absorbing the qualities of his opponent, a vampire Slayer, a woman of power. Like Buffy, Spike foils gender expectations. He puts aside the coat temporarily as he undergoes the change from soulless to ensouled, but reclaims it late in the seventh season. In doing so, he acknowledges the darker parts of his history and himself. Also late in the seventh season, in the fight against the First Evil, Buffy makes him her weapon, her stake: she refuses to reject him when he is manipulated by the First Evil; she gives him back his ability to fight humans and thus leads him to the moment when he is able to declare that he has free will—and choose *not* to kill a human who has almost killed him. If he is Buffy's weapon, he is a weapon with a will.

While Spike in "Tabula Rasa" steps into a name not his own, Buffy has no name at all. Her sister Dawn asks, "So you don't have a name?" Buffy replies, "Of course I do. I just don't happen to know it. [Tara's voice at the end of "Restless" has said, "You think you know what you are ... You haven't even begun." Buffy is still discovering herself. Here, in "Tabula Rasa," her sister offers to help.]" Dawn: "You want me to name you?" Buffy: "Oh, that's sweet—but I think I can name myself. I'll name me—Joan." When Dawn challenges this name as dull-sounding, Buffy asserts, "I feel like a Joan." The most famous Joan, of course, is Joan of Arc. When Buffy chooses her name, chooses the self to be, she chooses the name of a woman warrior who dies for her cause. In an earlier *Buffy* episode, the question is asked, "Who died and made her the boss?" Here, Buffy/Joan says, "I think I know why Joan's the boss." In the course of defending "Randy" from an attacking vampire, Buffy/Joan rediscovers her power: "I'm a superhero or something." After "Randy" bravely joins her in the fight, he announces, "I'm a superhero too!"—though they soon learn his strength is vampiric.

Buffy's choice to be Joan shows the distance she has come from, for example, the summer of 1999, when she ran away from home after killing Angel and began calling herself "Anne." (One might incidentally note that the name Anya is a variant of Anne—a variant of the name for an ordinary girl, or someone seeking normality.) It is Buffy Summers' middle name, and her choice of it suggests not only her wish for normality but also her wish to hide within herself and lose her pain. She becomes a waitress and avoids conflict even to the extent of refraining from objection when a customer slaps her on the behind. In calling the episode "Anne" (3.1), Whedon expresses Buffy's attempt to avoid heroism; whereas in "Tabula Rasa," when the characters' memories are blank slates, Buffy chooses not only heroism but also leadership: she is not only the muscle, but the one who plans and gives orders, though all of the Scoobies participate. Buffy's role in "Anne" is made clearer by contrast with the victim she helps—and helps move past victimization. Buffy is called on by someone who recognizes her: and recognizing Buffy means recognizing someone who will help others. The other in this case is a young woman who knew Buffy in Sunnydale, who lives on the street and has moved not only from place to place but also from name to name: Chanterelle, Lily, Sister Sunshine.

Spike's mercurial nature expresses itself in changes of name that suggest strength and choice: as Drusilla says just before she turns him, "your wealth lies ... in the spirit and imagination," and he imagines Spike—first in place of and later in addition to William. In contrast, Lily/Chanterelle seems to take on names by absorption of the attitude of those through whom she is trying to survive—whether it is a club of vampire worshippers (for whom she calls herself Chanterelle in "Lie to Me"), a traveling preacher (Sister Sunshine, "Anne"), or a boyfriend (Lily). Her request at the end of the episode to call herself "Anne" elevates her to the level of the everyday (and later, in the *Angel* series, we see that an everyday person can achieve a kind of heroism, as this same "Anne" runs a shelter).

The strength needed for the everyday claiming of self is made clear in the episode "Anne" by the demons who prey on the street people. They are taken to a hell of unending labor where claiming a name results in a blow; where the only acceptable answer to the question "Who are you?" is "I'm no one." When the FX channel broadcast rerun episodes of *Buffy*, a frequent promotional clip was the moment in "Anne" when Buffy reclaims her name, reclaims her self: "I'm Buffy—the Vampire Slayer. And you are?" In the battle that follows, she saves not only the leaderless lost souls, but also herself.

From the series' beginning, the name "Buffy" has stood out. The *Buffyverse Onomasticon* points out that Buffy can be considered a shortened form of the name Elizabeth (and the name Elizabeth, as in good Queen Bess, does, like Joan, have a heritage of power); but it seems unlikely that most viewers connect the name Buffy with Elizabeth. In common cultural currency, Buffy suggests an upper-middle-class girl who has few material problems in life. The dissonance in its joining with the term "the Vampire Slayer" makes for humor, of course; but it is also a witty defiance of stereotype. It is clear from the first episode that Buffy herself is not mocked but admired. As the third-season episode "Earshot" (3.18) declares, everyone—from popular cheerleader to excluded nerd—lives with pain. Claiming a self is always an act of heroism. Buffy's last name also suggests the heroic. As Chapter 2 explains, like the character Esther Summerson in Dickens's *Bleak House*, Buffy's surname connects her with the Persephone myth—the female who descends to hell, and whose reemergence brings summer and growth—with the distinction that Esther and Buffy, unlike Persephone, choose to enter the depths. (I'll also briefly note that in the first episode of Angel's own series, he establishes his power by defeating a vampire named Russell Winters.) So Buffy's last name suggests mythic power, while her first name suggests the ordinary, even silly person in whom that power can reside.

In the fifth-season episode "No Place Like Home" (5.5), the Scooby Gang prepare to face the biggest bad they have ever confronted—the one which will leave Buffy dead and buried. Though they come to know this hellgod as Glory (or Glorificus), in this episode they recognize her ineffable power when they discover that she is "That Which Cannot Be Named." In contrast, in the same episode, when Buffy wistfully asks her mom if she ever had a nickname, her mother tells her that she was "always just Buffy." The recognition of human limitation is central to this series, as James South, Stephanie Zacharek, David Lavery and I discussed in a 2003 PopPolitics roundtable. Fantasy though it is, *Buffy* does not recommend unattainable transcendence;[8] though the series recognizes the longing for it, it is not about the infinite unnamable. We must live in our single selves, and our free will is represented in the choice of the name we claim, the self we inhabit. Whether the name is accepted or created, this series repeatedly equates naming with existential choice. And in a series with characters like Faith, Angel, Dawn, and Will, perhaps the most significant symbolism is that the given name of its greatest hero is irreducibly human.

In a fourth-season episode of *Angel*, a character which seems ennobling and beautiful but is actually what might be called a demon of control has the following conversation with the Willow-like series regular Fred, who is under the demonic spell:

Fred: You don't have a name. ... I can't imagine one word,

> you know, summing you up. I mean, you're a superior being. Shouldn't you... Don't you want to choose it yourself?

Beautiful Evil Being Later Known as Jasmine:
> No one born to this earth can choose their own name.

Here again we have the issue of naming as a representation of identity. The demon's view should not be automatically dismissed; as Anya says in a seventh-season *Buffy*, "I told the truth all the time when I was a demon"; the devil can quote scripture. But does this mean that Spike is really William? That would be far too simple an answer.

Jasmine, of course, is not her true name; when she begins to take over the world, she can only be stopped when Angel, having discovered her true name at great cost, binds her with it. This storyline seems on the surface to represent the essentialist use of naming, and to follow the earlier Le Guin *Earthsea* representation of naming. But in *The Other Wind*, Le Guin's 2001 *Earthsea* sequel, her hero Ged/Sparrowhawk speaks to Alder about Alder's dead wife:

> "We who have true names keep them. When we die, it's our use-name that is forgotten. ... This is a mystery to the learned, I can tell you, but as well as we understand it, a true name is a word in the True Speech. That's why only one with the gift can know a child's name and give it. And the name binds the being—alive or dead. All the art of the Summoner lies in that. ... Yet when the master summoned your wife to come by her true name, she didn't come to him. You called her by her use name, Lily, and she came to you. ... I do not understand it. All I know is that it is changing. It is all changing." There was no fear in his voice, only fierce exultation (44–46).

Mary Alice Money (citing Golden and Holder) argues that in the Buffyverse, the ability to change is the mark of being human (99, 102). And Buffy tells Spike in Season Seven that he is alive because she saw him change. While a name may trap and bind someone with an inhumanly unchanging self, a being who chooses a self may also choose a name; and the symbolism is commutative, it works both ways.

Buffy, when she comes to herself, does not keep the name Joan—does not keep the name of the woman warrior who dies for the people; does not follow the Elisabeth Bronfen pattern of the death of the woman required for her civilization, but instead lives on. As Buffy's mother says, she is "always just Buffy." But in another, very important, sense, she *has* named herself: the character she has become has changed the meaning of the name, both within and outside of the text. The name "Buffy" does not mean today what it meant the night before the series began. So Buffy has in effect chosen her own name. Self-determination can exist within human limits. And in that sense, all of us can name ourselves.

Chapter 4

When Harry Met Buffy

Buffy Summers, Harry Potter, and Heroism[1]

A young person who has suffered parental loss moves to a new location and enters a new school, at the same time plunging into a world of magic and danger. This young person is forced to accept a role as a uniquely powerful challenger of dark forces, but is aided by an older advisor and both a male and a female friend. Humiliated in the everyday world, the young hero nonetheless grows stronger year by year fighting the dark forces in the hidden world of magic.

In 1997, the first book of the Harry Potter series was published. In 1997, the first episode of *Buffy the Vampire Slayer* was broadcast. As fans of the books and the show will realize, the narrative summary just given applies to both Buffy and Harry. The phenomenally successful Harry Potter books by J. K. Rowling and the highly admired Joss Whedon television series are worth analyzing in tandem for the many qualities the two share. Both provide us with heroes in some ways quite traditional: as Joan Acocella says, Harry Potter follows Vladimir Propp's 1928 *Morphology of the Folk Tale*, and part of the continuing story of Buffy Summers follows Joseph Campbell's chart of the hero's journey and return (see Chapter 2). Buffy and Harry also provide us with heroes who are famous in one realm (as the Vampire Slayer and the repeller of the wicked wizard Voldemort, respectively) and who, more like Clark Kent than Cinderella, must continue to endure everyday humiliation in the workaday world: he is threatened with expulsion, she actually is expelled. Both texts incorporate social problems symbolically: in *Buffy*, for example, internet predators are actually demons; in Harry Potter, racism is transmuted to a conflict between Muggle and non-Muggle (those without magical ancestry and those with). Both Buffy and Harry have shadow figures with whom to grapple, antagonists who bear striking similarities to the heroes: Harry's Voldemort and Buffy's Faith.[2] Buffy and Harry both live in worlds where most people do not recognize the existence of magic and its supernatural dangers: in both these texts the implication is that our world today is much more dangerous than we want to know, and Buffy and Harry are heroes in part because they have confronted that fact. But they do not confront it alone. Harry and Buffy are both heroes for whom friendship is crucial: Buffy survives in part because of her "Scooby Gang" of friends, and Harry depends on schoolmates Ron and Hermione. Perhaps this is the most important commonality for a hero of our technologically connected but socially strained time.

Both stories open with an annunciation of heroism. In the first Harry Potter book, *Harry Potter and the Sorcerer's Stone* (or, in the UK, ... *the Philosopher's Stone*), Harry is living very unhappily with his obsessively normal aunt, uncle, and wicked-stepsister-style cousin Dudley, all of whom consider Harry odd and unlovable: they force him to wear hand-me-downs from the grossly overweight Dudley and make him sleep in a cupboard under the stairs. His parents were killed when he was an infant; only on his eleventh birthday is he told of his magical heritage. The half-giant Hagrid, gamekeeper for Hogwarts School of Witchcraft and Wizardry, comes to fetch Harry to attend the school and in the process informs him that Harry is the only person ever to have survived a death curse from the tyrannical dark wizard Voldemort, whom most witches and wizards fear to name aloud. Though his parents were killed, the infant Harry somehow repelled the curse so that it rebounded upon Voldemort who, crushed, went into hiding. Thus Harry, who in the regular world does not even get a birthday cake, is famous in the magic world, difficult though he finds this to believe. The heroine of the first episode of *Buffy the Vampire Slayer* too is about to enter a new school—in this case, Sunnydale High: normal on the surface, but actually, as she soon learns, situated on a Hellmouth, which attracts a wide variety of dangerous magical creatures. Buffy has already (in the 1992 movie of the same name) had her initial encounter with the supernatural, but she is now trying to forget it and start a new life. Though neither of her parents is dead at this point, she has lost one through divorce; and the other, as it turns out, seems imperviously ignorant of the dangers Buffy faces (as so many parents are these days). Buffy has also lost her social status as high school cheerleader, May Queen, etc., because of the disruptions caused by the magic world (and for magic disruptions we may read teen problems). She wishes to regain normality in her new school. Sunnydale High has no gamekeeper to tell her she's different, but it does have a librarian, Rupert Giles. He announces that he's her new Watcher, her advisor, and that she must take up her sacred duties as the one girl in all the world who can fight the vampires, the demons, and the forces of darkness.

Many critics have commented on the realism to be found in Buffy's depiction of high school social relationships; similarly, many have commented on the realism of school life in Harry Potter. Their audiences relate to Buffy and Harry in part because they both long so desperately to be accepted. Yet neither of them is willing to go over to the social dark side, as two school opponents make clear early on. In the two-part opening ("Welcome to the Hellmouth", 1.1, and "The Harvest", 1.2), Buffy is helped out by Sunnydale High's social queen Cordelia Chase, who gives Buffy an oral quiz to determine her "coolness quotient" and finds her acceptable at first. When they encounter the shy, smart redhead Willow Rosenberg, however, the wealthy Cordelia shows her social colors as she mocks Willow's unfashionable clothes for their "softer side of Sears" look, and warns Buffy, "You want to fit in here, the first rule is know your losers. Once you can identify them all by sight, they're a lot easier to avoid." The next scene, however, shows Buffy approaching Willow, and Cordelia subsequently comments on Buffy's "downward mobility." By the end of "The Harvest," Cordelia is warning others about Buffy.

In Harry Potter's world, a similar function is performed by Draco Malfoy. Harry and Draco encounter each other at a wizards' robing shop, and Draco seems condescendingly willing to accept Harry as an unnamed new boy. On his way to Hogwarts, Harry encounters the Weasleys, a poor but friendly clan of redheads who help him board the train to school. As he is making friends with Ron Weasley, another eleven-year-old entering Hogwarts, they are intruded upon by the wealthy Draco, who will be in their class as well, and who wants to give the famous Harry Potter some advice: "You'll soon find out some wizarding families are much better than others, Potter. You don't want to go making friends with the wrong sort. I can help you there." But, like Buffy, Harry refuses social patronage: "'I think I can tell who the wrong sort are for myself, thanks,' [Harry] said coolly" (Sorcerer's Stone, 109), and thus begins a feud that lasts for years. Draco, whose name means dragon, and queen Cordelia show that Harry and Buffy fight social dragons, not just physical ones.

In that fight, they are soon joined not only by their redheaded friends Willow Rosenberg and Ron Weasley (WR and RW),[3] but also by one other best friend apiece. Tanya Krzywinska (189) has noted that Buffy's friend Willow can be paralleled to Harry's friend Hermione Granger because they are both bookworms and witches: although her parents are so non-magical as to be dentists, Hermione has been identified as magical and so is now studying as a witch at Hogwarts, in the same class with Harry and Ron— and she is the best student in their grade. So too is the brilliant Willow, who starts the series as non-magical but later studies magic and becomes a witch. Willow and Hermione both aid their heroic friends with their schoolwork and supply helpful information for fighting evil—Hermione through her exceptional knowledge of spells and Willow first through her exceptional skills with a computer, and later through spells (an equation of technology and magic which deserves fuller exploration).[4]

Buffy's other best friend is Xander Harris. As Willow's and Hermione's roles correlate, so too do those of Xander Harris and Ron Weasley. Like Ron, Xander comes from a less affluent background; Cordelia mocks his parents for their lack of money. Like Ron, Xander feels that he is ignored and slighted in school. Although Ron is a wizard, in his own world he is nothing special; neither Ron nor Xander perceives himself as having special powers. As Cordelia says to Xander, "It must be hard when all your friends have, like, superpowers. Slayer, werewolves, witches, vampires, and you're like this little nothing. You must feel like Jimmy Olsen" ("The Zeppo," 3.13). Or as Hermione says to Harry on a rare occasion when Ron and Harry are angry at each other, "… you're really famous—[Ron's] always shunted to one side whenever people see you, and he puts up with it" (Goblet of Fire, 290). Their lack of special gifts accentuates the loyalty and bravery that Ron and Xander each offers as a friend to a character frequently placed in abnormal danger.

Thus, in each world, there is a triumvirate of friends: Harry and Buffy each have a modest, normal male and an unusually intelligent female as friends. All of them are at odds with the social elite, and are burdened as well as excited by dangerous adventures. And these adventures are not shown as magically managed in the sense of being cost free. "There was a lot more to magic, as Harry quickly found out, than waving your wand and saying a few funny words. They had to study the night skies through their telescopes every Wednesday night at midnight and learn the names of different stars and the movements of the planets. Three times a week they went out to the greenhouses behind the castle to study Herbology ... where they learned how to take care of all the strange plants and fungi ..." etc. (*Sorcerer's Stone*, 133). Harry practices the Patronus Charm after school hours with Professor Lupin (*Prisoner of Azkaban*, 237) and the summoning charm with Hermione during lunch hours (*Goblet of Fire*). And as for Buffy, in episode after episode she is shown training and exercising with Giles, then patrolling when she'd rather be out on a date (see, e.g., "Never Kill a Boy on the First Date," 1.5).

Also noteworthy is the time these friends spend with books. Buffy's Scooby Gang enlarges over the years, always including Xander and Willow, but also sometimes including Buffy's Angel, Willow's Oz, and even, eventually, Cordelia, who by some hormonal miracle ends up dating Xander. (Not to mention the social conversion; see Mary Alice Money.) In later years, Anya, Tara, Dawn, Spike, and even Andrew join in. Time and again, as a number of critics have noted, the Scooby Gang gathers in the library, hitting the books so that Buffy can hit the right demon. Of course, Buffy's mentor is a librarian (see DeCandido and Blake). After the school library is blown up, the Scoobies consult the extensive book collection in his magic store. And Ron, Hermione, and Harry are also shown bonding over long searches through lengthy tomes—trying to find a solution for a Triwizard Tournament clue, or investigating a famous wizard (Nicolas Flamel) to prevent the theft of an important magical object (the Sorcerer's Stone). Furthermore, Harry's most important mentor is the Hogwarts Headmaster, Albus Dumbledore. For both Harry and Buffy, heroism depends on a work ethic which is intertwined with bookwork, if not always precisely schoolwork (cf. Wall and Zryd 54). Although both Buffy and Harry occasionally have magical dreams (prophetic or clairvoyant),[5] these are relatively rare aids to problem-solving: the work, on the other hand, is more or less constant. As Buffy says, "They're already piling on the reading, and Giles fills any free time I have with extra training ... [I] thought it was going to be like in the movies. You know—inspirational music; a montage: me sharpening my pencils, me reading, writing, falling asleep on a big pile of books with my glasses all crooked—'cause in my montage I have glasses. But—real life is slow ..." And she notes, "I'm starting to think this working hard is hard work" ("Out of My Mind," 5.4).

A corollary to work is will, and it is another important element of the heroism of these characters. A cursory examination of either text might suggest that they promote essentialism or determinism, but that is not the case. The first Harry Potter book explains that when students arrive at Hogwarts, they are "sorted" into one of four "houses," each of which emphasizes particular character traits—Gryffindor for bravery; Ravenclaw, cleverness; Hufflepuff, loyalty; and Slytherin, ambition. (All the dark wizards have come from among the Slytherins.) The student puts on an ancient magic hat which announces the proper house; the student does not do anything for this apparent evaluation of essence. In the second Harry Potter book, however, Harry tells Dumbledore he is concerned because the Sorting Hat wanted to put him in Slytherin, like the major villain of that book, Tom Riddle (as well as Draco Malfoy). And Dumbledore responds, "'Yet the Sorting Hat placed you in Gryffindor. You know why that was. Think.' 'It only put me in Gryffindor,' said Harry in a defeated voice, 'because I asked not to go in Slytherin ...' '*Exactly*,' said Dumbledore, beaming ... 'Which makes you *very different* from Tom Riddle. It is our choices, Harry, that show what we truly are, far more than our abilities'" (*Chamber of Secrets*, 333). Hermione, who would seem by nature suited to Ravenclaw because of her intelligence, is in Gryffindor because time and again she chooses to act bravely; the loyal Ron, who would seem suited to Hufflepuff, is in Gryffindor for the same reason.

Similarly, in the second and third seasons of *Buffy*, the show overtly addresses the issue of choice. It is often noted that Buffy is "the Chosen One," and she sometimes resents being destined to this fate. When Californian Buffy gets accepted at Northwestern University, she asks to leave Sunnydale. Her Watcher says, "But you're a Slayer." And Buffy replies, "Yeah, I'm also a person. You can't just define me by my Slayerness. That's—something-ism" ("Choices," 3.19). Even within the framework of her destiny she does make choices, as Xander points out. In "Inca Mummy Girl" (2.4), "Ampata," a young woman who was chosen to be a sacrifice hundreds of years ago, returns to life, but is only able to stay alive by taking the lives of others, ultimately even trying to take the life of Xander, whom she loves. Buffy sees the parallel in this other "Chosen One," but as Xander points out, when Buffy was confronted with the choice, she gave her own life in order to save others: in the last episode of the first season, Buffy briefly dies ("Prophecy Girl," 1.12). She dies again (much more thoroughly) at the end of Season Five, once more choosing self-sacrifice. As she says to cancer victim and vampire wannabe Billy Fordham, "You don't have a good choice, but you have a choice" ("Lie to Me," 2.7).

The nature of these heroes' choices is explored through the use of dark doubles, Jungian shadows—of which the Inca Mummy Girl is only a minor example. Roz Kaveney has pointed out that the early Cordelia is what Buffy could have been (9). Similarly, the blond, gray-eyed, over-mothered and offensively fathered Draco Malfoy is a clear foil to the dark-haired, green-eyed orphan Harry. Draco is fathered by the wicked Lucius, whose name suggests Lucifer; their surname, of course, means "bad faith," which is appropriate for their treacherous natures.

Buffy, as most of her viewers will know, has her own bad Faith: the anomalous extra Slayer. When Buffy briefly dies, her death activates the first second Slayer, Kendra; when Kendra dies, another Slayer, Faith, is called. Like Buffy, Faith is fatherless; while Buffy's mother is generally clueless, Faith's was alcoholically neglectful. When Faith accidentally kills a human being, she begins a downward spiral that leads to her offering herself to serve evil. In the episode titled, appropriately for this discussion, "Choices," Willow (or "Will," to recall her significant nickname) is captured by the fallen Faith, who prepares to turn her over to the major villain of the season, the mayor of Sunnydale. Will says to Faith, "You know it didn't have to be this way. But you made your choice. I know you had a tough life, I know that some people think you had a lot of bad breaks. Well, boo-hoo. Poor you. You know, you had a lot more in your life than—than some people. You had friends like Buffy. Now you have no one. You were a Slayer and now you're nothing. You're just a big worthless, selfish waste." Buffy's continuing relationship with her shadow Faith is a complicated one. For now, suffice it to note that it highlights the element of free will or, as these texts prefer to term it, choice.

Certainly that is also the case with the ultimate incarnation of Tom Riddle, the opponent Harry mentioned earlier: Harry has only faced a magical memory of Tom Riddle, because Tom grew up to be the darkest of wizards, Lord Voldemort. And Voldemort is Harry's darkest shadow. Even in the first book, Harry is surprised to learn that the magic wand which responds best to him is the only one which shares core elements with Voldemort's wand. (And just give a mental glance to Harry's wand and Buffy's stake.) And in the second book, Riddle/Voldemort says to Harry, "There are strange likenesses between us, after all. Both half-bloods, orphans, raised by Muggles. Probably the only two Parselmouths [speakers of Snake-language] to come to Hogwarts since the great Slytherin himself. We even look something alike ..." (*Chamber of Secrets*, 317). Repeatedly through the books, Malfoy scorns Harry for not having chosen the right side; but Harry probably knows better than anyone what he has rejected in rejecting Voldemort, whose name (in the latinate fashion used throughout the books) can be parsed as Vol-de-mort, or will of death, or death-wish.

(Voldemort, who declares he seeks immortality, is focusing on death.) By the end of book four, Harry has seen Voldemort's true face, and knows the ugliness of depravity.

Riddle/Voldemort's comment about half-bloods touches on another level of meaning invoked by both Harry and Buffy, and that is their use of social symbolism. While Fredric Jameson has argued that in magical narratives the symbolic "historical reality [is] ... defused by the sense of moonlit revels dissolving into thin air," (149) neither Buffy nor Harry delivers traditional happy endings which return us to the social status quo; instead, as Acocella notes, Rowling "asks her ... readers to face the hardest questions of life," (78) as do Whedon and Co.—and both the books and the series frame those questions symbolically. The symbolism of *Buffy* is so endemic that Kathleen Tracy, after its second season, was able to write a book with episode summaries each one of which is followed by an explanation of the "real life horror" correlating to the episode's events. For instance, Xander's being magically turned into a hyena in a pack correlates with the cruel laughter of high school cliques ("The Pack," 1.6); an episode with a Jekyll-Hyde boyfriend corresponds to an abusive relationship ("Beauty and the Beasts," 3.4); a witch who takes over her teenaged daughter's body is carrying vicarious living to the magical extreme ("The Witch," 1.3), and so forth.

Though less multitudinous, the social symbols in the Harry Potter books are no less important. Early on, we learn that Albus Dumbledore is famous for defeating a dark wizard in 1945, a date which leads to thoughts of Hitler. Voldemort himself suggests Hitler in his pursuit of pure blood—in this story's terms, only magical parents; he also recalls Hitler in his own lack of such "purity," because of his "filthy Muggle [father]" (*Chamber of Secrets*, 314). Draco Malfoy's detestation of Hermione as a filthy "Mudblood," or child of a Muggle, is an early indication of what will become a major plot motivator—the division between dark and good wizards falling generally along the lines of those who consider "pure blood" important or irrelevant. In the fourth book, wizards hooded like Ku Klux Klan "wizards" display their racial prejudice against Muggles: "A crowd of wizards ... was marching slowly across the field ... Their heads were hooded and their faces masked" (119). In the fifth book, those secretly working against Voldemort hide like Jews in Nazi Germany; Sirius Black is as housebound as Anne Frank.

For both texts, the racial/ethnic implications are debatable: Kent Ono argues that in *Buffy*, the vampires and demons represent the Other and are callously killed; Mary Alice Money argues that many are undemonized, made human, over the course of the series' years. Even young readers recognize that the Harry books deal with "prejudice" (Hulbert A17); it is also true, however, that Ron and Hermione argue over whether or not house-elves are happy as, in effect, slaves.[6] Ron believes they chose their path gladly; Hermione argues that social tradition brainwashes them into accepting their situation (and in fact Ron, unlike Hermione, has grown up in that tradition too). The matrix of individual and social forces is not simple. Harry, Buffy, Faith, and Voldemort have all made their choices; does Dumbledore's comment about our choices "show[ing] what we truly are" mean that choice is free?

Dumbledore himself is part of a larger construct, as is Buffy's Watcher Giles. Each of them can be seen as fulfilling the function of Propp's Donor character—the Obi-Wan Kenobi for the story, in greater or lesser degrees. In each case, the character is one of those rare adults who can see what is really going on in the younger character's world. Buffy can trust Giles, and Harry can trust Dumbledore. But still, the larger power structures are questioned. The largely patriarchal Council of Watchers, to which Giles belongs, submits Buffy to humiliating tests, unnecessarily risks her life, and—unlike Giles—presumes she should have no input into her situation. (Because he rejects their tactics, Giles is fired by the Council; and, in the seventh season, the Council headquarters is destroyed immediately after a hubristic comment by its leader.) And the local Sunnydale government is run by Mayor Wilkins, who has actually sold his soul for power. Similarly, while Dumbledore is insightful and trustworthy, the Ministry of Magic (which at one point removes Dumbledore from office, as Giles was removed by the Council) is not merely fussily bureaucratic, but—it turns out by the fourth book—led by a man who prefers purebloods and is in the gold-lined pocket of Lucius Malfoy and his crowd. Government influenced by money! A fantasy world indeed.

Perhaps most frightening, however, is the larger symbolism of the hidden magical world. In many traditional magical narratives, from the Odyssey to Snow White to the Lord of the Rings, magic soaks the world; it is ubiquitous; it can pop up anywhere. In other stories, such as the original tales of Superman, superpower seems to reside within one character. But in the stories of Buffy and Harry, there is an entire magical world which is unrecognized by an entire "normal" world. To put the case extremely briefly, the world is a much stranger—and more frightening—place than most of us are willing to realize: there is a whole world of dangers and wonders which most of us do not see. And in both Buffy's and Harry's worlds, the men (yes, men)[7] in power are aware of the dark and dangerous world of magic but publicly pretend it does not exist: the British prime minister, informed by the Ministry of Magic, is aware of the prison escape of a murderous wizard, and the principal of Sunnydale High and the sheriff (as well as the mayor) pretend that rampaging vampires are gangs on PCP. Again, the metaphor is clear: those in power choose not to deal with problems they know to be too frightening,[8] whether those problems are dark wizards or Medicaid funds. "I'd be kicked out of office for suggesting it!" says the Minister of Magic (*Goblet of Fire*, 707).

Perhaps most hopeful, on the other hand, is the representation of the modern hero's response. Buffy and Harry, unique in their powers and ordinary in their insecurities, have one major strength in common: their friends. When Buffy briefly dies, it is her friend Xander, not her boyfriend Angel, who brings her back: the undead, being breathless, are not good at mouth to mouth resuscitation.[9] And time and again the Scoobies work together to save the day—most notably in the episode "Primeval" (4.21), in which Buffy, Xander, Giles, and Willow join as one being. Similarly, Harry is repeatedly helped by his friends: at the end of *The Sorcerer's Stone*, for example, they have to get through a magical obstacle course which requires Ron's knowledge of chess and Hermione's powers of logic to enable Harry to face Voldemort. Even at the end of Book IV, when it seems Harry is alone among dark wizards, his wand conjures the ghostly echoes of his classmate Cedric, his mother, his father, and others to help him out, so that he is able to escape Voldemort again. And the dissension within the Order of the Phoenix, like the seventh-season dissension among the Slayers and Potential Slayers, shows that such cooperation is not simple; it requires labor and self-knowledge, only gradually gained as these long stories progress.

Both of these long stories work with and move beyond traditional forms. Propp's structures include a category for helpers, but as he defines them, they are often animals or objects. The goal in the structures he describes is marriage. But in the Harry and Buffy stories, friendship is not merely a means to an end (as the helper categorization would suggest); it is an end in itself. Every Harry Potter book thus far has ended with the rejoining of the friends and their subsequent separation for the summer holidays, with Harry's longing to return to school and friendship. And while Buffy and Angel (and later Buffy and Spike) provide plenty of romantic steam, the series does not end with her matched to either. An examination of the structure of the episodes would show that those with happy endings are most often those which conclude with a group of friends. In "When She Was Bad," for instance—the first episode of Buffy's second season—Buffy is struggling emotionally with her reaction to having been killed, however briefly, by the Vampire Master. She is cruel to each of her friends in turn. Near the end of the episode, she comes to emotional terms with her problems as she hammers into fragments the bones of the Master, and Angel puts his arms around her in comfort. A typical television series would probably have ended with this shot. But this show follows Buffy into the next day, when she reveals to Giles her dread of facing the friends she has hurt. When she slowly enters the schoolroom, Buffy is accepted back by Xander and Willow, who have saved her a seat in class. Only two season finales close with an image of Buffy alone (and one of these, from Season Two, is desperately sad); four out of seven finales close with a scene of the friends rejoined. Cindy Bowers has written of this series' representation of a younger generation, arguing that social research suggests teamwork is important to this age group. I have also argued elsewhere that Buffy, despite the voiceover which intones that she is the only one, actually repudiates patriarchal succession and the role of the lonely hero in favor of communal effort ("Who"; and see Playdon, Rose, and South, "All Torment"). The same can be said of Harry Potter. Put simply, these new heroes value and count on friendship as part of their heroism.

The Harry Potter books and Buffy have a rough correlation with real time: each Harry book covers a year at the Hogwarts school, and the first four books came out more or less once a year; each season of the Buffy series has covered a year of her life, too. The fifth Harry Potter book was published in 2003; in 2003, Buffy finished its seventh season, the second since the last Harry Potter book. In that time Buffy has died and been buried—and, as might be expected of a Campbellian hero, has returned—at the hands of her friends, and at great cost. She has also (in true Bildungsroman fashion) grown notably older in many ways: having dealt with her mother's death, having explored her sexuality and reacted to attempted rape by her ex-lover, having become a single mom to her sudden sister, having been forced into a drudge job to make ends meet—while Harry has gone to the movies. The fifth Harry book was delayed while Rowling participated in the creation of the enormously popular (if not critically acclaimed) movie versions of the early novels. Faithful fans await Harry's next step in what Rowling has said she plans to be a seven-book series. The promised publication date for Harry the sixth is 2005.

Buffy in its seventh year thus moved ahead of Harry in time (and of course

Harry started at age eleven, Buffy at sixteen). Both the series and the books, however, have through the years braved more and more of the dark. At the end of the fifth season, in "The Gift" (5.22), Buffy sacrificed her life to save the world and to avoid allowing her younger sister to make such a sacrifice. It is worth noting that Rowling has wondered aloud why fans assume she won't kill Harry; his fate may be similar to Buffy's in this regard as well.

In any case, it is clear that either of them is willing to die for others, to die for the right. The two texts recognize, however, that death is not the worst (in fact, in a seventh-season episode, the battle-weary Buffy calls it "dessert" ["Potential," 7.12]). Fighting evil requires a power in and of itself both necessary and dangerous—morally dangerous. As Acocella says, "There is much for Rowling to resolve in the remaining volumes, above all the question about power—is it reconcilable with goodness?—that she poses in the first four books" (78). (Of course, if Rowling is able to resolve that question—more power to her.) *Buffy* has already been asking that question, too, and in the seventh-season opener the issue is framed in a way that should provoke unease: In the opening scene, Buffy, training her younger sister Dawn in self-defense, says, "It's about power." In the closing scene, the First Evil (introduced in the third season's "Amends," 3.10, as the ultimate motive of evil, something akin to the cause of Original Sin) tortures the newly ensouled vampire Spike and, in the process, morphs successively into the forms of six major villains ("Big Bads") from each season, in reverse order—finally settling into the form of Buffy herself. And with the face of Buffy, the First Evil says, "It's about power."

There is always the danger that you will reflect what you oppose, that you will become the thing you fight. And the very first, primeval Slayer has told Buffy, "No friends—just the kill" ("Restless," 4.22), just the violence. But as Spike tells Buffy in "Fool for Love," she draws power from her loved ones—her "ties to the world"; it is what allows her to resist the darkness; for "Every Slayer's got a death wish—even you" (5.7). And as Dumbledore says, Voldemort—the death-wish in Harry's world—is best fought through the "bond of friendship" (*Goblet of Fire*, 723). Power must be balanced with the mercy borne of human connection. And the lesson is not just for the hero, but for us all. As Xander, now a carpenter,[10] tells Will (whose misuse of power has been apocalyptic), we must hammer out our fate using power in balance with control ("Help," 7.4). The depth of forgiveness in *Buffy* can be measured in part by the degree of wrongdoing committed by major characters (Xander leaving Anya at the altar; Buffy battering Spike; Spike's attempted rape; Willow's deadly vengeance for her beloved Tara's murder—among other grim events); how far the Harry characters might go remains to be seen.

In this short chapter, only a few of the similarities between Buffy and Harry can be touched on. These heroes work with knowledge, not just with physical force; they question social structures; they emphasize the individual's choice, but also validate friendship. Both Harry and Buffy are in some ways traditional magical heroes; neither, however, represents simple Freudian wish-fulfillment. At the turn of the millenium, the hero is much more than a wielder of a wand or a stake.

Chapter 5

Every Night I Save You

Buffy, Spike, Sex, and Redemption[1]

For Godsake hold your tongue, and let me love …
Call us what you will, wee are made such by love;
Call her one, mee another flye,
We'are tapers too, and at our owne cost die,
And wee in us find th'Eagle and the Dove.
The Phoenix riddle hath more wit
By us, we two being one, are it.
So to one neutrall thing both sexes fit,
Wee dye and rise the same, and prove
Mysterious by this love.

> John Donne, lines from "The Canonization"

When I kiss you, I want to die.

> Buffy to Angel, "Reptile Boy" (2.5)

If I kiss you, it'll make the sun go down.

> Dream Riley to Buffy, "Hush" (4.10)

The sun sets, and she appears.

> Spike to Buffy, "Once More, with Feeling" (6.7)

Every night I save you.

    Spike to Buffy, "After Life" (6.3)

Love, death, rebirth, redemption—the connection of these is certainly not new to *Buffy the Vampire Slayer*. In the late sixteenth and early seventeenth century, the wordplay equating sex and death was a favorite of John Donne and other Metaphysical poets. The relation of sex and death might be causal—a *carpe diem* appeal to a mistress—or metaphoric—a representation of the transcendence of the intercourse of lovers. While the Metaphysical poets' striking conversational style and exuberantly noticeable metaphors suggest that they are part of *Buffy*'s distant literary lineage, the connection of love and death runs throughout literary and cultural history. The physical act of love and the physical experience of death can both be seen as threshold events, as scholars such as Victor Turner and Joseph Campbell have acknowledged; they can both be seen as transformative, involving a sometimes transcendent change of condition.

Most of these terms can, of course, be applied to vampires, those liminal creatures who revisit, night after night, the edge of life and death, and whom many scholars see as representing the id, the unconscious, repressed urges let loose. The pre-vampire version of the character would then represent the ego or conscious self. We recognize this two-sidedness as metaphor; but those with a knowledge of literary history may also at this point find themselves thinking of the strange case of Dr. Donne, a very two-sided personality: Jack Donne, the wild young author of bawdy love poetry, who was converted to the Reverend Dr. Donne, Dean of St Paul's, a famed and powerful preacher. The metaphor resonates because it touches reality. And today, the text in which this metaphor and reality converge most powerfully is *Buffy the Vampire Slayer*.

Not only horror scholars in general but *Buffy* scholars in particular, such as Diane Dekelb-Rittenhouse, Tanya Krzywinska, Roz Kaveney, and Mary Alice Money, have discussed the vampire/human versions of characters in *Buffy*. Multitudes of vampires in *Buffy* are fated to be nothing more than dust, but for a few we know both the human and the vampire version, and those few are generally allowed to live. They are thus also allowed to display the ego-to-id relationship of the human-vampire elements of the personality.

As has often been noted, when the alternate-universe Vamp Willow makes her appearance in Sunnydale, we get our first inkling of Willow's lesbian leanings. And, in a variation on the order of the change, the vampire Angelus's cruel obsession with Buffy is a transmutation of the love of Buffy borne by Angel, the vampire with a soul: as Willow says to Buffy, "You're still the only thing he thinks about" ("Passion," 2.17). Drusilla, the chaste nineteenth-century girl who was to have become a nun, the bride of Christ, becomes instead the sadistically sexual paramour of the vampire Spike. The alternative world's harder side of Xander feasts on Cordelia with Will—clearly a vampiric extension of the urges the normal Xander felt for Cordy ("The Wish," 3.9). We also see vamp/non-vamp versions of both Darla and Harmony—who, however, seem to have lived their lives in fuller expression of their ids, since the change is not marked for either: Darla goes from colonial prostitute to bloodsucker, Harmony from high school ditz to vampire ditz. Only briefly, in the episode "Nightmares," do we see the vampire face of Buffy—and so briefly, in fact, that we do not see any evidence of a vampire personality (1.10).

We do, however, see an extensive exploration of Buffy's dark side through two other characters: Faith and Spike. And, as we move to this variation, we will move from Freudian analysis to include Jungian. To quote a very simple expression of the idea by Jung, "the realm of the shadow ... is ... the negative side of the personality" (147). The dark-haired, violent, promiscuous Slayer Faith is Buffy's Shadow figure (see, e.g., Keller). In Faith, Buffy has battled the dark side of herself, and they struggle to come to resolution—though, interestingly, Buffy's Shadow Faith has taken Angel as her Virgilian guide through hell in her search for atonement on his eponymous series. And Buffy has at least recognized the need to allow that search, because, as Faith says to her, "[You] kill me, you become me" ("Enemies" 3.17). Less obvious but even more interesting is the relationship with Buffy's second shadow, Spike.

It is not until the fifth-season episode "Fool for Love" that we see the late Victorian human version of the vampire we have known as Spike, or William the Bloody (5.7). Certainly the living William qualifies as an exemplar of repression of the id: when asked to join a conversation about a rash of recent, presumably vampiric, disappearances, he remarks, "I prefer not to think of such dark ugly business at all ... I prefer placing my energies into creating things of beauty," such as his poetry, which his acquaintances term "bloody awful." The Spike whom viewers have come to know since Season Two is a cheerfully vicious black-leather-wearing punk with peroxide blond hair, starting out as half of a Sid-and-Nancy set, with the raven-haired Drusilla, and later sidetracked by the implantation of a chip in his head which prevents his harming humans. The Victorian William, however, is dressed in a foppish suit that recalls not only the three-piece outfit Spike wears in "Tabula Rasa" (6.8), but also the one in Xander's dream in "Restless" (4.22), when Xander imagines Spike training to be a Watcher under the guidance of Buffy's mentor Giles (and in fact in the last three seasons Spike performed some of a Watcher's informative functions). Furthermore, instead of white-haired, William is as blond as Buffy.

In the excellent short essay "Spike as Shadow," Delores J. Nurss argues:

> Spike has devoted a century to acting out William's shadow [and also], Spike particularly reflects Buffy—he forces her to confront the fact that she is as much of a killer as he is, however much of a good guy she tries to be. But [the] Shadow doesn't just hold the bad things you've suppressed, but also the good you've turned your back on. When Buffy has difficulty relating to her Mom [sic], she comes home, to her horror, to find Spike sipping tea with Joyce and crying on her shoulder. When Buffy fears to ever fall in love again, Spike falls in love with her. In the context of [the] Shadow, Spike has not made one inconsistent move, ever.

These remarks on Spike as Shadow are, I think, very illuminating. Certainly Jung's words about the Shadow seem very apt: it "behaves more or less like a primitive, who is not only the passive victim of his affects but also singularly incapable of moral judgment" (146). However, if we wish to be strictly Jungian, we might note that Jung says that "the shadow ... is always of the same sex as the subject" (147). For a "contrasexual figure," "we meet the animus of a woman, and the anima of a man, two corresponding archetypes," (147) a male element of the female, and a female element of the male. Spike might be seen as Buffy's animus, and Buffy as Spike's anima. I find it interesting that one of the terms Jung mentions for the anima is the phrase "My Lady Soul" (though he dislikes the term as "too vague," 150–51—and it sounds a bit like Barry White). It is a phrase which seems poignantly appropriate if we see Buffy as representing Spike's, or William's, anima. Despite the occasional felicity of application, I choose not to be too strictly Jungian, since that would involve acceptance of declarations such as Jung's remark that "In women ... Eros ["the function of relationship"] is an expression of their true nature, while their Logos ["cognition"] is often only a regrettable accident" (152). With comments such as these in mind, I am more than willing to overlook Jungian gender specifications and stretch a point to call Spike Buffy's Shadow as well. As Ursula K. Le Guin says, "Jung's terminology is notoriously difficult, as he keeps changing meanings" (58). In fact, if one employs the connection of the animus to the "paternal Logos," (152) it seems hardly Spike-like at all. But using another emphasis in the definition of the animus, Spike (not William) as quintessential masculine seems quite appropriate. The name Spike is clearly phallic; the whole Spike persona seems a highly masculinized compensation for the relatively feminized poet William. Whether animus or shadow, it is still true that it is dangerous to ignore it, destroy it, or be seduced by it (Nurss).

And thus we return to love and death. In "Fool for Love," the episode in which we first see William, the softer side of Spike, we also see Spike kill two Slayers. As he describes their deaths at Buffy's request, he explains to her that "Every Slayer has a death wish—even you." He warns her that she's "just a little bit in love with it," that someday she'll feel the desire and "the second that happens, you know I'll be there—I'll slip in." In this emotionally charged scene, the image of Spike "slip[ping] in" unquestionably joins visions of sex and death. So, of course, does Buffy, when she tells the ensouled Angel, "When I kiss you, I want to die"—not an idle comment, made to a vampire. When Buffy imagines Riley in her dream in "Hush," she has him say, "If I kiss you, it'll make the sun go down." As Don Keller suggests, the sun going down suggests the unconscious (170). I would add that, despite this statement's coming from Buffy's imagined sense of Riley, who is soon to be her boyfriend, still the combination of the kiss, the unconscious, and the setting sun evoke the image of a vampire again. Of Buffy's three major sexual relationships, two—the first and last—have been with vampires—the very notably named Angel and Spike (see Chapter 3). Angel can never make love with his beloved Buffy because he will lose his soul if he does; his absolute restraint puts him in the position of the superego, while Spike at first clearly expresses the id. And, of course, their names correspond to these functions. As for Riley, only in Buffy's dream does he make the sun go down, does he access the unconscious in his relationship with her; as Spike tells him, Buffy wants some "monster in her man" ("Into the Woods," 5.10), and Riley does not have in him that release of darkness (see Chapter 9).

As for Buffy herself, as Spike notes, "The sun sets, and she appears." The Slayer, who fights the forces of darkness, is, like the vampires, a liminal character, on the edge between light and dark. To fight for the light, she must move through the darkness; and, after her dream encounter with the first of all Slayers and her actual encounter with Dracula, she agrees that, as they say, her "power is rooted in darkness" ("Buffy vs. Dracula," 5.1)—i.e., her connection to the unconscious. In the context of the musical episode in which Spike says "the sun sets, and she appears," we are also aware of the fact that he means she has come to him again (though at this point their relationship is not actively sexual); in her unhappy state after her own return from death, she is drawn to his darkness. In sum, at this stage Buffy's desire for Spike and her desire for death are equivalent.

What are we to make, then, of the last epigraph—Spike's declaration that "Every night I save you"? It contains at least two thematically important points. The most literal and obvious, paradoxically, contradicts the direct statement, because Spike does *not* save Buffy. The context is this: he makes the statement in "After Life," the third hour of the sixth season. At the end of the fifth season, Buffy had sacrificed her life to save the world and, above all, her sister. In spite of the efforts of her friends the Scooby Gang (including Spike), a wound has been opened in the world, which Buffy has healed with her own body. Her sister Dawn (another of the significantly named characters) has been chained to the top of a giant tower (is there a Freudian in the house?) at which the opening is located, and into which Buffy flings herself. Despite Dawn's offer, Buffy will not allow her fourteen-year-old sister to take that plunge. The only other member of the Scooby Gang we ever see at the top of that tower is Spike, who has promised to protect Dawn and is flung down hundreds of feet to the ground, the fall of the white-haired vampire recalling the fall of Lucifer. The entire scene, with the tower and the glowing opening, can be seen as a Freudian representation of sexual joining. And Spike does come close to joining Buffy there, but he is not quite ready, not quite worthy; when she falls, she falls into the light; when he falls, he falls into the earth (literally, almost into the cracks of earthquake, though he pulls himself back just in time).

One hundred and forty-seven days pass (Spike tells it to the day), and Willow, Xander, Tara, and Anya cast a spell which brings Buffy back: they fear that, like Angel in similar circumstances, she has been suffering in a hell dimension, and indeed she seems withdrawn and unresponsive. She goes to visit Spike in his crypt, pausing on the way in front of a funerary angel statue which creates a visual of Buffy outlined by wings (foreshadowing the revelation at the end of the episode). Spike, in the lower level of his crypt, smashes his hand against the rocks as he thinks of her: he knows Buffy has smashed her hand as she "clawed her way out of her coffin," emphasizing again the mirroring of the vampire and this Slayer ("Done it myself," he says). These two are both emotionally wounded, and when Spike emerges from below to find her in the upper level of his crypt, they each acknowledge the other's wound. Then he begins a more formal speech. In "After Life," Sarah Michelle Gellar and James Marsters perform what I call "mutual soliloquies"—each delivers to the other a speech which is in effect (in terms of both length and revelatory content) a soliloquy, while the other actor silently responds. It is an acting challenge which few could meet with the extraordinary skill of Gellar and Marsters. Gellar's responses are muted because of Buffy's condition, which we only know for certain by the end of the episode after the second "mutual soliloquy" in which Buffy informs Spike that she thinks she was in heaven, and was "torn out" by her friends. But for now we hear Spike's confession:

> Uh—I do remember what I said. The promise. To protect her [Dawn]. If I'd 'a' done that, even if I didn't make it, you wouldn't have had to jump. But I want you to know I *did* save you—not when it counted, of course, but after that. Every night after that. I'd see it all again. I'd do something different—faster, more clever, you know. Dozens of times, lots of different ways. Every night I save you.

Of course literally, as he is very unhappily confessing, Spike does not save Buffy. I can remember, after the second season of *The X-Files*, actually counting up the times Scully rescued Mulder, and vice versa (and at that point they were actually about even). But Buffy is never completely rescued by a male. Sometimes males help her, or participate in a group effort, as Angel and Xander do in "Halloween" (2.6) or "Reptile Boy," or as Spike himself does (unseen) in "Family" (5.6) or "Blood Ties" (5.13); but Buffy is never simply rescued by a solo male hero.[2] In fact, as many viewers know, she began her existence as a reversal of the stereotype of the little woman in need of saving. It is thematically positive that Spike does not literally save Buffy. But listen again to his words: "Every night I save you." For this line's second thematically important point, we must return to the underlying pattern of Buffy's relation to the night, the unconscious, the id, the shadow, or the animus. The hero must embrace this darkness to become truly strong—to save herself; and as the sixth season proceeds, Buffy embraces Spike.

Even before her death, Buffy has been concerned about her deadening emotions. In the fifth-season episode "Intervention," she says to Giles, "Maybe being the perfect Slayer means being too hard to love at all" (5.18). At the beginning of the fifth season, she has asked Giles to help her investigate her roots in darkness; now he directs her to a quest during which she speaks with a Spirit Guide in the form of the First Slayer. Buffy asks if she's losing her ability to love—"not just boyfriend love"—and the Spirit Guide tells her: "Only if you reject it. Love is pain. And the Slayer forges strength from pain. Love—give—forgive—risk the pain—it is your nature. Love will bring you to your gift ... Death is your gift."

This cryptic pronouncement is given one resolution when Buffy realizes in the one hundredth episode, "The Gift" (5.22) that she can give her life in place of Dawn's. With this chapter's discussion in mind, however, I would like to propose another application, though the explanation may take some time. By the sixth season, it is generally accepted that Spike actually loves Buffy (though the quality of his love can be debated); his actions at the time of and after her death—a time when he, unlike the other Scoobies, was not planning for her return—show that he has not been motivated simply by lust; and, in "Dead Things," the wise Tara tells Buffy, "He does love you" (6.13). Buffy, however, repeatedly rejects this belief. In episode after episode, she says that, as a soulless vampire, he cannot feel anything. And in this view, of course, she projects her own emotional deadness on her shadow. Especially after her literal return from the dead, she has felt emotionally detached. In the musical episode "Once More, with Feeling" (and note the last word of the title), just before she and Spike engage in their first romantic kiss (which closes the episode), she sings, "This isn't real, but I just want to feel"—whereas he sings, "I died so many years ago; you can make me feel as though it isn't so." It is significant that in this episode a magic spell makes the characters sing their innermost feelings: we are hearing truth here.

Many critics who have discussed Faith's doubling of Buffy have cited the scene in which Faith has possessed Buffy's body and, in the shape of Buffy, batters the body of Faith, calling herself "disgusting, murderous" ("Who Are You?" 4.16). It is a powerful image of self-hatred. In "Dead Things," the scene is recapitulated with Buffy's other double, Spike. Again we see Buffy above, battering the figure that represents the hated quality—in this case, Spike. Why does she strike him until his face looks almost as damaged as it did after Glory tortured him? Because, in trying to save her, he has insisted that he loves her, whereas she says (punctuating the words with punches), "You don't have a soul— ... you're dead inside—you can't feel anything real." And yet at the end of this episode, Buffy is telling Tara that the only time she feels anything is when she is with Spike; and she sobs to her friend that Tara must not forgive her.

As the Spirit Guide says, Buffy does need to forgive; she needs to forgive herself; she needs to forgive Spike, and the side of herself represented by him; as the Guide says, she needs to "risk the pain." In "Hell's Bells," (6.16) the episode of Xander and Anya's failed wedding, a meddling demon comments, "Sometimes two people—all they bring each other is pain," just as we cut to a scene of Buffy and Spike meeting.[3] In the preceding episode, she has broken off their torrid affair with the words, "I'm sorry, William"; with the use of his human name, there is a rare acknowledgment of that other self in him. At the wedding, both of them are pained by their meeting; but the two are so genuinely kind to each other that there is as much caritas as eros in the scene. "Not just boyfriend love," indeed.

Despite the months of a passionately sexual affair and despite the apparent resolution of the kindness of the scene in "Hell's Bells," Buffy has not, at this point in the story, fully recognized her darker aspect; Buffy has not fully embraced her Spike. She cannot accept the possibility that he could change. In her essay on "The Undemonization of Supporting Characters in *Buffy*," Mary Alice Money expands on a comment by Golden and Holder to define the abilities to change and to feel as the primary criteria for humanity. In the sixth season, Buffy is barely beginning to conceive of the possibility of darker, even demonic elements in herself (see, e.g., "Restless"); and it may be even harder to contemplate the possibility of humanity in Spike; what would the implications be for her work as Slayer? Spike's is a metaphysically interesting case because of the difficulties it poses. As many critics have noted, *Buffy* is important in part because of the increasing moral complexity of its universe. The character Angel clearly contributed to the building of that complexity by being a vampire capable of good. However, since Angel is able to be good because he possesses a soul, he still represents an essentialist definition of good. Spike owns no human soul, yet repeatedly *does* good; if he can be seen as capable of change, capable of good, capable of *love*, then he can represent an existentialist definition of good. Even when he does, in the series' last season, own a soul, the character still pulls against an essentialist interpretation and towards existential choice because he, unlike Angel, acquires a soul as a result of his own agency: he receives a soul as a result of his personal quest (see Chapter 2). The chip which prevents him from harming humans can be paralleled to psychiatric medications which allow sufferers a respite and the chance to work through their psychological issues. The subsequent change is thus not simply physiological.

The change is indicated in part by the continuing metaphor of light and dark in the series. Just as coming to know the night within herself may help to save Buffy, so too Spike may need to come into the light of day. In "After Life," just before she confesses to Spike (and only to Spike) that she thinks she has been in heaven, Buffy comments with surprise on his being out in the "daylight", yet, as he says, "not on fire? Sun's low enough; it's shady enough here." As Chapter 2 explains, along with this serious scene, there are many comedic instances (beginning as early as the fifth season) when Spike bundles himself up under a blanket in order to be near Buffy—and hence in the daylight. "Normal Again" (6.17) provides another serious moment illuminated by light imagery: as Spike advises Buffy to "Let yourself live, already" and announces that he will tell her friends about them if she does not, he steps towards her but flinches and physically recoils: he has moved directly into the sunlight, and that is something he is not able to withstand. The expression on his face recalls his reaction to pain from the chip. He says that if her friends won't accept her having a relationship with him, Buffy can join him in the dark. However, the room in which he stands is actually lighter than the place he occupies in "After Life." As Buffy rests in the sunlight, he is unable to reach her, but he has tried—and it seems he is closer than he once would have been.[4]

Not only such imagery, but also words and actions in other scenes suggest some degree of change. In "Hell's Bells," when Buffy tells him that it hurts to see him with a woman they both know he has brought to the wedding solely to make Buffy jealous, his first, unthinking response is to say "I'm sorry," then he corrects himself to say "or—good." When (in "Smashed," 6.9) he believes his chip has completely stopped working (before discovering that it has stopped reacting to Buffy alone among humans),[5] he goes hunting for a human to eat; but when he chooses one, he seems to have to talk himself into the act, with a diatribe of some length in front of the intended victim. With remarks like, "Just 'cause [Buffy's] confused about where she fits in, I'm supposed to be too? 'Cause I'm not," he seems to protest too much. He appears intent on convincing himself that "I'm evil," yet he also delays the act: "I know what I am. I'm dangerous. I'm evil ... I am a killer. That's what I do. I kill. And yeah—maybe it's been a long time. But it's not like you forget how. You just do it. And now I can again—all right? So here goes." In the end, he almost apologizes to the intended victim: "This might hurt a little." In the next episode, "Wrecked" (6.10), he goes with Buffy to locate the floating hideout of a master of dark magic, Rack, to which Will has taken Dawn. Rack's place, Spike explains, can only be sensed by witches, vampires, and others "into the Big Bad." Interestingly enough, Spike never finds the hideout; he complains that Buffy is interrupting him too much; and after searching for some time, they simply hear Dawn scream. Why is it so hard for Spike to find Rack's place? Could it be that Buffy is affecting him—that he is no longer so deeply "into the Big Bad"?

It is also worth noting that Buffy and Spike do not make love until they discover that he *can* physically harm her—and though they do engage in their usual violent "dance" ("That's all we've ever done," he tells her in "Fool for Love"), he does not really hurt her.[6] One might certainly argue that she is drawn to him all the more powerfully because of the literal danger of death; "Every Slayer has a death wish." But one might also suggest that that there is an unacknowledged trust between them (as indeed Spike argues in "Tabula Rasa," though Buffy denies the idea in "Dead Things"). The breaking of trust in the attempted rape is so shattering that it propels Spike to earn his soul (see Chapter 2). In the seventh season, they slowly come to acknowledge their renewed trust even when others (such as Giles) fear the connection. Buffy recognizes both the darkness in herself ("Get It Done," 7.15) and the light in Spike—the fact that Spike has "changed": In "Never Leave Me" (7.9), she declares, "I believe in you, Spike." Her belief in him saves him when he is tormented by the First Evil ("Showtime," 7.11). His belief in her saves her when she has cut herself off from all others; her connection with him allows her to find herself, to be whole again ("Touched," 7.20; see Chapter 6). These two characters, who *could* kill each other and *have* each literally died, die in each other's arms only metaphorically. They "dye and rise the same."

John Donne would have enjoyed them. Donne was said to be ruined by his marriage to a woman above him; only after years of struggle and difficulty and, finally, conversion, did he emerge as the preacher who reminded us that "no man is an island" (a prime theorem in the Buffyverse)—and that the bell of death "tolls for thee," tolls for us all. Buffy and Spike, who have each physically died, have access to the unconscious, and their lovemaking is powerful—but sex and death are not enough. Spike tells Buffy that he knows her, that she is like him—and he is right; he knows her dark side in both its strengths and weaknesses. But he does not yet know all of her; and even more significantly, he does not know all of himself, any more than she knows all of him or of herself.[7] We can always imagine more of Spike and Buffy. The quest for self-knowledge is part of life and growth; as Joss Whedon says, "I think of *Buffy* as life ... Life doesn't stop ... We're always changing and growing" (Kaveney, cover). And as Ursula K. Le Guin says, "The shadow is the guide ... of the journey of self-knowledge, to adulthood, to the light. 'Lucifer' means the one who carries the light" (61). To the degree that we can live with the failure, face the darkness, and risk the pain, then we can find hope, faith, and maybe even love in the words, "Every night I save you."

Chapter 6

Show Me Your World

Exiting the Text
and the Globalization of *Buffy*[1]

Xander: We saved the world.
Willow: We *changed* the world.

Joss Whedon, "Chosen" (7.22)

From a news article titled "A Fear of Vampires Can Mask a Fear of Something Much Worse" by Ralph Blumenthal, *New York Times*, 29 December 2002:

> Rumors that the government of [Malawi, a] landlocked southern African country, was colluding with vampires to collect human blood in exchange for food sent terrified villagers fleeing, wire services reported last week. A suspected vampire helper was stoned or beaten to death; three priests were attacked; and a foreign aid encampment identified as vampire headquarters was destroyed.
>
> It didn't happen in a vacuum. Malawi faces widespread starvation and a severe AIDS epidemic, as well as an uproar over efforts by the country's first and only democratically elected president, Bakili Muluzi, to override a two-term limit and remain in office after 2004.
>
> "Vampires say a lot about our fears and hopes," said Nina Auerbach, an English professor at the University of Pennsylvania and author of "Our Vampires, Ourselves."

> For millenia, the storied undead that emerge from the
> grave to suck the lifeblood of the living have embodied
> power "and our fears of power," Ms. Auerbach said.

Globalization is about power. Which way does it flow? Is it a circuit, a connection—or draining blood-suckage? "It's about the power," says Dark Willow on her way toward world destruction at the end of Season Six. "This is about power," says Amy when she shows Willow "The Killer in Me" (7.13). "It's about power," says Buffy, teaching Dawn to protect herself at the beginning of Season Seven; and at the end of the same episode, "It's about power," says the First Evil to mad, unbad, and dangerous-to-know Spike.

Whether the power is good or bad depends on who is using it and how it's used; so, too, globalization. Attitudes towards globalization can be seen in two major clusters. Thomas L. Friedman, who in *The Lexus and the Olive Tree* discusses both views, expresses the negative as "forest-crushing forces of development and Disney-round-the-clock homogenization, which, if unchecked, [have] the potential to destroy the environment and uproot cultures, at a pace never before seen in human history" (18). As the reference to Disney indicates, globalization is often identified with Americanization, or Anglo-Americanization. David Rieff, in the liberal magazine *Mother Jones*, refers to the positive form of globalization when he speaks of "the dream of global citizenship" and "the idea of an international community" (37)—as Friedman puts it, "a world that is being knit together tighter and tighter by technology, markets, and telecommunications" (258). In this view of globalization, power connects both ways.

Before I started writing about *Buffy*, I had never been outside the USA. Then somehow I found myself talking about *Buffy* in Canada; and next in England; and, when I learned that Gerry Bloustien was going to be able to take me to Australia, I emailed my coeditor David Lavery and said "*Buffy* is showing me the world." (Perhaps I should have said the English-speaking world.) A short while later, he emailed me back and said that he got the reference—and cited Angel speaking to Darla just before she makes him a vampire: "Show me your world," he says ("Becoming," Part 1, 2.21). To quote Mae West, "I'm no Angel"—at least I hope not—and David was giving me credit for being deeper than I had planned (though I believe, like Robert Frost and Roz Kaveney, in taking credit for everything anybody finds in my stuff). But that exchange was the source of this chapter. *Buffy* certainly teaches about internal psychological struggles, but it also has a broader reach. Buffy can be seen as both a metaphor for and an enactment of globalization, contemplating both its negative and positive aspects. Through the text, through the community of scholars and fans, and through the text's closing invocation of the world—through the way we exit the text—Buffy shows us globalization.

As always, I am not trying to argue for a single allegory, excluding all other options of interpretation. Having said that, I hope the possibilities I suggest will be persuasive. The negative version of globalization can be seen as a sort of imperialist, colonialist vampirism. That people in Malawi identified a "foreign aid encampment as vampire headquarters" was probably no coincidence. In the late 1990s, a "man in the street in Baghdad" being interviewed by CNN "refer[red] to America as an 'international Dracula that sucks the blood of people around the world'" (Friedman 313). Fredric Jameson would alert us to such views. Jeffrey Pasley, in Buffy and Philosophy, refers to the attacks of the various Buffy Big Bads as "globalization from hell" (258). As Mr. Trick says ("Faith, Hope, and Trick," 3.3), "We stay local—but we live global. I mean, you get the hankering for the blood of a fifteen-year-old Filipino and I'm on the Net and she's on the way next day Express Air."

So—globalization equals vampirism, and Buffy fights vampires, right? Any Buffy reader knows it could never be that simple. The vampires in the single text of Buffy carry as many meanings as they do in a variety of texts worldwide—as Pasley, among others, acknowledges. Many of us have noted that they can suggest the id or the shadow (see, e.g., Busse; Dekelb-Rittenhouse); others have discussed them as embodiments of liminality; a number of critics (such as Kent Ono and Mary Alice Money, in their very different ways) have discussed vamps as representing the outcast or the Other in society; while others, such as James South and Brian Wall and Michael Zryd, discuss them (and associated demons) as the exact opposite—the Marxist representatives of capitalist power as displayed in the blood assembly line in "The Wish" (3.9) or the exploitation of the workers in "Anne" (3.1), with Buffy wielding the hammer and sickle to resist. Or picture Buffy with a rocket launcher shooting vampires and that big blue meanie, the Judge, in the mall.

But now notice how the meaning swivels. The vampires are invading the mall, that bastion of American commercialism and capitalist power—a piston in the engine of globalization. The mall is Buffy's place, and she protects it and the people in it. More interesting to me, therefore, is the subversion within the series text that implicates Buffy (and those of us who identify with her and hers)—that implicates us in the dangers of globalization. The wry consciousness of self-criticism can be seen in many different sly, significant moments; and it is always worth remembering that *Buffy* gives us meaning not only through the large arc of narrative, but also through significant visuals, music, and of course packed dialogue. For the first half of the chapter, I will focus on three illustrations which evince recognition of the negative aspects of globalization.

For anyone who believes that *Buffy* endorses the McDonaldization of the globe, I have two words: *Doublemeat Palace*. In the sixth season, after her mother dies, and after Buffy drops out of college, dies, and returns from the dead, Buffy is in such severe financial straits that she takes a job at a fast-food restaurant. At the time, McDonald's was actually sponsoring the series (I remember noticing this with some wonderment), and Joss Whedon has commented that *Buffy*'s advertisers were not happy with the Doublemeat presentation (Pasley 264). If one is to contemplate the global spread of the capitalist system, one should recognize the disadvantages for workers at the bottom rung—and "Doublemeat Palace" (6.12) and the succeeding episodes in which Buffy continues her job clearly show some of those disadvantages. It is, as Anya cheerfully recognizes, "subsistence level employment." Workers move with mechanical slowness and are encouraged, as Tara says, to "dedicate their productive cooperation" ("Dead Things," 6.13) while they, including Buffy, become imbued with the odor and encased in the grease of the Doublemeat Palace, wearing the uniform and working double shifts of sixteen hours, nourished by Doublemeat Burgers. (You are what you eat.) There are few grimmer scenes in the series than Buffy's use of sex as an opiate, avoiding eye contact with Spike as they grip each other upright against the wall in the alley behind the restaurant.

Jeffrey Pasley notes that the episode ends with "our heroine concluding that her fears of corporate conspiracy were unjustified and resigning herself to a career in burger-flipping" (264–5). But I would argue that the fact that Doublemeat is not involved in a conspiracy makes it clearer that there is a problem in the system—which, in the real world, does not have to be conspiratorial to be problematic. This is a system that "eliminates variation"; as Buffy expresses the Doublemeat philosophy, "Variety is the spice of bad"—one of the dangers of globalization being its potential to diminish diversity—one quality of McDonaldization. When Buffy complains that the workers "seem all brain-dead" and "just stare into space," Xander, who has himself "swum [the] murky waters" of fast food, responds, "I think you're seeing demons where there's just life." And

Spike, trying to persuade her to walk out, warns her, "This place'll do stuff to you ... This place'll kill you!" They are both right. Working at this kind of job does allow you to subsist, but it does so at a cost. Like Buffy, a number of us may have worked at such a job at one point or another, but what does it mean to be what Manny the Manager calls "a lifer"?

Not only economics but also elements of materialism and militarism are questioned by the series as well. In "Restless," the finale of the fourth season, the nature of the four central characters and their journeys of self-discovery are examined through their dreams; and the course of this examination is rich with implications both psychological and political. Willow's dream version of *Death of a Salesman*, Xander's *Apocalypse Now*, and Buffy's encounter with Riley and Adam are all highly suggestive. First, it should be noted that whatever else it is, Willow's dream version of *Death of a Salesman* is funny—with main characters of a cowboy Riley, milkmaid Harmony, and flapper Buffy—and who knows what Willow is (certainly not Willow). But it is also fair to remember that Arthur Miller's play is about (among other things) a hardworking ordinary man who failed to succeed in the capitalist system, the symbolically named Willy Loman (Low-man) (referred to in "Band Candy," 3.6). And, in its humorous way, Willow's (Willy-Low's) dream mocks the cowboy combination of sex and aggression that spread out over the globe when she has her dream-Buffy spout at cowboy Riley, his face Frasier-lensed right in the foreground (with less aggressive Xander dead in the background) the following words: "All groin no brain—three billion of you passing around the same worn-out urge—men—with your *sales*." In the dream of the intellectual lesbian, the cowboy's face is thrust close to ours, but it shows no reaction, no recognition.

In Xander's *Heart-of-Darkness*-y dream, he enters *Apocalypse Now* after the soldiers and scientists of the Initiative startle him by observing him en masse as he is about to urinate. Big brothers are watching you. But when the late Principal Snyder, as Kurtz, asks Xander if he is a soldier, Xander answers that he is "a comfortadore." And we know that when he is awake, also ("The Yoko Factor," 4.20), Xander rejects that other choice of the lower economic rung besides fast food—the enlistment option—and not just because, as Anya says, "they make you get up really early." Xander fights as a partner in Buffy's war, but he resists being commanded or, as Snyder puts it, "shepherded." Xander is not going to be one of the sheep, and the sheep metaphor is an important one throughout the series. Our heroes are not mindless followers.

Perhaps the most overt questioning of the militarism and materialism that can be associated with globalization comes in Buffy's own dream. In his commentary, Joss Whedon notes that Riley and Adam are the "All-American" guys. Buffy finds them together, with a gun on the table between them; its presence is highlighted because the table is transparent and, Hitchcock-style, the camera shoots the gun from underneath. Again, the dream is silly and funny; again, it drips meaning like a coffeemaker. Riley and Adam are dressed in suits; as Whedon says, they are the suits, the businessmen, who don't fully understand Buffy and her world view. Riley tells her, "We're drawing up a plan for world domination. The key element? Coffeemakers that think." Now let me apologize for ripping the wings off the butterfly of humor, but let me also note that "Coffeemakers that think" are perfect symbols for the globalizing spread of technology—including not only the materialism of such appliances, but also the implication of the "thinking" elements of technology, computers and all they do. Buffy replies, "World domination? Is that a good?" And Riley answers, "Baby, we're the government. It's what we do." Adam—whose name, of course, suggests the beginning of the Judeo-Christian myth (see Chapter 3) and is thus a powerful expression of a patriarchal story—notes, "She's uncomfortable with certain concepts. It's understandable. Aggression is a natural human tendency. Though you and me come by it another way." "We're not demons," Buffy insists; "Is that a fact?" asks Adam. The demon in Buffy is important to the series' story as a whole, and I will return to it later. But for now, note that in her dream, Buffy—and the series—are questioning the idea of All-American domination of the world, both through the spread of technological goods and through governmental aggression. Her views of the usefulness of such methods is made wonderfully clear when Riley and Adam climax their scene by deciding to make a fort out of pillows: it is the little boy way of dealing with the world.

A third potential negative element of globalization is its cultural presumption. Globalization can mean the spread of culture in many different directions. Willow, for example, contemplates taking a course in West African drumming. But her comment that it's going to change everything carries a fair amount of freight: her expression clearly shows pleasure at the thought of learning music from another culture, but the fact that "it's going to change everything" can be made as an at least half-joking statement suggests that the cultural playing field is not even. I would argue that the series recognizes this unevenness and criticizes cultural presumption. This occurs repeatedly in the context of translation. In

"Selfless" (7.5), the hilarious subtitles remind us of the difficulty of cultural transposition. Or consider Andrew's translation of "From beneath you, it devours," from the "Mexicoan": "It eats you starting with your bottom." Or note Dawn's complaint and Buffy's reply in the seventh-season episode "Get It Done" (7.15): "Did you know that ancient Sumerians did not speak English?" "They're worse than the French!" The humor comes in part from their pretense of an unwarranted expectation that ancient Sumerians (or the French) should speak English.

A notable example of droll critique of cultural presumption comes in Season Seven. Chao Ahn, a Potential Slayer from Shanghai, is first mentioned in the episode "Potential" (7.12) and first appears in the next episode, "First Date." The mall is once again invoked: Giles, who hates the mall and all it represents, has taken Chao Ahn shopping there. The British-born father figure (and of course if Giles is Britain and Buffy is America, it is appropriate that he is the parent) believes, however, that he has handled Chao Ahn's situation nicely by taking her shopping, feeding her ice cream and communicating with her (he thinks) in her language. I have heard scholars (e.g. Viv Chin) complain that the presentation of the Asian Chao Ahn can be seen as demeaning. Certainly, we are meant to laugh at the scene; however, I would argue that the object of our laughter is not Chao Ahn but Buffy's British Watcher Rupert Giles. Further, I would argue that this scene is part of a long thread which calls into question some of Giles's attitudes and choices, culminating in his choice to kill Buffy's ever-present and very significant Other, Spike. (That the choice is wrong is expressed not only by Buffy but also by the plot, given Spike's role in the final battle of the series.) Giles is of course one of the core four Scoobies, but such classification has never prevented a Buffyverse character from falling into wrong before. Giles is remarkable partly because he resists his indoctrination, turning against the patriarchal Watchers' Council when Buffy is dangerously tested at the age of eighteen. But it is only too believable that he is in part shaped by his past, as are all characters in the Buffyverse. So in this scene with Chao Ahn, he in his fatherly fashion believes her to be expressing gratitude to be in America and happy to have her new Anglo daddy feed her ice cream—when instead she is telling him she's sick to her stomach. The cultural presumption of some globalizers, well-intentioned though they may be, is gently mocked in this scene. Giles, burdened by shopping bags, says, "Dear lord, I hate that mall ..." But when Buffy, Xander, and Willow ask how he and Chao Ahn got along, he says, "As I suspected, ice cream is a universal language." Chao Ahn, supplemented by subtitles, states, "Like many from Asia, I am lactose intolerant. I'm very uncomfortable." Buffy, smile fixed in place: "What'd she say?" Giles: "She's grateful to be in a land of plenty." Even though Giles himself may hate the mall, and his comment may have an edge of sarcasm, still the passage overall indicates an Anglo-American presumption that Chao Ahn has enjoyed her exposure to our ways and goods. Because we are reading the subtitles, we in the audience know more than Giles does in this scene—one of the reasons it's funny, with the humor of the unexpected, because one does not, in this series, normally know more than Giles—though soon, in "Lies My Parents Told Me," (7.17) Buffy will tell him that he's taught her everything she needs to know. This shift in the power of knowledge indicates a critique of his attitude, not a mockery of Chao Ahn.

Altogether, then, the series shows a consciousness of the negative ramifications of globalization and the dangerous attitudes that can be associated with it. It displays a healthy concern from workers toiling in the vineyards of Hollywood, where the wine of cultural globalization is made.

Nonetheless, the series participates in and endorses globalization in other important ways. The series has activated (to use a Slayer term) a large community of scholars and fans. I, for one, never expected to visit Australia, but *Buffy* brought me there, in the incarnation of Gerry Bloustien. As her 2002 *European Journal of Cultural Studies* article notes (428), she has met face-to-face with fans from the USA, Australia, the UK, and Spain; and she notes that there are thriving websites originating in these countries and Holland, Portugal, Italy, Sweden, and Germany, and that the series has been screened, among other places, in Argentina, China, Denmark, Finland, Hungary, Japan, Norway, and Poland. A fan site I consulted in 2003 listed contributions from fans from thirty-eight countries. When David Lavery and I called for papers for *Fighting the Forces*, we received proposals from five different countries; and since we started *Slayage: The Online International Journal of Buffy Studies*, we have heard from many more. I've gotten to practice my anemic foreign language skills corresponding with scholars from France and aiding in the translation of an article from Italian. David Lavery recently invited readers of *Slayage* to send in brief reports of their way of "Discovering Buffy." We have received responses from viewers from all regions of the USA, from England, Canada, Australia, Wales, New Zealand, Sweden, Ireland, Scotland, Israel, and Latvia; from people who have viewed *Buffy* in Germany, Malaysia, Japan, and the Czech Republic. The Region 1 DVDs include *Buffy* with Spanish and French language tracks; Region 2 DVDs include subtitles in Danish, Finnish, Norwegian, and Swedish. The implications of the conversation among us are beyond the scope of this chapter, but *Buffy* is unquestionably a global phenomenon.

Why? Gerry Bloustien quotes Bessière's comment that "the impossible is a realm of polysemy," and argues that "speculative fictions such as *Buffy* can resonate with the adolescent experience—albeit nuanced by gender, ethnicity, race and class—even in social contexts far from their geographic origins" (428). I would certainly concur. Furthermore, as she and presumably most *Buffy* scholars would probably agree, the series reaches beyond adolescence: those who wrote of their experiences "Discovering Buffy" reported connecting to the show as early as age eight and as late as seventy-three. I contend that the show's linguistic, musical, and visual texture make it art, and here I want to focus on one important reason that people around the world have connected to its art: its mythic elements. Specifically, I want to discuss the myth's very direct connection to globalization.

I plan to work from the quotation with which I opened this essay, when in the closing scene of the series Xander says, "We saved the world," and Willow counters with, "We *changed* the world"—by her vocal emphasis clearly indicating that she considers this to be the more important accomplishment. Buffy, on the other hand, says relatively little; indeed, the very end of the series (in the person of Dawn) asks her to speak—and she says nothing in return; we see a close-up of her smiling, not speaking. Each of these three speech-acts or choices is significant in terms of the series' shaping of the Buffy myth.

At one time or another, Buffy has called both Spike and Willow her "big gun" or best weapon. Each of these characters, as I and others have said before, can be seen in some ways as foils and/or shadow figures for Buffy, and as completing her. (Curiously, though Faith can also be seen as a shadow for Buffy, Buffy has never referred to her as her "big gun.") The mysterious, ancient Guardian-Woman reminds Buffy in "End of Days" (7.21) that (as Buffy herself says in "Restless," 4.22) she "already has weapons." The series finale shows all of the characters working together, but Spike and Willow have special roles. As, in effect, different aspects of herself, Spike and Willow correspond to two of the emphases of the conclusion, indicated in "saving" and "changing" the world. And they continue the light imagery patterns I have earlier described.

We saved the world

In Chapter 2, I discussed light imagery in relation to the Joseph Campbell monomyth, particularly as it applies to the characters of Buffy and Spike. Recently, David Lavery let me know of an email from Richard Slotkin, who noted that Joss Whedon had studied Joseph Campbell with him at Wesleyan University. In Chapter 2, I argue that both Buffy and Spike, in their different ways, have followed the monomyth pattern, and that their achievement of enlightenment is imagaically shown as a painful process. Like Laurel Bowman, I consider Season Six to be for Buffy a representation of the monomyth's Difficult Return passage for the hero; clearly Spike endures a Difficult Return in Season Seven,[2] as he suffered possession, madness, and unwilling murder.

The culmination of Spike's light imagery occurs in the last episode, "Chosen." As Spike sacrifices himself to do what he calls the "clean-up" after Buffy's battle, he turns into a pillar of light. Of course, in true Spike fashion, he is a laughing pillar of light wearing Liz Taylor jewelry. Many of us have noted that his self-sacrifice echoes Buffy's in Season Five; and his final statement "I want to know how it ends" is a counterpoint to the message earlier given to Buffy: "You think you know what you are—what's to come. You haven't even begun," a message clearly applicable to the series' end which is her beginning (4.22, 5.1). In "Chosen," when Buffy holds Spike's hand as he prepares, in effect, to detonate himself, flames rise from their fingers. The flames may recollect the physical passion of their past, but the context of the scene is certainly not suggestive of simple lust. That Buffy at last tells him she loves him and that he replies that she does not, suggests that he does not act in the hope of gaining her love, but rather with genuine altruism—coupled with a sense of adventure, to judge from his final words. (He is released to be reborn, as many viewers knew, in the Buffyverse spinoff *Angel*, where Spike and Angel become the Ambiguously Good Duo.) It is also worth noting his final address to her— the only time that he calls her "lamb," recalling the Christian imagery of sacrifice which can apply to both of them.[3] On the other hand, another similarity to Buffy's sacrificial death rests in the ambiguity: Marti Noxon noted that Buffy's death in Season Five could be interpreted as suicide, and Spike's belief that Buffy does not love him could suggest that his death is perhaps too willing here. Yet another interpretation would be that, once she expresses her love and accepts her shadow, he disappears, now in effect part of her (see Chapter 5).[4]

The phallically named Spike is in some ways exceptionally male. In Season Seven, Buffy's interaction with Spike entrains her dealings with the traditionally masculine matter of fighting a war—here, the war against the First Evil. But Spike is also, along with Willow, a preeminently liminal character (see, respectively, Spicer and Battis). And he is at Buffy's side in spite of most of the other males who fight with her—Xander, Robin Wood, and Giles. Robin Wood, the son of a Slayer, was raised by a Watcher; and Giles, of course, has been one. Neither of them is fully identified with the Watchers' viewpoint—Giles, of course, has overtly rejected the Watchers at serious cost. But each of them has been influenced in some degree by the Watchers and all they represent. And the series very clearly disavows the Watchers again and again. As the Watchers prepare, in "Never Leave Me," (7.9) to fight The First (and they know it is The First, though they have not told Buffy), the head of the Watchers' Council, Quentin Travers, in the war room with a giant map of the world looking as though it should belong to Dr. Evil or a James Bond villain, says to his gathered Watchers, "We're still the masters of our fate, still captains of our souls." He alludes to W. E. Henley's poem "Invictus," which has often been identified with British imperialism. He concludes his speech by cloaking himself in biblical righteousness, providing chapter, verse, and proud self-reference: "Proverbs 24:6: 'For by wise counsel [Council], you shall make your war.'" He is then blown up—a rather emphatic textual reprehension of his viewpoint. Travers's patriarchal, hierarchical attitude is indicated by the fact that he still, after two potentially illuminating encounters with Buffy, refers to her as "the girl," denying her the significance of a name (or, in this case, even her title of Slayer).

Giles, in contrast, wants Buffy to be the general of the war. And his concern that Spike may be triggered as a sleeper agent by the First Evil is valid. But when Buffy decides that Spike's potential as a weapon for good outweighs the danger, Giles assumes that her judgment is clouded by her relationship with Spike, rather than trusting that her assessment of the risk is correct (as, in the end, it turns out to be). Furthermore, when Slayer-son Watcher-child Robin Wood—who admits having "maneuvered" himself and Buffy into their jobs at Sunnydale High before he is willing to let her know who he is—asks for Giles's cooperation in a scheme to kill Spike, Giles agrees even though he knows Robin Wood's judgment is at least as prejudiced against Spike as Buffy may be prejudiced in favor, because Wood is the child of the second Slayer Spike killed. Giles undermines Buffy's authority as "general" by going behind her back to make a decision he knows she disapproves of; and in that sense, like his Watcher predecessors, he is treating her as little more than a "girl." (In contrast, Riley, while willing to kill Spike, leaves the decision to Buffy in "As You Were," 6.14.)

This attempted killing is further significant because it parallels Giles's killing of Ben in "The Gift" (5.22). A number of people, notably Jacob M. Held in *Buffy and Philosophy*, have written that Giles's actions are justified for the sake of the greater good; that the ends justified the means. I would point out that a notable similarity in the two cases—the death of Ben and the attempted killing of Spike—is that they are based on the risk of future harm. President George W. Bush would certainly have gone along with Giles's reasoning.[5] Buffy, however, does not. Her declaration that "You can't beat evil by doing evil" ("First Date") directly repudiates the argument that the ends justify the means. Since Ben is killed, we are left to speculate whether or not a method (such as Ben's earlier suggestion of drugs) could have been found to control Glory; but since Spike is not killed, the series has the opportunity to demonstrate that Buffy's choice was in this case justified. One might compare Buffy's choice not to kill Spike to Bilbo Baggins' choice not to kill Gollum—a dangerous gamble on mercy, but one which the text endorses even at serious cost. Having faith in human relationships is not a simple matter; it sometimes requires the risk of pain and death.

Spike's self-sacrifice, then, is both the climax of his personal journey and a justification of Buffy as a leader. This comes at the end of a season in which Buffy's qualities as a leader have been understandably called into question; and here we turn to the second part of the quotation, Willow's.

We *changed* the world

Joss Whedon has repeatedly said that one of his main goals in *Buffy* has been to change attitudes in the real world—in particular, attitudes about women. If Spike represents one aspect of Buffy in saving the world, Willow, the other preeminently liminal character, represents another aspect of Buffy in changing the world. Saving the world is a battle that happens over and over again in the Buffyverse with grim regularity; it is only at the series' end, however, that Willow speaks of changing the world. And they do it, of course, through the globalization of Buffy's power.

A number of *Buffy* critics, among them Zoe-Jane Playdon, Anita Rose, and I, have talked about the importance of shared power, the community, and the group dynamic in the Buffyverse as part of the feminism of the series. In Season Seven, the *Buffy* writers go out of their way to show Buffy departing from that path. Eric Alterman, author of *What Liberal Media?* reports in his MSN weblog that a number of

> Buffyites [felt] the show had slipped this year, falling into a very administration-like (and un-Buffy-like) us vs. them moral schema. Several correspondents expressed grave disappointment and even anger. A few, while conceding that this seemed to be true, made the case that it was an intentional commentary on the Bush gang: that it's very much to be noted that Buffy, acting now as a moral absolutist [—] the Wolfowitz of the Scoobies, if you will [—] was in fact cast out by her comrades in the last episode ["Empty Places," 7.19]. Having been thus isolated and shunned, she will drop the preaching (the show[']s defenders anticipate) about good and evil, which has not rallied the troups and in fact only offended her potential allies (get it?), and just get on in a more pragmatic way with the business at hand; which is to say, the last episode will establish firmly that the entire season has been a critique of absolutism.

If we continue with this anthropomorphic representation of international politics, it should be noted that Buffy has succeeded in the past in part because she has, as Spike puts it, "ties to the world" ("Fool for Love," 5.7)—because she operates within a group of friends who support but can also question each other.[6]

Her interactions with the Potential Slayers, the Slayers in training, represent both problematic personal and political patterns. Except in age and gender, the Potentials are various—diverse in socioeconomic class, in race, in ethnicity, in geographic origin. We see Potentials not only from various parts of the USA, but also from the UK, Germany, Turkey, and China; Buffy, walking through a house full of sleeping Potentials in "Get It Done," peruses a table full of language dictionaries including Greek, French, Norwegian, and Spanish. But this is no "model UN—geek stuff," to use brother Lance's words from "Him" (7.6). Living crammed into a house full, or a world full, of very different people can be an uncomfortable business, and Buffy shows us how not to do it. In reversal of the Scooby "ties to the world" tradition, we see her failing to really get to know the Potentials— even to learn their names; she is not sure whether or not she's speaking to Chloe just before Chloe dies ("Get It Done"). In this she reiterates the lack of respect Quentin Travers shows her, when he fails to refer to her by name. And in case we did not recognize Buffy's failure, Faith points it out specifically in "Empty Places," the episode in which Buffy is cast out.

Throughout the season, Buffy's withdrawal has been charted. In the fifth episode, "Selfless," for example, she says, "You get down on me for cutting myself off, but in the end the Slayer is always cut off ... There's only me. I am the law." (Did anyone else think of Judge Dredd?) It is worth noting that open communication with loved ones in the past has led to Buffy's being incarcerated in a mental institution ("Normal Again," 6.17), an experience that might tend to chill the urge to communicate.[7] In the memorable seventeenth episode, "Conversations with Dead People" (in which, interestingly enough, Spike says not a word), vampire psychologist intern Holden Webster spends much of the hour leading Buffy to contemplate her lack of connection. (She stakes him.) She is not monolithically ungiving; in "Bring on the Night" (7.10) she, unlike the Watchers' Council and against Giles's recommendation to her, shares information with the Slayers in training, saying "Welcome to the War Room." And Xander's speech to the Potentials about Buffy's caring for them is eminently believable. But even Xander responds to Buffy with "Jawohl," indicating her Hitlerian, dictatorial tendencies, during what Anya calls Buffy's "Everyone Sucks But Me" speech.

It is when Buffy is living through this phase, this attitude, that Giles, trying to prepare her to accept the death of Spike that he has already planned, reminds Buffy of her refusal to allow anyone to kill Dawn when Glory threatened the world. Giles says, "Faced with the same choice now, you'd let her die." And Buffy says, "If I had to, to save the world." Even this declaration is a qualified one; putting aside Giles's inaccurate implication that Spike's case is exactly parallel, Buffy, even in her harshest frame of mind, still leaves herself a big "if." But Spike himself, in the same episode ("Lies My Parents Told Me"), says to Robin Wood, "I know Slayers. No matter how many people they've got around them, they fight alone. Life of a Chosen One. The rest of us be damned."

This is a paradigm for failure, both personally and internationally. Fortunately for all, Buffy is able to break the pattern, to reframe the paradigm. How does she do it? First of all, she has both the connection with her shadow to strengthen her alone and connection with community—friends and associates willing and able to tell her where to get off; she is, as noted earlier, rejected by the group and thus forced into self-contemplation, never a Buffy strength. Excluded by all but Spike, she admits that she has been "making excuses" for her failure to connect. The second step illuminates the psychological elements of the story: Buffy is able to come up with her world-changing plan only when she joins Spike in the basement, only when she accepts her shadow and connects with her dark side.

She creates the change through her other "big gun," Willow. And this change is the Campbellian hero's boon: her sharing of power with the Potentials from around the world. As early as the third episode of the season, this conclusion is foreshadowed when, at the end of the episode, Buffy and a wounded Willow clasp hands as Willow works on a healing trance ("Same Time, Same Place," 7.3). Clothing is often significant in *Buffy*, and here both women are dressed in a differing mix of white and gray: heroes do not have to be pure white in the Buffyverse. Trying to help the healing, Buffy says to Willow, "I've got so much strength I'm giving it away." In "Lessons," the first episode of the season, Giles has told Willow, "You're connected to a great power, whether you feel it or not"—and Willow's magic, in the end, enables people worldwide to participate in the connection by sharing her power.

And just as the liminal Spike has, nonetheless, some very masculine associations, so the liminal Willow has some strong female associations—the lesbian who works with the power of the prehistoric female Guardians. Buffy, through Willow, reiterates her earlier choices to eschew solo, stereotypically masculine heroics (and both Xander and Giles approve).

Significantly, Buffy is shown in a flashback in "Chosen" inviting the Potentials to choose whether or not to accept this power—whereas she and all before her in the Slayer line have been chosen; and as she says in "Get It Done," the first Slayer was "violated" by the Shadow Men because she had no choice. (Buffy knows her own Shadow.) Joss Whedon has said he had to work in shorthand for the series' closing, but the montage of Potentials being activated by Willow and Buffy is clearly meant to show young women of various natures and forms from around the world: it shows the globalization of Buffy's power. In this way, the world in the Buffy myth is not merely saved once more, but changed forever. In the last battle, set in the high school, Willow—Buffy's Will—acts physically and symbolically upstairs, while Buffy, Spike, and the other champions battle down below, uniting the conscious and subconscious. And Willow, like Spike, glows with light. In fact, at one point, his shaft of light breaks into her room (and I'm not sure it's necessary to follow out the imagaic implications there). It should be noted that Spike only begins to glow after Will has dispersed power to all the Potential Slayers, and the "rising music" has indicated their coming victory.[8]

Buffy has shared her power around the world; but what are we to make of the fact that not every young woman is a Slayer? (I won't attempt to discuss the young men here, except to say that men and women do fight together, in a communal effort, in the Last Battle of Sunnydale.) As Tanya Krzywinska said to me in an email after she saw the last episode, "I ... sat there waiting for the slayer power to hit me, but sadly it didn't ...." The episode called "Potential" actually focuses on Dawn and Xander and the bravery of working for the cause even if not in the "spotlight." Perhaps it can be argued that in the end of the myth, being a Slayer, then, means being a leader.

What qualifies one as a leader in the Buffyverse? Is there anything that the diverse Potential Slayers presumably have in common? Buffy, in "Get It Done," discovers that the Slayer line was begun when men forced a girl to accept within herself demonic power—"the energy of the demon, its spirit, its heart"—and then proceeded to hide the source of that power from future Slayers. Though the series does not have the characters deal with this discovery at length, one might note Cordelia's acceptance, in *Angel*, of being part demon; and fanfic writers such as Barb Cummings and A. J. Hofacre years ago picked up on the earlier hints (for example, in "Restless") of Buffy's part-demon nature and explored them in their writing. (And I refer you to Erma Petrova's essay in *Refractory*.) As Joss Whedon says in his commentary to "Restless," it is important that Buffy balances within herself the Slayer side and the Buffy side (or we might say the save-the-world side and the connection side—see Chapter 10). In "Get It Done," she refuses to accept "more power" because she "didn't like the loophole" of becoming "less human." But she has, in spite of the lack of original choice, come to accept the demonic as part of a balance within herself—psychologically, she accepts the power of the id; politically, she incorporates the Other. It is such a person who can become a leader, can be a Slayer.

For the First Evil, this means that Buffy is one of the "Dirty Girls"; for the Buffy myth, this means that the Dirty Girls will rule the world. Caleb, the vessel of the First Evil, expresses traditional patriarchal religious scorn of women (as Mary Wollstonecraft reminded us long ago, whether or not women had souls had been a matter of some debate). And, in Season Seven, the First Evil chooses to take the form of a Potential Slayer named Eve—clearly recalling the Judeo-Christian traditional casting of woman in the role of first sinner and sexual temptress (see Chapter 3). The Potential Eve is a short blonde woman; but the First Evil also spends much of Season Seven in the form of another short blonde woman, Buffy herself. In *Fighting the Forces*, I noted that Glory was "a parodic version of the overdressed blonde

bimbo some have considered Buffy" (17). The First Evil's presentation as
Eve and as Buffy continues this visual pattern, and is thus one element of
the text that suggests that Buffy must fight herself, must fight that inner
voice that calls herself a "Dirty Girl" and may reject power. The climax
of the battle, for Buffy, comes when she tells the whining, Buffy-shaped
First, in one of the best of the Buffy puns, "Get out of my face!" Slayers or
Potential Slayers who can choose to handle the demon within are capable
of becoming leaders, are capable of wielding power.[9]

So, now—we saved the world; we changed the world. What of Buffy's
silence at the end? Joss Whedon has said that one of his favorite novelists
is Charles Dickens; and I have made comparisons between Buffy Summers
and Esther Summerson of *Bleak House*. In a PopPolitics roundtable, I spoke
of my hope that *Buffy* would end in the fashion of *Bleak House*: narrator
Esther Summerson stops in the middle of a sentence; her last words are
"even supposing"—inviting the reader to fill in the blank. Just so, at the end
of *Buffy*, we are left with a question for readers to answer. As the Scoobies
joke about the destruction of the mall and the need to tell the world about
Starbucks (recall part one of this chapter), Faith, who sees herself as the
Second Slayer, asks Buffy how it feels now that she's no longer the "only
one"—in other words, now that Buffy is no longer the First. Buffy's
condition is ambiguous: during the fight after the power-sharing she has
seemed no less powerful, but Faith's question may imply a lessening of
power; or perhaps it simply means that she is now one of many. In any
case, Buffy's lack of an answer means that *we* get to answer the question.

Buffy has fulfilled the Campbellian monomyth right through to the giving
of the boons, by the time she is just past her legal maturity. In her end is her
beginning. The story is both complete and incomplete. The text invokes the
imagination of the reader—all those readers from around the globe whom
I spoke of earlier—to finish the story in their own fashions. In effect, it is
a blessing upon all fanfiction writers—the ultimate endorsement of reader
response. (And this open ending changes another part of the myth: Buffy's
story does not close with the traditional female happy ending of choosing
a mate; Teresa de Lauretis, take note and rejoice.) The story is unended
and alive. Repeatedly in episodes such as "Storyteller" (7.16) and "Lies My
Parents Told Me" and before them, "Superstar" (4.17) and "Fool for Love,"
we have been shown the power (as well as the danger) of storytelling. At
the end of "Storyteller," Andrew turns off his videocamera in mid-sentence,
ending the episode as he clicks the remote in our faces, dumping us into
reality in a prelude of the series' closing. In "A Religion in Narrative," David

Lavery argues that "It's about the power" refers to the power of narrative. *Buffy* the character shares the power and responsibility of the Slayer with Potentials across the globe; and her act is equivalent to *Buffy* the series' sharing of the power and responsibility of Buffy's unfinished story with viewers. As Walter Fisher says, humankind is the storytelling animal; we experience the world as stories. And as Buffy says in "Storyteller," and Joss Whedon says in many times and in many places, the stories must be true. In his conduct of the *Buffy* writing company, Joss Whedon has shared the power with such as Jane Espenson, David Greenwalt, and Marti Noxon. As we exit the text of the series, Whedon and Co. throw the end of the narrative out into the world so that it depends on us to conclude it. They have given us the power of the myth; now we must write, and live, our own stories.

May we write well.

Part II
Tight Focus

Chapter 7

Love and Loss:
It's Not Over

Time, Love, and Loss
in "Surprise"/"Innocence"[1]

The double grief of a lost bliss
Is to recall its happy hour in pain …
We were alone with innocence and dim time.

> Francesca, forever in torment with her lover Paolo
> in Dante's *Inferno*, Canto V, ll. 118–19, 126

Seize the moment, because tomorrow you might be dead.

> Buffy to Willow, "Welcome to the Hellmouth" (1.1)

Give me time.

> Buffy to Angelus, "Innocence" (2.14)

One of the best-known and most written-about episodes of *Buffy* is also
the one that Joss Whedon lists as his favorite: "Innocence," the second
half of a two-parter, in which Buffy deals with the consequences of
making love for the first time ("The Last Sundown" DVD feature). It is
the twenty-sixth episode of the series—i.e., it comes just past the point
at which a full season of (for this era) 22 episodes would normally end,
though it is actually just over halfway through Buffy's second season (the
first season having lasted only twelve episodes). By this point, the series
itself, like its heroine on some occasions, was displaying an extraordinary
maturity. Joss Whedon speaks of the two-parter as a unit (using a singular

verb): "'Surprise' and 'Innocence' deals with the pivotal moment in Buffy and Angel's relationship where they have sex for the first time and then the second half deals with rather appalling consequences of that act." It seems right, therefore, to discuss them together, though "Surprise" (2.13) was written by Marti Noxon (who went on to helm the series in the last two years) and directed by Michael Range (who later directed, for example, "Bad Girls," 3.14, and "Pangs," 4.8), while "Innocence" was written and directed by Whedon. As Whedon says, "'Surprise' and 'Innocence' represent the mission statement of the show more than any other show we've done because they operate on a very mythic level and a very personal level. On the mythic level it's the hero's journey—she loses this very important person to her—Angel goes bad and now she has to fight him ... But on a more personal level, this is a show about: 'I slept with somebody and now he doesn't call me anymore.'"

A number of critics (e.g. Tracy, Siemann) have written about the clear-cut metaphoric significance of Buffy's first sexual encounter. In effect, a young woman's worst fear is realized when, after they sleep together, her partner's behavior is monstrous. However, the two-parter engages the audience in the experience of love and loss not only through the central metaphor but through a number of subtle techniques, metaphoric and narrative, visual, aural, and temporal. Gerry Bloustien has addressed the constructed nature of time in Buffy from a sociological perspective. The use of time in "Surprise"/"Innocence" is also fascinating in terms of narrative and filmic techniques. Whedon, Noxon, and all the crew of Mutant Enemy build the Buffy/Angel relationship through series time—but they also prepare the audience through a series of foreshadowings both before and within the two-parter. Thus there is a complex tuning of emotional response, with attentive viewers recognizing both the strength of the relationship Buffy and Angel have built, and the adumbration of trouble (as will be discussed below)—not to mention, of course, the reiterated danger of "a vampire in love with a Slayer" ("Out of Mind, Out of Sight," 1.11). Furthermore, Whedon uses time displacement to signify and experientially convey the loss Buffy suffers. The audience is not shown images of the lovemaking until Buffy has already come to realize that Angel is lost. The two-part title, too, suggests this poignancy through displacement. Chronological order would typically suggest that "innocence" exists first and is then taken by "surprise." Whedon instead shows us that innocence is only fully realized after it is lost.

Do You Really Think You're Ready, Buffy?

Like the first episode of the series, "Surprise" starts with a prophetic Buffy dream (in "Welcome to the Hellmouth," the dream comes immediately after the teaser; in "Surprise," it is the teaser). And as is the case with all the Buffy dreams we see, it is extraordinarily resonant. Here, she dreams before awakening to her seventeenth birthday. The first English words in the dream and the episode are "Do you really think you're ready, Buffy?"— and the entire dream is a premonition of the transition Buffy is about to go through, the threshold of maturation she is about to cross. It is marked by birthday, battle, and sexual initiation. At first it is not clear that she is in a dream: in her dream, Buffy awakens in bed (as she will soon sexually awaken); she reaches for water, and finding none, goes to seek it. As dreamy music plays, dream-Buffy, in satiny, white pajamas of plain cut (with a black undershirt), opens and walks through a doorway that leads from her home to another psychological place—a dream-version of the teen night club, the Bronze. She has left her home and gone to a place where males and females meet. She, in her simple, innocent white, is followed by a woman in elaborate dark clothing, a woman with blood on her mouth: Drusilla, the once innocent victim of Angelus—she who is now the most lascivious and violent of vampires. She often operates as a double of Buffy (of this, more later) and does so here. Dream-Buffy does not see Drusilla following behind her; but of course it is Buffy's dream, so she knows Dru is there: Buffy is recognizing that there is a threat she is unaware of, embodied here as one of her own dark doubles.

Drusilla is one of three females important to Buffy who figure in this dream. The other two are Willow and Buffy's mother, Joyce, both of whom are concerned for her welfare. (In fact, even Drusilla has expressed sympathy: "Poor little thing," she calls Buffy in "Lie to Me," 2.7, when she anticipates what's to come for Buffy and Angel.) Buffy's supernatural powers mean that she has, through her dreams, access to knowledge unavailable to her on a conscious level. From each of the three females Buffy takes a hint in a different form. First Willow, smiling as she sits at a Bronze table with a monkey in a red hat and jacket, speaks words which may seem incomprehensible: "L'hippo a piqué tes pantalons." It is, as Nikki Stafford (212) notes, a reference to a conversation with Oz which was part of the beginning of their connection as a couple ("What's My Line?" Part 2, 2.10). Willow thus sets a context of male-female relationships. The use of the word "piqué," which Stafford translates as a "slang" way of saying "stolen," is a term that can mean "snatch" or also "prick"—so this no-pants monkey has a sexually symbolic way with him. Second, Buffy's mother asks if Buffy really thinks she's ready. Joyce is holding a large coffee cup and saucer, and she drops the saucer, which breaks. One might recall the Jewish wedding ceremony with the groom's breaking of the wine glass as a reminder that this is traditional sexual symbology, with the female as vessel (cf. the male/female symbolism of the sword and the Holy Grail, the holy vessel; just think of *The Da Vinci Code*). It should also be noted that when this part of the dream later comes true (when Joyce repeats the words, drops a dish, and breaks it), she and Buffy are, because it is her birthday, discussing another rite of passage: whether or not the now seventeen-year-old Buffy is to be allowed to get a driver's license. And driving can itself be a metaphor for sex (as Riley makes obvious in the picnic scene of "Something Blue," 4.9).[2] So, in this birthday dream, Buffy's best friend opens the sexual subtext with a smile; then Buffy's mother cautions her; and the entire time, Buffy's double Drusilla, the embodiment of sexual depredation, lurks, bloody-lipped, in the background. Last in this enchanted dream evening, Buffy sees Angel across the crowded room and moves toward him—only to see her substitute, Drusilla, dust him (as Buffy has more than once feared she herself might have to do). Angel dies as he and Buffy reach to each other, their outstretched fingers not quite able to touch (an image later echoed and transformed in "The Body," 5.16). When she awakens for real, Buffy is no longer wearing white satin, but only the black undershirt—the color hints at both sexual experience and mourning. The dream rehearses the experience Buffy is about to have: her choice to go through the sexual experience means that Angel will lose his soul, will die to her.

Guys! Buffy! Snake! Basement! Now!

Willow's line from "Reptile Boy" (2.5) is perhaps the most compact example of a pattern common in *Buffy*: smaller elements represent larger ones, a kind of semiotic synecdoche (using both sound and picture). In "Reptile Boy," there is a very Freudian fraternity which worships a phallic demon (acknowledged as such by the writers) and uses women to get ahead in the world; the frat boys seem admirable on the surface while engaging in wickedness in the basement of the subconscious (where the demon snake appears). Buffy allows herself to be ensnared by them and, after a struggle (woman breaking free of her chains here quite literally), releases herself with the gladly accepted help of not only her female friend Willow but also the outsider males Xander, Giles, and Angel (see Chapter 1). The whole plot and symbolic subtext is neatly summarized in Willow's telegraphic command: "Guys! Buffy! Snake! Basement! Now!"

Willow's "Reptile Boy" line comes towards the end of the episode, but the technique is often used as a method of foreshadowing; the opening dream in "Surprise" is an example, a small representation of the longer story. The technique also extends through multiple episodes. Certain tropes are established which parallel and symbolically foreshadow later events. Since Whedon and Co. knew the overall arc of a season, it is possible that the early versions of a pattern are purposeful foreshadowing; it is also possible that they are preliminary explorations or first inklings of an idea which the writers will choose to develop more fully later. Retroactive continuity allows for the effect of foreshadowing. Roz Kaveney has queried Jane Espenson about "inadvertent foreshadowing"; Espenson noted that Joss Whedon had on occasion asked, "'Were we planning this back then?' And even he didn't know for sure" (Espenson, 107–08). She also comments, "Some of it is conscious and some of it is not conscious, but it is clearly there anyway" (107). The method is not unlike that of Charles Dickens, who wrote his novels in serialized form, knowing the overall arc but creating week by week, following where the characters led.[3] In any case, some of these patterns serve as, to adapt literary terminology, types (a term used most often to refer to types of Christ, parallel figures which anticipate the messiah). Whether the reference is to a single character or a plot pattern, they are precapitulations, precaps (if I may put it that way) of what is to come.

In other words, the Buffy/Angel loss is long prepared for in the series, shocking though it nonetheless seemed to many viewers at the time: it has that wonderful quality of much great literature, of seeming both surprising and inevitable. It may have more preparatory parallels than any other element of the series. As of the seventh episode of the series, we know that Angel was given his soul through a gypsy curse in order that he might suffer the torture of guilt; in "Surprise," one of the many surprises is that Willow's mentor and Giles's significant other, technopagan computer teacher Jenny Calendar, is a member of that gypsy tribe who was sent to watch Angel. Her name is actually Janna Kalderash, and she is contacted by her Uncle Enyos. He tells her that a tribal elder woman ("never wrong") has seen Angel's torment lessening. He insists that Jenny's declarations of Angel's attempts to atone are irrelevant. He does not, however, tell her the specific consequences; she simply promises to "see to it," to prevent Angel's happiness by separating him and Buffy, and she takes the first opportunity to do so when she urges him to leave town to dispose of a body part from the Armageddon-inducing demon that Spike and Dru are planning to assemble (the Judge). It is only after Buffy and Angel have actually made love that Ms. Calendar (and the audience, and Buffy) learns the specific consequences—that "one minute's happiness" will mean the loss of Angel's soul, just as one minute's satisfaction would damn the soul of Goethe's Faust to hell.[4]

In fact, in the same conversation, she learns that this loss has already happened, and the audience knows it is because Buffy and Angel have made love. Her uncle's practice of the economy of knowledge with Jenny (he holds the capital) is similar to the relationship between the Watchers' Council and Giles; they are very parsimonious in their dispersal of knowledge, even to key agents in the field. (Giles, for example, was not told of the existence of the concurrent Slayer, Kendra, before her arrival in Sunnydale; nor was Kendra's Watcher Sam Zabuto apparently told that Buffy had been revived.) Knowledge (and its power) is one of the many themes often connected to sexual initiation. The snake leads us to the tree of knowledge bearing the apple of temptation; only afterwards do we know our nakedness. Nor is it only a matter of the participants' gaining sometimes painful perspective. The most private of acts is embedded in the social order. Buffy and Angel's lovemaking is not just a private choice; it is an act with consequences for the community, and knowledge of it spreads painfully fast (one of the many consequences for Buffy is, in fact, the lack of privacy). The eating of the apple expels us all from the garden.

But to return to the preparatory patterns: Buffy and Angel's first lovemaking in "Surprise" is precisely forecast by their first kiss in "Angel" (1.7). In "Angel," they are attacked by vampires sent by the Master; in "Surprise," they are attacked by vampires sent by Spike and Dru, the current masters of Sunnydale's vampires. In each case, they run through the night to escape; in the first case to Buffy's home, in the second case to Angel's home. In "Angel," Angel has been wounded in the attack, and so Buffy tells him to take off his shirt so that she can tend his wounds; the scene involves her discovery of his shoulder tattoo, and clearly involves sensual pleasure for both of them. In "Surprise," Buffy has been wounded in the attack, and Angel is the one who lowers the spaghetti strap from her shoulder as he tenderly checks her wound. They fight together and they care for each other both physically and emotionally before moving on to the next step. In "Angel," after a delay, Buffy and Angel face each other in her bedroom, and they kiss for the first time, the pair shot in profile before her slatted bedroom blinds—a visual echo of many a noir movie moment, the mixture of visual light and dark reflecting the mixture of light and dark emotion; it is a shot used many times in many places (including the series credits and trailers for the series in syndication). But the passion of the first kiss overcomes Angel to the degree that he loses control and vamps out, his face transforming to display the feral monster he carries within. The pattern predicts exactly his response to their first lovemaking (*le grand baiser*, the big kiss, the French call it): its passion, his happiness, results in his becoming fully monstrous when he loses his soul.

Though the first kiss is the most clear-cut precap of the first lovemaking, there are others. In the first episode of the series, for example, Buffy, in the Bronze with Willow for the first time, asks if she wants to hear her philosophy: "Life is short ... Seize the moment, because tomorrow you might be dead." The thought is reiterated near the beginning of "Surprise," when Buffy and Willow talk over Buffy's relationship with Angel. "To act on want can be wrong," Buffy realizes; but "What if I never feel this way again?" And "Carpe diem. You told me that once," says Willow; "It means 'seize the day.'" In "Welcome to the Hellmouth," while Buffy goes off in the Bronze to talk with Giles, she sees Willow leaving with an attractive dark-haired young man—"seizing the moment," as Buffy tells Giles, recalling her earlier conversation with Willow; but Buffy has just spotted this young man for a vampire, and he will soon turn on Willow just as, many episodes later, Angel turns on Buffy. Willow's "Surprise" comment "you told me that once" might remind us of the parallel between the two events. As Buffy says to Willow in "Surprise," "Once you get to a certain point, the seizing is sort of inevitable." Both Willow and Buffy find danger in seizing the moment.

"I want this moment to last," says the Master to Buffy in "Prophecy Girl" (1.12). The Master's biting of Buffy in this, the last episode of the first season, is—like many a story of a vampire's bite—a representation of a sexual encounter, and more specifically of loss of virginity: Buffy, in her white prom dress, lies dead after the bite—the symbolic death of maidenhood. But as Elisabeth Krimmer and Shilpa Raval point out, this story, in Whedon's version, is amalgamated with that of the hero's journey (158–9); Buffy (like Luke Skywalker before her) has entered the dark cave to face her destiny; and she is reborn more powerful than she was before, though her death was brief enough that her friend Xander could use CPR to revive her. (It will later take Willow and the others much more terrible effort when Buffy dies again.) And if we see this as one of the precaps of

Buffy's actual sexual initiation, then the pattern of regained strength bodes well. Her revival and empowerment in "Prophecy Girl" are a brief version of the lengthier struggles we see later.

Throughout the series, then, premonitory or echoing passages build to enrich key expressions of patterns such as we find in "Surprise"/ "Innocence." The writers also use not only parallel plot constructs, but parallel characters. In "Surprise"/"Innocence," we see variations on a theme through the couples in particular. Buffy and Angel are echoed, reflected, reversed, and recalled in Spike and Dru, Xander and Cordelia, Willow and Oz, Giles and Jenny, and even Joyce and Hank Summers. These pairings run through many episodes, of course, but are particularly highlighted here. For instance, after Buffy's dream, we see a scene of Buffy and Angel discussing the progress of their relationship, passionately kissing as they literally stand at a threshold (his apartment door), the setting expressing the relationship. After a succeeding scene in which Willow and Buffy discuss the latter's relationship with Angel, there is a scene in which Willow approaches Oz and they decide to date (specifically, to attend Buffy's surprise birthday party together); again, the setting reflects the relationship: their open, happy beginning is shot in the sunny outdoors. In the next scene, we see, in contrast, Xander quietly asking Cordelia to attend the party with him; she is coming ("Chips and dip girl!"), but won't accept him as a date. They have kept their sexually heated groping of each other secret (often literally in the closet), and their scene is shot from the inside of the school locker before which they stand, a claustrophobic physical representation of their secrecy. In a series filled with couplings, this two-parter is saturated with them, readying attentiveness to the romantic choices that can be made.

Opening the Box

In the candlelit dark we find Spike and Drusilla. One of the most interesting character parallels can be seen to involve a specific physical symbol as well. Many have seen Spike/Dru as a mirroring of Buffy/Angel: the light-haired Spike vs. the dark-haired Angel, the dark-haired Dru vs. the light-haired Buffy; gleefully violent Spike vs. conscience-ridden Angel, completely amoral Dru vs. the highly moral Slayer. In both pairs, their passion is notable: Buffy and Angel love each other though one is vampire and the other is the Slayer; Spike and Dru, though they are both vampires, "share affection and jealousy" and thus "stink of humanity," as we are told in this episode by no less an authority than the Judge. Dru has, in the past, been

Angel's lover (she was sired by him); Spike will, in the future, be Buffy's.

Some of the similarities between Dru and Buffy have been hinted at in this chapter's discussion of the opening dream of "Surprise." Angel—or Angelus—is the first sexual partner for each; each of them has psychic visions; each of them is preternaturally strong. In "Surprise" they are both shown having parties: Buffy's is a surprise birthday party; Drusilla's is a party to celebrate her return to health. Spike has arranged to rejuvenate her after an illness with an infusion of her sire Angel's blood in "What's My Line?" Part 2; Buffy will later save Angel by giving him hers in "Graduation Day." Soon after the credits in "Surprise," Angel asks what Buffy wants for her birthday gift; she tells him, "Surprise me." The surprise of the title is his gift, then—which turns out to be a claddagh ring, the sign of their union; their sexual union is another surprise gift (considering that he had agreed to leave town that evening); and, of course, the greatest surprise is the loss of his soul. Drusilla's party gifts are not a surprise for her; Spike allows her to peek in one of the boxes which hold the body parts of the Judge. In fact, one of her presents ends up at Buffy's party, because on her way Buffy ("sacred duty, yada yada") attacks a group of vamps and Jenny Calendar brings in a wooden box which they were carrying. When Buffy opens the box, a severed, armor-clad arm reaches out to throttle her. With Angel's help, she pulls it off her neck, and Angel and Giles identify it as belonging to the Judge, who, in his fully assembled form, will destroy the world (or, more specifically, all the humanity in it).

The woman's opening the box which leads to all kinds of trouble and woe recalls Pandora's box, "Pandora" meaning "the gift of all" (Hamilton 70). Dru, of course, wants to open that dangerous box; Buffy does so unwittingly—but then, of course, so does Pandora. The opening of the box is also correlated with sexual transition[5] both here and in the myth. Pandora is a beautiful young wife, and her box is a wedding gift from the gods. To move from the mythic to the linguistic, one needs hardly note the use of the term "box" in sexual slang; and it is difficult not to note that Spike says of Dru, "She can't have her fun without the box," which he also calls her "lost treasure." Like the story of the Garden of Eden, the story of Pandora connects the gaining of sexual experience with the gaining of knowledge of the world; a loss of innocence and an acquisition of trouble as a result of the woman's choice.[6] When Angel later tells Buffy "maybe we shouldn't," she says, "Just kiss me"; and here Buffy opens the box. Life before the apple is bitten, before the box is opened, is paradisaic—without real knowledge of death. But those who are conscious of self are also conscious of death. With adulthood comes the knowledge of both sex and death. Another French term for the climax of lovemaking is *la petite morte*, the little death. This episode shows us the movement from the prelapsarian eternal to the mortality of normal time and life; it shows us, and Buffy, the sorrow of the world.

In the Greco-Roman myth, Pandora is left surrounded by sadness—but still, in one corner of the box, there is the gift of Hope. Whedon gives Buffy a whole other box. In "Innocence," having decided she must fight the now devilish Angel, she is given a box of her own, not the sexually ravaged Drusilla's. It was provided—as so many things are in the Buffyverse—by the efforts of the community: Giles, Xander, Willow, Cordelia, and Oz working together. Xander having come up with first "a thought" then "a plan," the Scoobies sneak onto a nearby army base shortly after Angel turns. They use knowledge Xander acquired in his brief experience as a soldier (during "Halloween," 2.6). "Happy Birthday, Buffy. I hope you like the color," says Xander as Buffy opens yet another wooden box. In it is not an arm, but armament. Buffy has something to fight with.

The Water's Edge

Xander's "Happy Birthday, Buffy" echoes the deadly Drusilla in the last words spoken at the end of the opening dream. In the dream, Buffy has looked for water by her bedside; and going to seek it, what she has found is Angel. Like the symbol of the opened box, water symbolism repeatedly appears in the episode. From the Greek Sirens to Dickens's Steerforth, from the German Lorelei to the Russian Water Grandfather (Campbell 80), water has been linked to sexual seduction. It has also, of course, been used to signify transition, crossing over (e.g. the River Jordan, rebirth, baptism). "Surprise"/"Innocence" makes use of both of those meanings.

When Buffy and Angel plan to part from each other for months so that Angel can take away the danger, they do so at the water's edge. On the Sunnydale docks (Sunnydale has as many convenient geographical features as *The Simpsons'* Springfield), they stand at a marker of transition. They stand before a huge ship, a sign of a journey, and Angel says, "I should go the rest of the way alone"—but of course their lives are about to become more deeply entangled. And, just as surely, Buffy is on a journey of her own. As Krimmer and Raval say, Buffy and Angel are supremely conscious of the threat of death; "If you haven't noticed, someone pretty much always wants us dead," says Buffy (154–5). Equally, one might note, they are aware of the passage of time. As Philip Pullman writes of the symbols of truth in *His Dark Materials*, "in the hourglass range of meanings you get death. In fact, after time, which is the first one, death is the second one" (*The Golden Compass*, 143). And "Six months? A year?" of absence to dispose of a problem means something proportionally quite different to a seventeen-year-old vampire slayer and a 240-something vampire. But there at the water's edge, Angel gives her "a sign of devotion"—her birthday surprise, a silver claddagh ring to match his own. Donna Potts notes that claddagh rings (comprised of the hands of friendship, crown of loyalty, and heart of love) are often used for wedding ceremonies. Angel tells Buffy that when you "wear it with the heart pointing towards you, it means you belong to somebody." He shows her that he wears his in that fashion, and then tells her, "Put it on," leaving it to her to choose whether or not she will say she belongs to him. Like the "One Hand One Heart" ("Make of our hearts one heart") scene in *West Side Story*, this scene at the docks is, in effect, a wedding ceremony (both scenes taking place before the sexual act). As Golden and Holder put it, the giving of the ring "is as close to a wedding as these two are ever likely to get" (103). Immediately afterwards, when Buffy and Angel are attacked by vampires, the two lovers plunge into the water one after another (a visual displayed again and again in the repeated previews leading up to the two-parter). There is a physical and symbolic immersion—both sensually dramatic and emblematically ritualistic.

In the next scene the sensual elements are highlighted in a lighthearted way, Xander expressing jealousy when he learns Buffy and Angel had to change: "And we needed clothes because ...?" "We got wet," Buffy tersely answers. After a research session during which Buffy nods off and dreams again of Angel's death with killer Drusilla and herself in similar white gowns (the veil between herself and her substitute growing thinner), Buffy and Angel reconnoiter, searching for information about the Judge at Spike and Drusilla's place. They find the big blue demon to be fully activated.[7] Chased out by Spike and Dru's vampires, they escape through the sewer tunnels and emerge through a manhole into the pouring rain. This emergence gives another visual suggestion of transition. They run through the rain to hide at Angel's; and their wet sensuality is a felt element of the ensuing scene, during which Angel finally says in words that he loves Buffy. The two are shown with wet hair and clothing; the dim light from Angel's window casts a shadow of water trickling down the wall behind the bed on which they sit. Tears and rain mix as they sink out of frame, Buffy's head above Angel's—one more sign that she is not forced, that she, like Angel, has made a choice. But this choice, of course, leads to the next scene of water and transition—Angel's soul washed away in the rain, as he falls to the ground, crying out Buffy's name. This is the end of "Surprise."

It is perfectly appropriate that, at the end of "Innocence," there is a sound-and-sight echo of the scene in the rain. After Buffy and Co. dispatch the Judge during his attempt to suck the life force from the patrons of the Sunnydale Mall, they leave him in flaming pieces and thus engage the water sprinklers. When Angelus runs, Buffy chases him. "We rained the heavens upon it, poured it all over the actors for several hours there," says Joss Whedon in the "Innocence" commentary. Buffy and Angelus fight their episode-ending battle with clothing and hair just as wet as they were in the moments leading up to their lovemaking. Sex and death come together: "Come on, Buffy—you know you want it," taunts Angelus. And he laughs, "You can't kill me." "Give me time," says Buffy. Their physical interaction ends with a kick to the wet Angelic balls.

Whedon refers to Buffy's experience as an "adolescent baptism of fire," the old image joining fire and water. Transition, the rite of passage through time to the next threshold—this is indicated, then, in many ways throughout the text: the precapitulations (dream or not), the imagery—the opening of the box, the water immersion, even the images of thresholds in the art prints on Buffy's stairwell, distinctly visible for the first time in "Surprise"/"Innocence." The effect of transition is also expressed in the text's interface with the world. Whedon chose (with the assent of the WB Network) to construct Buffy's sexual initiation as a two-part episode: "Surprise" ends just after the sexual act, and "Innocence" proceeds with the consequences. Furthermore, the two parts were shown one night after another (19 and 20 January 1998). "Surprise" ends with the ominous shot of Angel in the rain, and viewers were left in intense suspense, perhaps the more intense because the story was to continue the following evening. Of course, this scheduling was brilliant in practical terms: the series was moving from Monday nights at 9:00 pm Eastern time to Tuesday nights at 8:00 pm, and the January showings ensured that the audience would travel with the story. But the effect was also to link Buffy's transition to an external transition—both to the move to a new night and time and, more simply and directly, to the experience of moving from one episode to the next on the day after—as Buffy was about to experience the day after. The external presentation thus underscored the theme.[8]

Did Anything Happen Last Night?

Perhaps the most poignant of all the techniques, however, is Whedon's choice to postpone showing Buffy and Angel's lovemaking until after the painful break between the two. It is in "Innocence" that we see the full cruelty of Angelus, the "guy who won't call." "Surprise" starts with Buffy awakening within her dream, only to see Angel killed; the first scene of Buffy in "Innocence" is her awakening in Angel's bed to find him gone. The audience knows that Angel has, indeed, gone, has turned; the episode has opened to show Angelus killing a blonde prostitute ("a pro") in a crude parallel to Angel's sexual interaction with the blonde Buffy. The hooker has offered to help him, and the help he accepts is her blood: he grabs her, bites her, drains her—and then, as if to emphasize the coital nature of the encounter, blows smoky air from his lips. As almost every serious Buffy fan learns, Angelus, unlike Angel, smokes. When, in a long sustained shot, we see him rejoin Spike (whom we have seen cigarette in mouth from his very first scene), Angelus draws a match the long length of a table in prelude to lighting up. There is a mixture of unhealthy evil and sexual burn in the imagery (cf. Chapter 2). Angelus is dangerous.

The scene in which Angelus first emotionally wounds Buffy is preceded by a scene of a similar emotional wound for Willow: she discovers Xander kissing Cordelia in the library. Granted, Xander has not lost his soul and, further, he does not plan to emotionally eviscerate Willow; but she nonetheless perceives the experience as a sexual wound: "It just means you'd rather be with someone you hate than be with me," she says. The character parallels help build to the emotional crescendo of the coming scene between Buffy and Angel.

Joss Whedon says he realized, after trying to shoot the first Buffy/Angelus scene outdoors, that this had to be "a bedroom scene" (like the first kiss, we might note). "We had to play this in the bedroom where they had made love. And he had to be semi-nude—it had to be as intimate as it possibly could." Angelus's being shirtless means that the audience sees the tattoo which was shown just before their first kiss. When Buffy comes looking for the missing Angel, she steps towards the bed, not seeing him walk behind her—but the audience knows that she is in unwitting danger (though it's not yet clear what kind)—and that knowledge is underlined by a brief musical response in the score. The sense of touch is invoked as well; he allows her, in her relief that he's alive, to embrace his naked torso; he leads her to an even more vulnerable emotional state before he strikes:

Angelus: You got a lot to learn about men, kiddo. Although I
             guess you proved that last night.

Buffy:	What are you saying?
Angelus:	Let's not make an issue of it, okay? In fact, let's not talk about it at all.
Buffy:	I, I don't understand. Was it m-me? Was I not good?
Angelus:	You were great ... Really. I thought you were a pro.
Buffy:	How can you say this to me?
Angelus:	Lighten up. It was a good time. It doesn't mean like we have to make a big deal.
Buffy:	It is a big deal!
Angelus:	It's what? Bells ringing, fireworks, a dulcet choir of pretty little birdies? Come on, Buffy. It's not like I've never been there before.

Buffy, of course, had never "been there" before. When next she and Angelus meet, in the school hallway where he threatens Willow's life, we are shown an extreme close-up as he grabs her in a silhouetted, shadowed kiss and flings her aside as callously as the "pro" he drained in the teaser. Buffy, almost always silvertongued, is speechless in her pain. As Angelus soon tells the wheelchair-bound Spike, "She's stronger than any Slayer you've ever faced. Force won't get it done. You gotta work from the inside. To kill this girl, you have to love her." When the Scoobies frantically regroup, Giles tries to imagine what "triggered" Angel's "change." "Did anything happen last night?" he asks, in fatherly ignorance.

Only Willow, among the Scoobies, fully realizes the cause as Buffy runs from the library and Giles's questions. Alone in her room, Buffy fingers the large silver cross (on her dresser) that Angel gave her to wear in the series' first episode, and removes, but still clutches, the silver claddagh ring. She falls to her bed, wordlessly weeping. It is at this point of utter loss that we are shown the images of their lovemaking, in all its poignancy. Buffy recalls her "lost bliss ... in pain." The notes of the quiet, slow score music descend as the scene ends, echoing /reflecting the sense of loss; solo oboe-like tones float sadly.[9] We see a moving, rich red coverlet—the color of passion—and shots so close up that it is difficult to tell what curves of the body we are seeing: lips, hands, shoulders, silhouetted profiles, lighted curves—"tiny, almost abstract pieces," Whedon says he asked Director of Photography Michael Gershman to provide. In the scene of the first kiss, there were stripes of light and dark through the slatted blinds behind them; here, in their lovemaking, Whedon arranged that "the light would change constantly," creating a sense of evanescence, ephemerality.[10] There is, as Whedon says, "a Lynchean sort of darkness to it," but it is also shot through with ever-departing light. It is her memory, and it is as beautiful and sad as any memory of joy that is lost.

More than anything else, Whedon's choice to present this scene in "Innocence" rather than "Surprise" makes the show cohere around the theme of love and loss. Krimmer and Raval speak about the infinite deferral of pleasure central to the Buffy/Angel relationship, and in the long run that is an important element of the text. But in this episode we see the joy of transcendent love—only after it is gone.

That Was Then—This Is Now

Krimmer and Raval (157) also point out that Buffy transforms the traditional metaphoric death of the maiden (at the death of her maidenhood) by making it the male who, in effect, dies: "Your boyfriend is dead," says Angelus to Buffy. But Whedon makes sure that Buffy (as well as Buffy) has another way to resist: as I mentioned before, he gives her another box. One reason Buffy's heroism does not seem unattainable is that she keeps getting knocked down—and keeps getting back up again, an experience many viewers can relate to. Here she gets back up from one of her lowest places—and a place many lovers have been. As Whedon says in his DVD commentary, "The politics are complicated." Lorna Jowett notes that Executive Producer Gail Berman said in an interview, "When Buffy and Angel have relations, it is not a good thing." Joss Whedon, in the commentary, says, "I believe that Buffy and Angel were in love and that what they did wasn't bad." He adds, "I don't want to be saying, 'all teenagers must boff—you must boff now ....'" As Catherine Siemann reminds us, this is a horror show, and part of the horror is fearing such treatment at the hands of those we love (128).

But part of the heroism is fighting back. And so Buffy stands, feet astraddle atop a moral kiosk, the Atlas of the mall. She will wield the "man-toy," as Whedon calls the rocket launcher ("not my other man-toy")[11] to defend decent mall-going people everywhere (see Chapter 6). We know Buffy is back when she regains her linguistic power, calling the bright blue Judge "the Smurf." "You're a fool," says the stolid blue demon; "No weapon forged can stop me." "That was then," says Buffy, as Xander hands her the rocket launcher; "This is now." And Buffy, as faithful viewers know, "lives very much in the now," as Giles told Joyce in their first meeting ("Angel"). Here we see another kind of seizing the moment. Whedon has us truly suffer with his truly suffering heroine, but we get to rejoice as she fights back, as well. Judge kibble scatters everywhere. There are few more satisfying moments in the series than watching the slow-motion TV-Peckinpah flying leap taken by Angelus and Drusilla (who has started flirting with her "Daddy").[12] As giant black clouds roll back, Buffy announces to Xander: "Best present ever."

It's Not Over

A simpler series would have stopped with that explosion of power (followed by Buffy's well-aimed kick of Angelus). This is not, of course, a simple series. As Buffy and Jonathan agree in "Superstar," 4.17, you can't solve everything with one big gesture; life must carry on, and so does this series. In Philip Pullman's *His Dark Materials* trilogy, Dust is the sign of Original Sin (*The Subtle Knife*, 75); and in Buffy's dream of her "original sin," Angel is dusted: the vulnerability of the mortal body is realized after sex. We return to everyday life, and Buffy's doorstep, in a rather rattley gray Citroen, Giles's car. "It's not over—I suppose you know that," Giles tells her. Buffy will have to continue to struggle through both everyday difficulties and the enormously painful emotional aftermath of her choice to connect with this man "who wasn't, you know, stable," as Whedon says in the interview on "Welcome to the Hellmouth."

In "Surprise"/"Innocence," Whedon, Noxon, and Co. take on the myth of Original Sin, the conflation of sex, knowledge, and the stain of evil. Our culture is far too complicit in this mixture for mature art to ignore it. ("This is not happening," says Principal Snyder in "School Hard," the first Spike/Dru episode. "Well, then, I guess the crisis is over!" says Joyce, 2.3.) To pretend that sorting out the feelings should be a clear-cut, rational process would be mere propaganda for a certain social view. Despite her rocket launcher, Buffy will need to work through the feelings for many a long year; "It's not over." Buffy has made a sexual choice for which the consequences were far more severe than seems fair—as often happens in real life.[13] In episodes to come, such as "I Only Have Eyes for You," 2.19, she voices her self-condemnation; and, in fact, it might be said that she never again allows herself to be as open as she was with Angel. But for the here and now of the episode, in its penultimate scene, the fatherly Giles refuses to call her a sinner: "If it's guilt you're looking for, Buffy, I'm—I'm not your man. All you will get from me is my support and my respect."

These words work against the power of the ancient myth. Even stronger, however, is the final scene, which operates both within and against the pattern simultaneously. The plot admits the entrapment of our sexual mores and the sorrow thus generated; the closing words and images resist the cultural propulsion to guilt. The scene with Buffy's father-figure is followed by a scene with her mother. In the "Innocence" commentary on this scene, Whedon says, "Yes, the title actually did mean something; it meant not just a loss of innocence, but the fact that the innocence isn't lost—that Buffy is in this sense an innocent, that she hasn't lost anything of herself, even though she has gone through a painful maturing process and that's why her mom says, 'You don't look any different to me' here as a way of stating that, she's still the same good person that she was." The phrase "lost her virginity" never occurs in "Surprise"/"Innocence." The morning after Buffy first makes love, her mother *does* note something different about her; but here, in this final scene, as Whedon says, she asserts that her sad-eyed daughter looks the same.

Mother and daughter are watching an old black-and-white movie together as Joyce brings in two cupcakes, one with a candle, to celebrate Buffy's birthday (which, like her lovemaking, is already past). In the movie the woman (Alice Faye) is singing about love, dancing in the arms of her beloved. I could not help noticing (as I dare say third-generation TV writer Joss Whedon did too) that the "sweetheart" Alice Faye sings to is Robert Young, best known for his title role in *Father Knows Best*.[14] And for me his face served as a reminder that Buffy's father was not there; Joyce, like Buffy, is no longer with the man she once loved. That Robert Young is the man in the movie suggests a lost world of naiveté.

But Joyce—no epic hero—carries on, as Buffy will. And the visual presentation supports them: in stocking feet, dressed casually, Joyce is nonetheless all in white, down to her socks; Buffy, with a blue-green sweater, is mostly in white too, down to her socks. Goodness is stained only with sorrow: When her mother invites Buffy to blow out the candle and make a wish, Buffy, it seems, feels too much sorrow to imagine wishing for happiness: "Let it burn," she says, her last words in "Innocence."

In an episode about seizing the moment, the burning candle is the emblem of the passing of time, the candle slowly dying in the night. The flame is also the emblem of passion, and sometimes the light of knowledge. Time, passion, knowledge: the elements of Original Sin. Buffy, with her rocket launcher, has resisted the social construction of her sin as expressed through the evil Angelus: "That doesn't work any more," she tells him when he taunts her. But Buffy deals in reality, so we know she will pay a price, innocent or not; we know she will not stop feeling for the man she slept with. And a lover does not have to be as monstrously cruel as Angelus for the words to cut—for one to feel paradise is lost, to feel cast out from timeless bliss. For Buffy, as for most of us at some point in life, the pain is wedded to the passion; and they both still burn.

Chapter 8

Laughter:

For Those of Us in Our Audience Who Are Me

Xander, Laughter, and "The Zeppo"[1]

Laughter is a protest scream against death.

Mel Brooks

I laugh in the face of danger—then I hide until it goes away.

Xander to Buffy, "The Witch" (1.3)

Giles: There's something different about this menace,
            something in the air—a stench of death.
Xander: Yeah, I think it's Bob.

"The Zeppo" (3.13)

Dissecting humor … is an interesting operation in which the patient usually dies.

A. A. Berger[2]

What we laugh at tells us who we are. Humor and laughter are part of the *Buffy* mix from the start; critics in print and audiences at home immediately expressed enjoyment of the series' skilled mixture of many genres, with a hefty dose of horror/comedy. Every regular *Buffy* character participates in the comedy (Overbey and Preston-Matto *passim*), but certainly none more so than the first Sunnydale teen to learn of Buffy's secret identity: Alexander Lavelle Harris—Xander.

My own strongest early memory of Xander comes from the moment in the pilot when, emerging from the library stacks having overheard Giles's classic "You are the Slayer" speech to Buffy, Nicholas Brendon's Xander, speaking only to himself and us, emits a heartfelt, "*What???*" Karen Eileen Overbey and Lahney Preston-Matto note that "he is the one at whom his friends and we, as audience, laugh," and they call him "the typical American teenager" (76). In a first-season episode, Xander asks for a translation of one of Giles's more arcane explanations with the prompt "And for those of us in our studio audience who are me?" ("I Robot, You Jane," 1.8). Xander often takes the Greek choral position of the everyday person expressing an everyday point of view; in the pilot, for instance, he is the one saying, "I have a problem, see, because we're talking about vampires. We're having a talk with vampires in it." However, as the years progress, he steps into the role of Tiresias, too, as the Seer of the series— though he loses only one of his eyes ("Dirty Girls," 7.18). "I see more than anyone knows," he says in the seventh season ("Potential," 7.12). It is no surprise, then, that while Joss Whedon says he sees part of himself in all the characters, he nonetheless identifies most closely with Xander ("Welcome to the Hellmouth" commentary). "I'm Joss in high school," says Nicholas Brendon of his character (Tracy 49). Whedon notes that, in high school, he shared Xander's status as un-cool; certainly we know that Joss Whedon uses humor even more notably than Xander does,[3] and as the creator and prime writer/director of the series he is also, in effect, its seer. Given the role of Xander and the role of Whedon, it seems right to discuss *Buffy*'s use of laughter in an episode focusing on Xander—and "The Zeppo" seems an irresistible choice.

There are earlier Xander-centric episodes. "The Pack" (1.6), for instance, has its fair share of horror/humor. "The Pack," in fact, contains a touchstone moment of knowing who you are by what you laugh at: Buffy knows something is seriously wrong with Xander (he is possessed by a hyena spirit) when her normally kind friend laughs at a cheap, cruel, Goodyear blimp joke: "Kid's fat." But "The Zeppo" stands out. In 2002,

Robert Hanks wrote that "four or five episodes of *Buffy* would be on my list of the ten best pieces of television drama ever made," and the first he lists is "The Zeppo." "The Zeppo" was written by Dan Vebber, who wrote only one other *Buffy* episode. However, that episode was "Lovers Walk" (whose title constitutes a declarative sentence)—an episode many fans consider memorable: it is the episode in which the drunken and broken-hearted Spike, dumped by Dru, returns to Sunnydale to wreak havoc on every romantic relationship within his range, while delivering the extraordinarily moving "Love's Bitch" speech to a chastened Buffy and Angel (3.8). The fact that one writer could create both "Lovers Walk" and "The Zeppo" is a testament to extraordinary talent. Vebber did not stay with the series; he went on to write for another of television's artists, *Simpsons* creator Matt Groening, on the *Futurama* series. As for his work on *Buffy*, it deserves careful attention. However, it is also important to realize that every *Buffy* episode has something of Joss Whedon in it—not just because he decided the overall seasonal and series narrative arc (Kaveney), but also because, as Jane Espenson says, highly paid script doctor Joss Whedon "usually makes his own last pass, you get the shooting draft and find the bits he has changed and what is stunning is how uniformly amazing his stuff is" ("Writing", 106).[4] So "The Zeppo" is the creation of Dan Vebber and (to a degree we can't completely know) also of the Xand-man's creator and alter-ego, Joss Whedon.[5] And in some senses this episode represents Whedon's relationship to the series as a whole.

"The Zeppo" is exceptional in part because it is presented largely from Xander's point of view. His is the main plot, while the apocalyptic battle in which the other Scoobies are engaged is presented as secondary—as befits the perspective of a teenage boy. In the series pilot, Buffy's mother tells her, "I know—if you don't go out, it'll be the end of the world. Everything's life and death when you're a teenage girl!" Apocalyptic battles are equated with Xander's teen trauma as well, though with a different technique. The series makes frequent use of a type of cutting on sound—what I like to call stitched segues, in which a cut from one scene to another moves from a question to an answer or a subject to a predicate, or some other direct response or commentary.[6] Here, for example, Willow's boyfriend Oz advises Xander, "You've got some identity issues. It's not ..." and the scene cuts to Giles solemnly saying "The end of the world." As the episode proceeds, the two strands of story will converge, and Xander's private problems will impinge directly on the larger threat. For both Buffy in the pilot and Xander here, it is a matter of identity crisis, of finding one's self. But the difference here, of course, is that we are not viewing events through the hero's, Buffy's, perspective (as we in large part do in a typical episode). Hence both Steve Wilson and Nikki Stafford point out that this episode can be compared to Tom Stoppard's *Rosencrantz and Guildenstern Are Dead*, in which the childhood friends of Hamlet, minor characters in Shakespeare, take center stage for Stoppard: ordinary folk give their view. And, as with Stoppard's play, the results are not only alarming and disconcerting but also funny.

The varieties of types of humor in "The Zeppo" are staggering—puns, slapstick, bathos, irony, parody, to name a few (see Wilson). Words, visuals, and music carry the humor. The variety itself is carnivalesque, boundary-breaking, absurd in its excess. The episode starts out with a serious battle with stereotypical visual accoutrements—mist, wind, cave, candlelight, swords, demons—but as soon as Xander appears, the humor begins. In contrast to the dramatic warriors, we have the physical comedy of Xander scrambling out from under the debris of battle. As Alan Dale says in *Comedy Is a Man in Trouble*, "The loss of dignity ... can result in our identifying with the victim [of] the mishap" (5). Nicholas Brendon handles the physical humor in a way that suggests vulnerability. The character also counters by quickly displaying verbal facility (it seems less harsh to laugh a little at his physical mishaps because in other ways he shows us he is not weak). With Buffy, Faith, and Giles having battled the demons physically and Willow and Giles having contributed through arcana and magic, Xander stumbles up (when they finally realize he's missing) to offer two thumbs up and a congratulatory "Good show, everyone," which he then slides into punning TV-series reflexivity with "I think we have a hit." He also quickly moves into defensive self-deprecation: "If anyone sees my spine laying around, just try not to step on it." As Jana Riess reminds us, the use of humor can show control (42–6), and Xander is attempting to assert some control.

Buffy is nevertheless concerned about the safety of her non-superhero friend. Her comments to him, in contrast to her use of zingers against villains (Overbey and Preston-Matto 76), display at first gentle linguistic diffidence; she worries that he will get "hurt," or (as Faith says) "killed," or, to quote Buffy, "Both. A-and, you know, with the pain and the death, maybe you shouldn't be leaping into the fray like that." Then she can no longer hold back from an agile little linguistic leap herself, advising Xander that he should in future stay "fray-adjacent."[7] Willow also displays her status with the type of humor she evokes. At this point in the series, Willow is just beginning to explore her strengths in magic; she has only shown flickers of the dark power we later know her to contain. She is still most notably the very self-conscious outsider intellectual— and like her friend Xander, extremely self-deprecating. All of these elements flavor the laugh she invokes when Buffy asks of the dead demons, "What do we do with the trio here? Should we burn them?" and Willow answers with quiet cheer, "I brought marshmallows." To the baffled and slightly revolted looks from the others, she responds, "Occasionally, I am callous and strange." As Overbey and Preston-Matto point out, the language of each of the main characters reflects the personality, and the same can be said of the type of humor.

Flugelhorns, Failure, and Xander's Toole

But Xander is unsuccessful even with humor in the early part of "The Zeppo." As the opening scene ends, he makes a joke based on an allusion which Giles fails to understand: "But gee, Mr. White, if Clark and Lois get all the good stories, I'll never be a good reporter!" Of course, he is trying to suggest that he does not want to be excluded from the demon-fighting action as if he were a junior partner in the enterprise. But with the comment "Jimmy Olsen jokes are pretty much going to be lost on you, huh?" Xander accepts the failure of the joke and Giles's lack of comprehension. Most in the audience would stand with Xander here in more ways than one—both getting his joke and sympathizing with his sense of exclusion.

The next scene (the first after the credits) follows through with both the embarrassing physical comedy and the directive use of allusion, with the addition of another element: the invective stylings of Ms. Cordelia Chase. We see Xander the next day at school, jumping up and down on the quad, shirt-tail flapping under his sweater (again, signing lack of control) as he pleads to be thrown the football that a few guys in letterman jackets are tossing about. Cordelia, sharply dressed in red and black (clothing showing her in social control), watches from a distance as, of course, he misses the throw and it lands in the lunch of the lowering Jack O'Toole, the man with the ludicrously phallic name (see Chapter 3). The animate phallus Jack (even his hair pokes up) immediately threatens our boy Xander with yet another phallic symbol, a knife ("I oughtta cut your face open"). When Xander tries to defuse the situation with humor, his movements are awkward and his attempts at allusion, as in the scene with Giles, fail. Jack asks if he wants a fight, wants to be "starting something," and Xander replies with words as out of control as his throwing hand, "What? Starting something? Like that Michael Jackson song, right? That was a lot of fun. 'Too high to get over, yeah, yeah ...' Remember that fun song?" Allusion depends on the speaker and listener willingly sharing a cultural base of information, and Jack, asking "Are you retarded?," refuses to accept a united perspective with Xander.

So even his humor has failed Xander when he is confronted with another incarnation of his failures: Cordelia. From the beginning of the series, Cordelia and Xander had cheerfully flung Beatrice and Benedick barbs at each other, neither holding back the verbal weaponry (cf. Spike and Buffy). The writers realized they had been writing them as a couple, and in "What's My Line?" Part 2 (2.10), the kisses begin. Buffy in the fourth season speaks of having held back a little in her physical sparring with her boyfriend Riley, but one of the pleasures in Xander-Cordelia interactions is that they don't verbally hold back. Freud would have no trouble recognizing the sexuality and aggression being released in their interchanges (115). In effect, high school princess (or, as it says on her license plate, Queen) Cordelia treats Xander as an equal by sparring with him, even while expressing her scorn of him in other ways. One of the series' notable moments of social bravery comes when Cordelia chooses to publicly claim Xander as a boyfriend, "no matter how lame he is" ("Bewitched, Bothered, and Bewildered," 2.16). It is all the more painful, therefore, when she finds him kissing Willow in "Lovers Walk." Spike has kidnapped Willow and Xander, threatening Xander's life unless Willow will make Spike a love potion to reclaim Drusilla, and, left alone, Willow and Xander kiss, as he puts it, under threat of "impending death." That Oz and Cordelia burst in intending to rescue Xander and Willow only makes the situation worse; and worse still is the fact that Cordelia is seriously injured in a fall as she rushes out of the room. Flowers and apologies do not right the situation, and Xander is left unforgiven.

In "The Zeppo," then, when Cordelia proceeds to clinically slice open Xander with a gleam in her eye, her invective has emotional weight for those familiar with the back story. It is more acceptable for us to laugh at her wit, even while we sympathize with Xander. Even if one does not know the back story, there is enough apparent truth in her commentary to make it painfully amusing. "Boy, of all the humiliations you've had, that was the latest," she tells him; the change from the expected phrase is cruelly funny not merely because it is unexpected but because it implies a long series of humiliations for Xander—and because it's true. As Cordelia says elsewhere, "Tact is just not saying true stuff" ("Killed by Death," 2.18). When Xander says of O'Toole, "I could've taken him," Cordelia responds, "Oh, please. O'Toole would macramé your face." Her wording is effective not only because of the visual image, but also because facial macramé is probably the only kind of macramé the macho O'Toole would do. The quintessence of her denunciation of Xander comes when she displays her shared knowledge of his base of allusions: "It must be really hard when all your friends have, like, superpowers—Slayer, werewolf, witches, vampires—and you're like, this little nothing. You must feel like Jimmy Olsen." The fact that she knows him well enough to choose the same reference he had himself used makes it hurt all the more. And it is Cordelia, again using a cultural allusion that pulls Xander to her as she inserts her knife, who calls him "the Zeppo"—"the useless part of the group," the Marx brother nobody knows.

In the two opening scenes, then, we have been led to identify with a character who has had both his life and his sexual status threatened. What is there to do but laugh? Mel Brooks and Sigmund Freud would expect no less. Xander turns to Oz for advice and continues to be painfully funny in a way that suggests lack of control: he turns into (to use his friend Jesse's phrase from the pilot) "a bibbling idiot," dithering on at embarrassingly uncontrolled length in response to Oz's laconic comments—one of the many scenes in which Xander is connected to qualities stereotypically seen as female (see Jowett). In his search for "cool," he asks Oz, "Is it about the talking? You know, the way you tend to express yourself in short, noncommittal phrases?" "Could be," says Oz, expressing himself in a short, noncommittal phrase. Xander theorizes that Oz is cool because he's in a band—"That's like a business-class ticket to cool with complimentary mojo after takeoff!" Xander's phrasing in this one spot in the conversation exemplifies the verbal wit that Overbey and Preston-Matto praise, and it also suggests cultural literacy. In contrast, he shows the gaps in a naïve young man's cultural awareness when, a few sentences later, he fails to understand why his eighth-grade work on the flugelhorn would not have the same social currency as Oz's work on lead guitar for a rock group. He comes out of the conversation with, as Oz says, "an exciting new obsession." He wants to find his "thing." Mr. Freud, bear with us.

When he drives up to Willow and Buffy the next day in a gleaming '57 Chevy convertible, he introduces it to them as his "thing." "Is this a penis metaphor?" asks Buffy; the viewers are certainly not smarter than the show. Brett Rodgers and Walter Scheidel explore at considerable length the humorous application of the car/driver/sexual power metaphor that runs through this episode (among others). It also seems worth noting that, since Xander immediately uses the car to go for doughnuts, we seem to be having fun with female sexual imagery as well. An attractive blonde asks him how the car handles; "Like a dream about warm, sticky things," he answers outside the doughnut shop. (To quote Buffy from another episode, "Raise your hand if 'Eww.'" And to quote Xander from "Once More, with Feeling," 6.7: "Respect the cruller. Tame the doughnut!")[8] The car (rented from his uncle) has given Xander enough confidence to respond to Cordelia with his own hyperbolic invective: "Cordelia. Feel free to drop dead of a wasting disease in the next twenty seconds." And we may laugh at her, the former victim, because she has lately been "the surgeon of mean" to him. Her scorn seems undercut when the beautiful blonde drives off with him.[9] Xander's clumsiness as he jumps into the car is not as marked as it is in the opening two scenes, but it still makes him faintly laughable. And Cordelia's view is justified in the very next scene when at the Bronze that evening, the blonde details a list of ex-boyfriends (and more importantly, their cars) almost as long as the Iliad's catalogue of ships. Xander is so bored that he even greets Angel, whom he dislikes, as "Friend! Buddy!" However, like Buffy, Willow, Faith, and Giles, Angel goes away to fight off the apocalypse, leaving Xander to his boring blonde.

Moments of uncomfortable physical humor come to a climax when Xander complains to his blonde that he has in the past done "quality violence for those people," but "they act like I'm, like I'm some sort of klutz." With inevitable irony, he then hits the car parked ahead of them, out of which steps, just as inevitably, Jack O'Toole. At the moment Mr. Metaphor emerges from the other car, Xander is saying "Oh God! Stay calm—little fender-bender. It's not [long pause as he sees Jack] ... the end of the world." So the identity-crisis phrase returns. He has to learn to deal with Jack O'Toole. All of the scenes of Xander's physical comedy in one way or another suggest (among other things) a young man's uncertainty as he grows into his adult body. It's not the end of the world, but the world will change for him.

In the ensuing scene, the emotional gravity starts to shift. Jack pulls out an appropriately giant blade which he calls Katie. Even with Katie in his face, Xander cannot resist a socially apt observation which conveys his own aggression: "You gave it a girl's name. How very serial-killer of you." That Xander can make such a remark in such a situation does give us the pleasurable laughter of verbal control after a series of uncontrolled physical mishaps. And even as Xander is being threatened with death, meanwhile, back in the library, Buffy and Giles are commenting on how important it is that Xander be kept safe. After a bit of what passes for repartee from Jack, he offers the blade to Xander, telling him that the difference between them is not who has the blade, but "who has the least fear"; and he taunts

Xander for his humiliation with "your woman lookin' on." But of course Xander does not want to attack someone else unnecessarily, even when he has been taunted. With knife in hand, he uses not the blade but sarcasm to attack not Jack but the blonde. He stops caring what he looks like to the trophy girl who doesn't care about him.[10] And when an authority figure, a cop, approaches and gives Xander the chance to turn in Jack, he instead chooses to continue dealing with the situation himself. Jack, pleased by Xander's choice not to "narc" on him, now wants to hang out; and so Xander, his blonde, and his Jack O'Toole drive off in the '57 Chevy.

Did I Mention That I'm Having a Very Strange Night?

Up to this point in the story, Xander's control of his own physicality and language has been erratic and often weak, and the humor has therefore been frequently painful. In the subsequent scenes, events seem wild and uncontrolled, but Xander's actions are less out of control, and the humor is less painful for a viewer identifying with Xander. The excesses of coming events are carnivalesque in the Rabelaisian sense Mikhail Bakhtin celebrates—rule-breaking, hierarchy-shifting, and grossly physical, laughing at fears about sex and death. The long tradition of the carnivalesque starts before the sixteenth-century comedy *Gargantua and Pantagruel* by Rabelais—and continues after: the episode also, quite naturally, evokes the Marx Brothers, though the upcoming scene is less a night at the opera and more a night at the cemetery. In this part of the story, the dead will come to life and be killed without guilt; Xander will have sex for the first time; he will triumph over the antagonist who has threatened both his life and masculinity; and that antagonist will be eaten. To quote Xander: "Yay?"

It should perhaps not surprise us that in Sunnydale, Jack's idea of a place to go for fun is the cemetery. There he raises the other members of his gang, who have been underground for different lengths of time and are in varying states of decay. Henri Bergson notes that mechanicalism—the inhuman in the human—is a basis for comedy, and Linda Badley (2) notes that zombies, particularly in "splatter comedy," display this characteristic joined with Freudian psychological implications: "Zombies descend from Dr. Caligari's Caesar, Wegener's Golem, and Karloff's Frankenstein monster, inheriting their mindlessness, speechlessness, and lurch, all of which suggest ... the 'repetitive compulsion' of the death drive." But the zombies in "The Zeppo" are funny precisely because they reverse these expectations. They move and talk like typical high school boys. When

Jack raises the first one, Bob, he says, "You big, hideous corpse—come here!" and they jump into a bear hug. Bob calls being raised "so awesome!" Xander's blonde shrieks and runs away; Xander, more schooled in the ways of horror, maintains some semblance of social normality as he raises his voice to her fleeing figure: "I'll call you!" he says, recapitulating many a young man's miserable attempt to pretend it's all okay as he sees the girl receding.[11] Bob is most concerned to make sure his favorite television show has been taped in his absence—*Walker, Texas Ranger*, a work of banal violence appropriate for Bob; and of course it's also appropriate enough that the audience of *Walker, Texas Ranger* would be made of faithful zombies. Jack assures Bob that he has taped "every ep," using the online fan's abbreviation for "episode" in another wonderfully colloquial incongruity from the rotting dead. When they raise the other two members of Jack's gang, Dickie and Parker, they are set on getting "beers" and cruising for girls at Taco Bell.

The humor does come from the reversal of zombie expectations. But the lessening of the mechanical qualities means that these are more like real high school boys—so when, in the end, Xander defeats them, the joy of his triumph can be seen more clearly as a defeat of the type of male which represented a threat to Xander.[12] Bob wears a Sunnydale letter jacket just like the ones worn by the football tossers in the second scene.

And the wildness on the way to their defeat is humorously cathartic for Xander. As Northrop Frye (43) says, just as tragedy results in a catharsis of pity and fear, so comedy results in a catharsis of sympathy and ridicule (and we might note that fear is covered fairly well in "The Zeppo," too). Jack's gang, with Xander as "Wheel-man," proceeds to rob a hardware store for bomb-making supplies. Xander's relative innocence is shown when he notes, just before they break the shop window, "This time of night, I'm pretty sure nothing's open." Xander's disbelief at his involvement in the wildness is part of the humor: "I'm the criminal element!" he says as they burglarize the store, just as, later, he keeps interrupting himself to say, "I can't believe I had sex."

In fact, he breaks his sexual boundaries as a result of trying to avoid breaking legal barriers. As he escapes Jack, Bob, Dickie, and Parker, he encounters Faith fighting one of the Sisterhood of Jhe, the apocalypse-cult demons of the first scene. Xander initiates the scene of sexual barrier-breaking by using his phallic car as a weapon, ramming the female demon—which, however, in jack-in-the-box fashion, pops back up to chase them. Leaving the demon behind, they land at Faith's hotel. Long-term *Buffy* viewers have known as early as the fourth episode ("Teacher's Pet," 1.4) that Xander is a virgin. It is also well-known that Xander is enamoured of Buffy, though he found himself attracted to Cordelia as well. In "The Zeppo," Xander's blonde might be looked at as a pale Buffy-substitute; a more direct Buffy-sub is the woman with whom he has sex for the first time, the other Slayer and Buffy's dark, sexually promiscuous double. In Faith's hotel room, for those unfamiliar with Xander's history, his puns reveal his sexual inexperience simultaneously to her and to viewers. Without the release of having killed the demon, Faith wants the release of sex; and when she puns, "Are you up for it?," he admits he's "Never been 'Up with People' before." The incongruity and mockery of the squeaky clean performance of "Up with People" allows Xander some wit, some verbal control, while acknowledging his lack of worldliness. As Faith straddles him, offering to "steer him round the curves" (and Rogers and Scheidel note the continuation of the car metaphor), he gazes up and asks, bemused, "Did I mention that I'm having a very strange night?"

Slow music which opens with descending notes—music suitable for adult romance or porn—plays as Faith and Xander have sex; and afterwards they gaze into each other's eyes—for a few seconds, until Xander finds himself gently pushed outside the hotel room door with his clothes in his hand as Faith says, "That was great. I gotta shower." In typical television parlance, the approximately five seconds Faith and Xander spent gazing at each other would represent a significantly longer period of time. "The Zeppo" draws attention to the televisual construct because here, the scene apparently represents the actual time spent on deep, meaningful gazes (no Mulvey intended).[13] And the realization surprises us as much as Xander. As Xander dances around the boundaries of behavior, the episode plays with boundaries of consciousness, too—nudging us towards consciousness of the episode as episode, but not so far that we truly lose suspension of disbelief and connection to the characters.

The carnival proceeds as Xander, back in his car, realizes that the materials Jack's gang had stolen would make up a bomb—and he realizes he needs to stop them. When he goes hunting for them, we get to see one of several Keystone Cops-style chase scenes, as Xander in the '57 Chevy chases the zombies down the street. He grabs the closest and deadest one and, holding him to the side of the speeding car as he drives one-handed, asks about the bomb's location—until, moving too close to a mailbox, he accidentally decapitates him and ends the interrogation. We can be shocked and then can laugh, in release, because, of course, the zombie is already dead. At the same time we are enjoying Xander's casual disposal of the gang members who threatened him.

Even more Keystone Cops-like is the scene in which Xander goes to the high school—which, naturally, is what teen zombies would like to blow up (and which, in fact, the Scoobies do—for unimpeachable reasons, of course—blow up at the end of the season). With Giles, Faith, Willow, Angel, and Buffy fighting the Hellmouth beast in the library and Oz in his werewolf form tucked away in a closet, Xander alternately chases and is chased by the zombies. After we see them run past the round window in the library door one after another, in cuckoo-clock formation, the Bergsonian mechanism gets its switch flipped and they all come running in the opposite direction, chased by some enthusiastic members of the Sisterhood of Jhe. But Xander fights valiantly, completely ignored by the heroes in the library: he wields an axe and squashes the threatening Bob with a soda machine. Xander's allusions now working at full power, he frightens off Dickie with a Clint Eastwood quip. He then proceeds to stand off Jack at the bomb site, winning the day essentially with his words, using his body only to block Jack's exit till Jack turns off the timer. Xander leaves the room warning Jack to stay away. The carnival is closed when Jack, who has been revealed to be a zombie of more recent date, is attacked by werewolf Oz after Jack, muttering a threat to Xander, opens a door marked "Door to remain closed" (hence his demise is fully his fault). The next day, in the episode's last scene, the unwitting Oz notes that he is "oddly full today."

> "Buffy, this is no laughing matter."
>
> "Hence my no laughing."

So: virginal sex, bombs, decapitation, robbery, car wrecks, and cannibalism—what could be more fun? Knowing what we're up to while we're at it. "The Zeppo" is an extraordinary combination of visceral release and high consciousness. At its best, laughter requires consciousness and releases consciousness. The Rabelaisian carnival elements of "The Zeppo" provide the release. But Bakhtin notes the ambivalence of such laughter (12), and notes too that carnival is often paired with parody (4–5). He cites medieval comic dialogues, whose two-sided presentations (the "sententious" posed against the "debased") parallel the two-sided nature of "The Zeppo"'s story (20). As noted earlier, the episode can be seen as a *Rosencrantz and Guildenstern* view of the *Buffy* world. Interwoven through Xander's adventures are scenes from a standard *Buffy* apocalypse-stopping episode, delicately heightened to the point of parody, using a variety of techniques. And it should be remembered that the *Rosencrantz and Guildenstern* role in "The Zeppo" is played by the character who represents the primary author of the series: Xander stands for Joss Whedon—and, again, for every normal person lost in a mad, mad world. It is in an early episode that Xander uses the phrase "And for those of us in our ... audience who are me" to ask for an explanation in normal terms. Not just at the beginning but throughout the series, and certainly here, he is clearly the normal man who sees the strangeness of the world.

Part of the self-consciousness of the episode comes within Xander's storyline. The sex scene has already been mentioned. In a further example in the same scene, Faith tells Xander, "Just relax. And take your pants off," and he responds, "Those two concepts are antithetical." This use of elevated language in a less-than-elevated situation is typical of Dickens (when Pip tells us that his sister/guardian throws him at her husband, he describes himself as "a connubial missile," for instance, in *Great Expectations*, 41). Bakhtin takes numerous examples from Dickens to describe this use of heteroglossia, and notes that "this varied play with the boundaries of speech types, languages and belief systems is one of the most fundamental aspects of comic style" ("Discourse," 308). The wit of this shift of language gears is well within Xander's capability. In a second-season episode, for example, he asserts, "Ho-Hos are a vital part of my cognitive process!" and Overbey and Preston-Matto note, "There are not too many teenagers, we think, who would be able to construct such a sentence on the fly, wrapping yummy SAT-words in chocolatey self-deprecation" (76). Their comment could equally well apply to this scene. And Xander's crafted, intellectually well-formed phrase (worthy of the author he represents) is itself antithetical to the simple sex Faith is offering. The reflective nature of Xander's remark, followed by his equally reflective "Did I mention I'm having a very strange night?" is paralleled by the presentation of the sex scene. On the one hand, it is part of the carnival, but on the other, the sex act itself is visually presented at a distance, as a reflection in a turned-off television screen, partly covered by clothing draped over it (the "real" world intervening before the image). And of course, Xander's whole "strange night" is a backwards image, a mirror reflection of the typical *Buffy* episode we see on our screens.

However, most of the episode's self-awareness comes in the sorted-out Scooby story, the apocalyptic tale to Xander's sub-apocalyptic one. While usually Xander is at the heart of (and sometimes is the heart of) the Scooby enterprises,[14] in this episode he is extruded. Time and again, members of the gang—Angel, Buffy, Giles, Willow—tell him that he should stay out of the fight in order to be safe, ironically oblivious to the deadly danger he is in. When Xander encounters Giles in the cemetery and attempts to find a way to avoid Jack and company, Giles performs the standard parental obliviousness routine and waves him back to the zombies in order that he should "stay out of trouble." Xander's next scene finds him confronted with the opportunity to join Jack's gang—the only problem being that the ritual requires the death of the initiate. (It is at this point that we learn Jack has been dead for three weeks.) Xander does not want to belong to Jack's gang, but he has been excluded from his own; and as Frye (43) says, "the theme of the comic is the integration of society, which usually takes the form of incorporating a central character into it"—here, Xander—but not yet. And his and our vision of the deconstructed society is an important part of the laughter along the way.

Music, plot, and parody help us see how easily *Buffy* could go over the top—though, in fact, it normally does not, largely because of the humor which is regularly integrated in the series rather than separated out as it is here. One of the stitched segues, for example, has Buffy comforting a wounded Willy (the barkeeper), who seriously advises her, "If I were you— I'd go find Angel—go somewhere quiet together. I'd be thinking about how I wanna spend my last night on earth." Then the scene cuts to Xander and the zombie gang, Bob standing in the back of the convertible yelling, "Let's get some beer!" Apocalypse Budweiser.

One of the deconstructive cues critics have noted is the use of music in the episode. When Xander moves into the carnivalesque zombie scenes, we hear the episode's theme—pizzicato strings. Their light, quick sound makes clear that we can view these segments without serious fear, even though some of their elements seem quite alarming. The slow, descending tones of the sex scene are cut off as Xander is thrown out, and the pizzicato strings begin again. When the Scoobies discuss the aftermath of the apocalyptic battle, choral music rises (as it has during a few earlier elevated moments). One of the most hilarious uses of music comes in perhaps the clearest moment of parody, and its nature is clarified by its plot placement. As noted earlier, after Xander is deflowered by Faith, he finds the bomb materials and realizes he must stop the zombies. He decides to ask Buffy's advice and finds her with Angel. The symphonic, rhapsodic tones of their love theme swell as they vie for the right to sacrifice self for the good of all and the sake of love; we see their fire-lit, tear-streaked faces as Xander clears his throat and the music stops. This moment of high romance is brought to you immediately after the anti-romantic Xander-Faith coupling. All Xander can manage in the face of their elevated mode is, "Hey. I've got this, um ... there's this, uh ... It's probably a bad time." Kindly persevering, he asks, "Can I help?" before leaving in response to their faintly shaken heads. They do not say a word to him; they are not even speaking the same language at this point. (We might also note that the episodes in which Buffy and Xander, respectively, have sex for the first time also seem to speak different languages; Buffy is multilingual.) As soon as Xander turns to leave, as Steve Wilson says, the symphonic music starts again (91).

And yet we know that these folks are not heroically different in kind: they eat doughnuts like the rest of us. Bathos is another of the tools of self-consciousness the episode employs: the juxtaposition of the elevated with the low. In a scene often cited by critics, a desperate Giles, refused contact by the Watchers' Council which has just fired him, decides to attempt to reach the Spirit Guides. Standing in the library, he explains to Buffy and Willow: "They exist out of time, but have knowledge of the future. I have no idea if they will respond to my efforts, but I have to try. All we know is that the fate of the entire world rests on it [and he peers into the doughnut box]. Did you eat all the jellies?" Yes, they did (Buffy ate a heroic three). The leap in level of import is a hilariously dangerous play with self-consciousness of the plot's potential for silliness, a play which just barely does not thrust us completely out of our suspension of disbelief. After all, a jelly doughnut is sometimes a very important thing; and the simple physical pleasures are often what keep us grounded, as C. S. Lewis explains in The Screwtape Letters (60) and Spike admits in "Becoming," Part 2 (2.22). What's the world without Happy Meals?[15] And Xander, who has spent the episode immersed in the carnival of the physical, is also the purveyor of jelly doughnuts.

In fact, the closing scenes of the episode show the overlapping of the stories: not only are the heroes doughnut-eaters, but also Xander is clearly a hero. As Giles and Willow work on a binding spell in the library, Giles says, "Who knows what's going to come up from beneath us?" The camera cuts not to the earth below the Hellmouth, but to the boiler room, where Jack and the gang are placing the bomb, and where Jack and Xander will have their face-off. They are in the basement of the school; as Greg Stevenson (100) notes parenthetically, "Notice Xander's moment of heroism takes place in a basement." Though he does not comment further on this point, faithful viewers re-viewing the episode know that Xander, after graduation, was forced to live in his parents' basement and (as "Restless," 4.22, shows), feared he would never get out of it. The basement represents his low social status; and even in a first viewing, the basement is also the architectural equivalent of the subconscious (cf. mad Spike in the school basement in Season Seven). What better place for a face-off with the id-like Jack O'Toole? This is what lies beneath the highly intellectual Giles and Willow in the library. The struggle in the subconscious is often at the base of an act of heroism.

Another architectural image (more symbolic setting) shows the connection between storylines. As Xander is on his way to his final confrontation with Jack, the hydra-headed Hellmouth monster smashes one head through the wall right next to Xander (and okay, one more in-your-face phallus). The walls between the worlds are breaking down and the battle is the same. Flashing lights, shrieking monsters, swords and heroes above; Xander, Jack, and the quietly ticking bomb below: the battle with the primitive in oneself, in the subconscious, is at the base of all those larger wars. And as more than one writer has noted, Buffy and company cannot save the world unless Xander saves the school they are in: the battle with self must be won first.

And Xander wins. Just as, in the sixth season, Xander saves the world by talking Dark Willow out of destroying it ("I saved the world with talking— from my mouth!" he later says),[16] so now he saves the world by using his words to make Jack see "who has less fear." Again, this warrior of words is the character who most clearly represents Joss Whedon. Jack argues, "I'm not afraid to die. I'm already dead." But as Xander expressively replies, "This is different. Being blown up isn't walking-around-and-drinking-with-your-buddies dead. It's little-bits-being-swept-up-by-a-janitor dead, and I don't think you're ready for that." Nicholas Brendon's face as he waits—wide-eyed, mouth slightly open—conveys a layering of real fear controlled under play-it-cool determination. Rogers and Scheidel rightly point out that he achieves his heroic deed after his sexual encounter (par. 41). However, the increased confidence derived from that encounter is just one element of his triumph here. Placed mid-plot, the sex is one event of many in the wild carnival. Another difference in his first and last confrontations with Jack is what's at stake. Cordelia calls him "the boy who had no cool"; Xander finds it difficult to face a social challenge such as Jack offered early in the episode. But, to paraphrase Lorelei Lee, he can be brave when it's important. So when his friends' lives are in danger (they are the world to him), he is willing to give his own.

The other Scoobies do not know what he has done. As they sit outside the school congratulating each other the next day, he modestly offers to get them snacks. Greg Stevenson argues that the most important theme of this episode is that "the integrity of moral actions does not require an audience for approval" (101). Cordelia (now less sharply toned in red and gray) taunts him at the episode's very end, asking if he is going on another "life or death doughnut mission." However, the usually loquacious Xander is content to remain silent. The narratives have been re-sutured, the stories have come together again, but we now know another version of "what's beneath." In fact, his heroism in this episode—his having saved the world unknown by the greater community, and his being looked at as a "loser" by the world at large—all this parallels exactly the role that Buffy and the entire Scooby Gang play in a typical episode: they save the world again and again without recognition or even, in many cases, respect.

While Xander's actions are unknown to the others in the story, he does, of course, have an audience: us. The world will never know all that the Scoobies do; the Scoobies will never know all that Xander does. But even Xander, the secret Seer, does not know all that the audience does. We and the creators are the only ones who know the Rabelaisian fate of Jack O'Toole, the fullness of which is sprung on us in the last scene. Jack has died threatening to sneak up on our hero in a cowardly attack "the minute your back is turned." No one has things finally under control; in *Buffy*, you never know when the werewolf will come out of the closet. The wildness is always there, whether it comes from inside us or out in the world. The wildness is part of what we laugh at, and it can make for joy or fear. When we watch *Buffy*, we get to contain the whole thing, with a Gargantuan swallow as big as Oz's. What we laugh at does tell us who we are. And if Xander is Whedon, and Xander is us—we are laughing together at ourselves.

Chapter 9

Fear:
The Princess Screamed Once

Power, Silence, and Fear in "Hush"[1]

Willow: Okay, say that I help [you with Buffy], and you start a conversation. It goes great. You like Buffy, she likes you. You spend time together; feelings grow deeper, and one day, without even realizing it, you find you're in love. Time stops, and it feels like the whole world's made for you two, and you two alone—until the day one of you leaves and rips the still beating heart from the other …

Riley: Yep, that's the plan.

> "The Initiative" (4.7)

Fortune favors the brave.

> Aeneas in Virgil's *Aeneid* (Book X, l. 284);
> Buffy in Whedon's "Hush" (4.10)

A symbol is not a sign of something known, but an indicator of something not known and *not expressible*, otherwise than symbolically.

> Ursula K. Le Guin, *The Language of the Night* (71, emphasis added)

Horrors beyond speaking of.

Joss Whedon's script of "Hush"

"Hush" is a *Buffy* episode embraced by fans and appreciated by those outside the *Buffy* circle: it is the only episode to have been nominated for an Emmy for its writing. This widespread approval may be because much of its meaning can be accessed even by those not familiar with the full series: it is dead scary, it is romantic, and it is ultimately unsettling, thought-provoking. The approval may also be in part because it is the epitome of polysemy: it allows, more markedly than many *Buffy* episodes, a traditional fantasy response but at the same time clearly invites a counter-reading.

As most *Buffy* fans will recall, "Hush" is the episode for which the characters speak no dialogue for approximately twenty-nine minutes. There is an opening dream sequence in which Buffy sees herself kissing graduate teaching assistant Riley Finn—whom she has yet to really kiss—in peculiar circumstances. He does not know of her identity as the Slayer, nor does she know of his work as a secret government agent who fights demons with the military-scientific organization the Initiative. She also sees a young blonde girl singing a nursery rhyme about "the Gentlemen" and holding a carved wooden box; and finally, Buffy sees a monstrous, bald, ghastly man dressed in an old-fashioned suit of clothes. After Buffy awakens, the episode moves through various domestic scenes involving regulars (Buffy, Willow, Giles, Xander, Spike, Anya)—and the arrival of a British visitor for Giles, Olivia. Next, monsters such as we have seen in Buffy's dream arrive and occupy a clock tower, magically drawing the voices away from all the sleeping townsfolk, and holding those voices in the box from Buffy's dream. They then proceed to cut the heart out of a young man, a girl, and unspecified others. Inspired by a drawing by Olivia, who has seen the monsters, Giles shares his research with the Scoobies: fairy tales tell him that when the princess screams, the monsters, the Gentlemen, will die; no sword can kill them. Unknown to each other, both Riley's secret government group the Initiative and the Scoobies attempt to deal with the situation. Buffy and, separately, Riley and the other Initiative soldiers patrol, while the Initiative scientists and the Scoobies separately research. Tara, who has met Willow at a Wicca meeting, also researches, and comes to try to work with Willow to cast a spell to restore speech. Buffy and Riley discover each other's secret identities as they fight the monsters; Tara and Willow are attacked by the monsters and resist. With Riley's help,

Buffy recovers her voice and destroys the monsters. The various couples confront each other in the aftermath.

"Hush" is generally acknowledged (e.g. by Sarah Skwire in *Fighting the Forces* and Joss Whedon himself in the DVD commentary) as a fairy-tale episode, with the implicit hierarchical world of the fairy tale. When the wise man, Giles, indicates the need for a princess, all the characters (including Buffy) and presumably viewers alike immediately assume that Buffy, the Chosen One, is that princess. The moment comes when the wise man is formally dispensing his wisdom, in Giles's touching and humorous overhead projector expository scene, accompanied by his own choice of soundtrack, *The Danse Macabre*—diegetic music which sounds thin and limited in terms of the texture of the recording, the rhythm, and the instrumentation—in contrast to the sweeping, surrounding sound, vocal and instrumental, that is Chris Beck's non-diegetic score. The old music and the old technology—overhead projection (which is itself a bit beyond Giles's technical expertise)—is appropriate for the problem's diagnosis: the attackers in this episode are fairy-tale monsters. When Giles indicates they were killed when "the princess screamed once," Buffy's response is to write on her message board, "How do I get my voice back?" She expects to take the role of the princess—and in fact she does. After she and her hero have their first kiss (to Christophe Beck's wonderful Buffy-Riley theme), the monsters are defeated, the world is temporarily righted once more, and the heterosexual couple end up together.

But just as Beck's score is more complex than Giles's presentation of the music of the macabre, so too the episode's story is more complex than the surface of the fairy tale. (And in fact I would suggest that this is one implication of the humorous lecture scene: we are only getting part of the story—a very useful part, but comically incomplete.) Certainly, as Bettelheim, Cashdan, and others have shown, any fairy tale can perform important emotional functions through its underlying psychological implications. If "Hush" were as simple in its presentation as my description above (princess, hero, kiss, kill, happily heterosexual ever after), then it would be a highly conservative text. But there are many more signs pointing down a different path in the forest of "Hush." Whedon, in his commentary, has said that he wants children to remember the fear of "Hush": in effect, he seems to be saying that he wants it to have the impact of a good fairy tale on children in working out their emotional world. And of course, sophisticated adults can appreciate more consciously the implications of a depth-plumbing fairy tale. "Hush" operates on this level; it also has the richness of text that can be found in almost any Whedonverse episode, constructed with care by an extraordinary group of artists and artisans collected by Whedon, including, for example, production designer Carey Meyer, costume designer Cynthia Bergstrom, and of course Emmy-winning musician Christophe Beck.

So let us examine a few more elements of the text. I will note that the fact that I am selecting certain elements automatically reveals my own interests; others would note other elements. "Bring your own subtext," as Whedon says. Whedon is also an avowed admirer of film critic Robin Wood (source of the name for the seventh season's nicely complex character of the new principal of Sunnydale High School) and has spoken in particular of Wood's term "the incoherent text." To quote Wood, "so many things feed into art which are beyond the artist's conscious control—not only his [sic] personal unconscious ... but the cultural assumptions of his [sic, indeed] society" (47). Wood is right, of course—and a true artist's work will say more than can be known by any one mind at any one time, more than can be articulated by any one critic or even by the artist, except through the work (as the opening epigraph by Ursula Le Guin asserts). It is also true, however, that television is often denied the status of art, as Camille Bacon-Smith says, because it is not recognized as aesthetically purposeful. I suppose that in all my writing on Buffy I am in a sense using the deist's model of the universe as clock to argue for a higher power here—in this case, the power of the artist: like a good clock, this fictional universe is too complex, it operates too smoothly, to have happened by accident. With the DVD commentaries, as David Lavery has pointed out, we can also find external support for the many levels of meaning conceived by the artist,[2] and I will occasionally draw on those in this discussion.

So. Buffy is a princess. Yes, she is beautiful; yes, she is willing to die for her people; yes, in this episode she ends up with the hero (though not, I happily note, at the end of the series). But "Hush" undercuts many of the fairy-tale tropes defined by scholars such as Vladimir Propp and Bruno Bettelheim. Visual images often carry the weight of this meaning. Instead of being the princess imprisoned in the tower, Buffy literally breaks into the tower: she crashes slow-motion through the wooden-slatted window of the monster's place of ritual, the Gentlemen's clock tower. Instead of being swept off her feet to be saved by the hero (cf. Errol Flynn, or Luke Skywalker swinging on that rope with Princess Leia), Buffy herself grabs a rope and swings through the air feet first in battle. Buffy and Riley reveal their secret selves to each other at the moment when they aim their weapons directly at each other (Freudians take note). When they whirl into position, it is the closest Buffy and Riley ever come to truly dancing with each other. And when Princess Buffy screams in order to destroy the monsters, it is not, as Darin Morgan once had Scully say to Mulder, "a girly scream." Nikki Stafford, in *Bite Me*, complains of the sound and expresses the wish that the producers had overdubbed (272); however, in the DVD commentary Whedon specifically notes that they did overdub. Rhona J. Berenstein devotes an entire chapter of *Attack of the Leading Ladies* to "The Interpretation of Screams": I would argue that this one is purposefully not princess-like. These images, visual and aural, all work towards the presentation of the empowered female who is characteristic of the Buffyverse, but—as is also typical of the series—there are not simply exhortations to young women to stand up for themselves, but also broader implications about the social system, too.

"Hush" has possibly the most frightening monsters in the Buffy series— and they look for all the world like dead white males. Instead of being the monster in/of the mansion, the Gothic female space, they are associated with a phallic tower, and float through the streets to cross by force the threshold into various homes (in contrast to the invited vampire), and, of course, to violently enter various bodies. In much horror, the house and the body are symbolically equivalent, and these monsters are carrying out a symbolically male role. Whedon, in the DVD commentary, repeatedly calls them "my boys." The script description of the first one's appearance in Buffy's dream is as follows: "He's old, bone white, bald—Nosferatu meets Hellraiser by way of the Joker. Actually he looks kind of like Mr. Burns, except that he can't stop his rictus-grin." For those of you who have been living on the dark side of Mercury for the last fifteen years, Mr. Burns is *The Simpsons'* quintessential capitalist—ancient, greedy, the powerful owner of the town's nuclear power plant, barely kept from death by medical science; and he looks like—well, he looks like one of the Gentlemen (only shorter). The very name of the Gentlemen, of course, evokes class associations, as does their clothing: these are the upper class, the monied bourgeois. The audience can see that they have servants (and these are called the Footmen in the script). The Footmen hold down their victims because, as Whedon says, the Gentlemen "would not sully themselves" by struggle with these lower beings. They are literally above us; they float six inches from the ground. In the DVD special feature on "Hush," Whedon directly refers to class difference: "It was like a class thing, almost." While in many episodes Buffy faces a single major antagonist, the Gentlemen are a group—they are a class; they are almost identical ("most similar," says the script); they are representative types, not individuals. Most viewers would probably assent to Whedon's comment that they are a "beautifully realized" version of "what [he] was going for": "very specifically, a Victorian kind of feel, because that to me is very creepy and fairy-tale-like—the politeness, the suits." The term "the suits," of course, indicates the monied male power structure. The Victorians (and the Gentlemen do look Victorian) are generally seen as the epitome of colonializing white male power.[3] We are shown these dead, white, well-to-do, upper-class, old-fashioned males spreading out across the town and taking over. If that's not patriarchy, I don't know what is.

Well, maybe I don't; I'm not saying they don't suggest patriarchy, just that there is not a simple one-to-one allegorical equivalence. To say that in "Hush" the monsters that Buffy destroys (head-first) are symbols of the patriarchy would be a terrible oversimplification. These monsters would scare the bunny tails off just about anyone, conservative or radical, and it's best to remember that. Maybe that's because they are not just political symbols; they also symbolize mortality and something about sex, something we can all relate to—the kind of basic foundational experience and fear that make the bones of a good fairy tale. So let's look at some other signs on the forest path of "Hush."

During Giles's show-and-tell on the Gentlemen, he asks on his transparency, "What do they want?" When Willow points to her chest, meaning "heart," Xander mouths silently, "boobies?" The rest look exasperated, but the connection with sex is appropriate—and not surprising, coming from Xander. For good measure, the audience is exposed to the sexual connection again in the same scene. When Xander writes, "How do we kill them?" Buffy makes a plunging hand gesture towards her lap, meaning to suggest the working of an invisible stake. (She proceeds to explain by demonstrating with a real stake.) The visual double entendre and the humor in the others' response calls attention to the sexuality of the context.

Narrative also gives us cues. "Hush" takes place almost exactly halfway through the run of the seven-year series, an arc during which Buffy makes the heroic journey from adolescent to adult. Sarah Skwire points out that, unlike the fairy-tale episodes "Gingerbread" and "Killed by Death," in which Buffy is represented as linked to childhood, here Buffy is in the budding adult state of the first-year college student, living in the emotional halfway house of the college dormitory. Although faithful viewers know that Buffy and Angel made love (with literally catastrophic consequences) on her seventeenth birthday, she does not have sex again after that until she reaches college and encounters Parker the "Poop-Head" Abrams. In terms of the general pattern of life for many young people in this culture, college and sex are associated. (And should I say "duh"?)

More specific narrative cues suggest more specific sexual awareness. Viewers who watched either the series or the DVDs in sequence will see the episode "Something Blue" (4.9) immediately before "Hush." In "Something Blue," Willow, grieving over the loss of Oz (who has left to protect her and others from his werewolf side) does a spell to have her Will done, and Buffy is suddenly betrothed to bad boy Spike. As Justine Larbalestier has noted, the episode in some ways played with prior fanfic conjoining of Buffy and Spike. It is also worth noting, as the Dancing Lessons fanfic authors point out, that Willow wills them to marry, not to become enamoured of each other; and of course the episode presages their later connection. But at the end of the episode, out from under the magic spell, Buffy tells Will that she is "totally" over the "bad boy thing."

"Be a good boy," says Professor Maggie Walsh to Riley in Buffy's dream at the opening of "Hush," the very next episode; i.e., Buffy's subconscious calls Riley a good boy, the kind she plans to focus on romantically. Buffy may think she's over the bad boy thing, but when she contemplates the good boy thing, that's really scary. If we don't want a bad boy, what would a "good boy" be like, the kind of boy that would have the mother Maggie seal of approval? If the structure of the episode as a whole is a fairy tale, then not only Buffy's dream but the whole fairy-tale episode lets her—and us—explore that question.

And again, narrative cues point to this focus: what brings the Gentlemen to Sunnydale? In most Buffy episodes, there is some suggestion of a cause for the arrival or revelation of the Monster, but the Gentlemen simply appear. If we wish to say they have come because Sunnydale sits on a Hellmouth, then we are ignoring Giles's transparency statement that "They come to a town," implying that they can come to any town (which would of course be appropriate for a fairy tale). Even if we allow that they could just show up, why do they show up now? It's not the unholy feast of something or other, as Jonathan says in "Superstar" (4.17).

The first time a Gentleman shows up is in Buffy's dream. Buffy occasionally has prophetic dreams. Is this dream prophecy or invocation? Or both? In her dream, the single Gentleman shows up right after she has kissed Riley. It would seem that Buffy's attraction to Riley is in some sense the cause for the arrival of the Gentlemen. Her sexual focus on Riley is the symbolic catalyst; not a logical plot cause, but a dream cause, a cause in terms of dream logic—and the only cause given in this episode, which, as Whedon notes, is itself like a dream. And, in fact, in Buffy's dream the single Gentleman is made equivalent to Riley: we see first Riley's hand on Buffy's shoulder, then a cut to the Gentleman with his hand on her shoulder. As Don Keller says in *Fighting the Forces*, "Riley ... become[s] a monster" (169). And what kind of monster? Consider the sexual implications. These are very white guys in suits, guys that all look alike; they are Victorian, noncommunicative, polite; they penetrate you and take your heart while trying not to get their hands dirty with you, touching you as little as possible. Instead of a real knife, they use a scalpel—not the passion of the knife but the physiological necessity of the medical device. In their first visual after Buffy's dream, Whedon shows only their feet, "shoes flat and together, very prim," says the script. In Buffy's dream lecture on the importance of communication, the chalkboard has clearly shown (among other scribbled notes) the phrase "Body language," a language in which the Slayer is adept. These monsters, in their body language, speak repression. Robin Wood writes of the monster in horror cinema as representing "the return of the repressed" (77); but these monsters represent the return of repression.

In her opening dream, the first Gentleman appears just after she and Riley have kissed, but when she awakens, they are once again unable to kiss. What Buffy fears in a relationship with a man like Riley takes shape in these monsters. "This feels very strange," she says, just before they kiss in her dream; and she recognizes that, though he (and she!) may not like it, for him it will take place with the necessary approval of authority, the woman who is at once a representative of the power of mother and of institutions: Professor Maggie Walsh. (I wish I had time to do an entire piece on mothers and fathers in "Hush.") In Buffy's dream, Professor Walsh instigates an interaction between Riley and Buffy. Though Buffy does not yet know of the existence of the Initiative, the Slayer already knows that Maggie is an authority figure, particularly in Riley's life. And let me note that one of the creepiest of many creepy scenes in the series occurs when Maggie Walsh watches on a monitor screen as the unaware Buffy and Riley make love for the first time in a later episode ("The 'I' in Team," 4.13). Furthermore, Buffy and Riley, in the "Hush" dream, kiss in front of a room full of people—in part, of course, just to add to the dream-weirdness (and Whedon notes that he pulled as many extras into the room as he could find). But it could also be said that a man like Riley acts always with awareness of society in mind—or at least Buffy's dream might suggest that this is her perception of him. The others in the room disappear when they kiss; and darkness falls. Dream-

Riley has said, "If I kiss you, it'll make the sun go down," suggesting a connection through the dark side, the unconscious level. And when the darkness comes and the others disappear, a smiling Buffy utters the words "Fortune favors the brave" for the first time. It seems in her dream they have dared to make a connection in spite of the inhibiting circumstances (a schoolroom, even a college lecture hall, cannot be described as Buffy's happy place). But almost immediately afterwards the single Gentleman, the monster of repression, appears, and she awakens to the inability to kiss or communicate with Riley.

"Fortune favors the brave," she again mutters, this time in irony and disgruntlement as she walks away from her tall, handsome hunk of useless. Whedon makes a point of mentioning in his commentary that "Fortune favors the brave" is "a phrase I got from Rick Griffin, a Grateful Dead artist, who had it plastered over one of his surfboard drawings." Whether or not it has further implications for him, Whedon does not say, but Don Keller identifies it as a phrase from Virgil (171). Keller notes that "whatever its general applicability, it specifically refers to Buffy and Riley's apprehension about kissing" (171). I will note further that it is a phrase from the *Aeneid*, one clearly well enough known to be recognizable by many (many academics, anyway). It is the sort of phrase that announces itself as a quote, and invites looking-up. It could hardly be more apropos. It connects Riley with the myth of Virgil's Aeneas, the hero of the *Aeneid*, one of the three great Greco-Roman epics. (And I refer you to C. W. Marshall's article on Giles and Aeneas in *Slayage* to suggest the further applicability of this particular source.) Aeneas is perhaps the most purely patriarchal of the classic heroes. This (to me) dull and duty-bound hero is an excellent parallel for Riley, the least liminal of Buffy's significant others.

Virgil wrote the *Aeneid* as, in effect, back story for the power of Rome; this epic is a grand-scale origins episode for the Roman state, the epitome of imperialism. Aeneas is a prince of Troy who, justified by the loss of his home and the loss of his women, founds the new Roman civilization through war. For Aeneas, the good of the state is more important than personal relationship—a defensible or even sometimes praiseworthy view in theory, but one often shown to be dubious in practice. Those familiar with the Buffy story beyond the standalone "Hush" episode can see further parallels: after Aeneas and Queen Dido's love affair, he leaves to fight for his (future) country and she kills herself. Just so, Riley eventually decides to invest his identity in being a fighter, not a lover; he rejoins the Army and departs the Hellmouth, leaving Buffy to kill herself during the battle against Glory (and consider the military implications of that phrase: the battle *against* Glory). Granted, Buffy's action is unquestionably a sacrifice made to save the world (while Dido's act is conspicuously not meant to help her people); but always, this series operates on many levels simultaneously and, as Marti Noxon says, her death can be read as suicide as well. Though the loss of her lover is not, as for Dido, the immediate cause, nonetheless it can be seen as a contributing factor; and both of these leaders, Buffy and Dido, leave those behind adrift without them. As with the appearance of the Gentlemen, the emotional substructure provides connections.

At this point I can't resist indulging in a brief digression. The other two major Greco-Roman epics are, of course, the *Iliad* and the *Odyssey*; their heroes are Achilles and Odysseus, respectively. Aeneas, Achilles, and Odysseus certainly represent three very different types of hero. And it seems to me that they correlate to the three main romantic interests in Buffy's life. Achilles, who sulks and broods in his tent, is an extraordinarily powerful warrior who sometimes fights for the right and sometimes does not, and gloomily ponders his own curious form of immortality—Achilles is of course Angel. Odysseus, who has a wonderful facility with language, who is a trickster in both word and deed, who is a great fighter but does not seem to take that as his defining characteristic, who enjoys having sex and is more or less kind to the various women he encounters but is basically a one-woman man, who actually enjoys hanging out with and fighting alongside the goddess of defensive warfare (Athena)—Odysseus, my favorite, is Spike.[4]

But to return to the fearfulness of Riley. That phrasing ambiguously allows two implications: that Riley is fearful, and that Riley is to be feared. And I would argue that this episode suggests the same—and applies the fear to all that Riley stands for. Riley is both Aeneas and the Gentlemen. Heroic self-denial and repression—with all the attendant miseries. Yes, the episode is not just a political manifesto: this is a fairy tale that, like many fairy tales, deals with sexual fears. This is personal. But of course the personal *is* political. Riley's attitudes towards his relationship with Buffy are woven within the fabric of his attitudes towards the world—as are hers in response. When Buffy and Riley really kiss for the first time later in this episode, the audience hears some of the most beautiful music scored for the entire series (Whedon says that he finds it more beautiful, more "adult," than the Buffy-Angel theme.) So, too, when Buffy gives her life at the end of the fifth season, we are uplifted by some of the series' most beautiful music. Sex and death can be inspiring. But this series does not allow the audience to rest in those moments of transcendence. We are carried on to work through the world; and that pattern can be seen within the episode of "Hush." The transcendent kiss occurs in Act 2 (with elemental fire and water in the background in the form of a broken, spewing hydrant and a trash can fire);[5] the revelation of their secret selves occurs at the end of Act 3; but, at the end of Act 4, Buffy and Riley sit silently facing each other, unable to talk. From Riley's friend Forrest we have heard, earlier in the episode, that Riley is not supposed to talk about his connection to the government; and that fact is reiterated by Riley at the beginning of the next episode, which starts with a continuation of the scene that ends "Hush." Their personal problems are embedded in their political attitudes, and vice versa.

Hence the fearfulness of the Gentlemen, who operate on a take-over-the-town global/political level and a psychosexual level; and they are made real to the level of the body, as well. As noted above, house and body can often be read as symbolically equivalent. The threshold of the building can also be a threshold of experience, as Joseph Campbell (among many others) makes clear; Keller, in discussing "Hush," points out that the Buffy-Riley kiss signifies "crossing a threshold" (171). I would note that Whedon, who both wrote and directed "Hush," recreates the thematic experience for audiences by repeatedly showing the Gentlemen literally crossing thresholds, "looking in windows, knocking on doors," as the little blonde Buffy-surrogate sings in her dream. When they are first shown after her dream, the shot is of their feet emerging from a doorway. When they take their first victim, we do not just see the aftermath, or the horror of the cutting itself: we see their approach and the young victim at his doorway in symbolic preliminary to their violent entry of his body. The monsters at the door—that is the horrid image. They are shown floating down corridors in an extension and suspense of the visual symbol of bodily penetration. One of the most frightening moments of the episode comes when Giles's visitor Olivia—to use Anya's term, his "orgasm friend"—puts her face close to the window. She thinks she observes the danger at a distance—a monster floating across the street—but suddenly sees it looking right at her, a Gentleman inches from her face, gazing straight through the window. The thought of unwanted entry is horrifying; the entry itself even more so. It is equivalent to rape. In the first instance of the Gentlemen's entry of a victim, we see them penetrate the young man's room from his point of view. And when their servants hold him down, we see the Gentlemen from the victim's point of view as they cut out his heart. Whedon has said that "this is an image from a dream of my own—the man floating at me as I lie in bed," and the fact that this heart-rending does take place in bed grounds the sexual, bodily imagery. When the climax of the scene comes, the bedded body is penetrated and we hear the *sound* of the cold scalpel's entry—one of the more horrifying symbolic representations of unwanted sex. The victim cannot scream, but the wound speaks.[6] In this conflation of sex and death, death is the more powerful image, but both are there. These Gentlemen are much less kindly than the one who stopped for Emily Dickinson.

The threshold imagery is also key to another important scene in the episode. "Hush," as most Buffy fans will remember, is the first episode in which Tara appears. She and Willow notice each other at a Wicca meeting which all the other participants seem to be using merely as an opportunity for display; only Willow and Tara seem open to a genuine search for new knowledge and experience. After the silence descends, Tara researches "spells of speech" and looks for Willow to help her do a spell. As one of the few people out this evening, she is pursued by the Gentlemen. When she finally reaches Willow, both of them are pursued into the dorm laundry room. Willow is physically damaged, having sprained her ankle, but she attempts to use her nonphysical power, her magic, to move a drink machine to block the doorway. Only when Tara joins hands with her (and one could do an entire essay on hands in "Hush") are they able together to block the threshold and stop the monsters.

This scene is also central to the main theme of "Hush," the difficulty of communication; and it is the first of many fourth- and fifth-season scenes to parallel the relationship of Tara and Willow with the relationship of Buffy and Riley, much to the latter's detriment. The scene is also preceded by a parallel humorous scene of communication in the Xander/Anya relationship, in which Xander at first mistakenly believes Spike has somehow vampirically drained Anya. While Xander has been unable to communicate his feelings to her through words when she asked him to earlier in the episode, he now clearly demonstrates the depth of his caring by beating up on Spike. Xander's counterattack for the non-attack and his joy at Anya's being alive—he hugs her—earns him romantic non-diegetic string music, tacit acceptance of his shrugged apology to Spike, a smile from Olivia and a smaller one from Giles. The romantic moment is immediately undercut by the happy Anya, whose bluntness of communication carries through to hand gestures: she cuts to the sex with a very lucid finger movement indicating her intention and dismaying her observers (except for Xander, of course).

The success of Xander and Anya's nonverbal communication is succeeded by Willow and Tara's. Willow and Tara run into the laundry room and, because of Willow's ankle, fall to the floor and sit there together. Willow at first tries to move the drink machine alone. Because she can shake it a little, Tara understands immediately what Willow is attempting. Tara watches her, and it is Tara who offers to join with Will, reaching her hand out in a silent gesture which Willow accepts. They look each other in the eyes and with perfect understanding join their power to move the machine "like a cannonball," the script says; it has become a defensive weapon, and they block the monsters banging at the threshold. They breathe deeply and gaze into each other's eyes, continuing to hold hands as they realize what they have accomplished together.

In contrast, consider the concurrent scene in which Buffy and Riley fight others of the Gentlemen in their headquarters, the clock tower (not only a phallic place but a place of machinery, gears, works—a set specially made for the episode; cf. the operations and set of the Initiative). Buffy and Riley both fight valiantly and effectively, helping each other out at various stages. But they kick, punch, and swing on opposite sides of the room. Whedon notes that he framed the scene thus for the spacing of the fight sequences; but the effect, of course, is quite different than the visual of Tara and Willow hand in hand: Buffy and Riley are apart. Even more noticeable is a moment of failed communication in the scene. Buffy sees the box from her dreams and knows that it must be destroyed. Held back by the monsters (it is she, not Riley, whom they have "deigned" to stab with a scalpel),[7] she gestures to Riley to smash the box. With slow-motion build-up and melodious horns of triumph, Riley whacks the wrong thing. (Take that as you will.) Afterwards, he smiles in proud expectation of her gratitude. (Take that as you will. Tara and Willow aren't the only ones who can have crypto-sex.) Buffy rolls her eyes and tries again. The moment is faintly sad, and certainly humorous. It is also a fair indicator of their relative skill in ... communication—clearly not as successful as Willow and Tara. At the beginning of the episode, Riley asks Buffy to tell him about her dream, and their brief conversation ends with her response, "I'm not saying a word," in a sing-song, childlike, nursery rhyme voice. What we have here is a failure to communicate. And certainly that, too, is represented by the Gentlemen.

The Gentlemen seem to understand each other very well; however, they do not bother to speak or listen to those literally beneath them, as they float through the town. For anyone who has ever felt unheard by the powers that be, this is a bad dream; and surely most of us have had times when we felt we were screaming and no one heard. The episode does not limit this kind of failure to the male gender: Willow's Wicca group provides some spectacularly unsuccessful communication to balance out the Gentlemen. A number of us have written about the connection of language with character, with heroism and power, in *Buffy*; in contrast, a failure of language can mean a failure of character. When the Wicca group leader says in response to Willow's request to try spells, "Oh, yeah, then we could get on our broomsticks and fly around on our broomsticks," regular Buffy-watchers would recognize the repetitious phrasing as a "feeble banter" attempt; the form of the failed witticism indicates a lack of intelligence while its content indicates, in this fictional universe, a closed mind. And when the stuttering Tara (who has too much to say and knows how little most people hear) attempts to comment, the Wiccan leader's officious silencing of the group in seeming attentiveness effectively silences Tara herself. The whole experience is succinctly mocked by Willow as "blah, blah Gaia, blah, blah moon, menstrual life force power thingy." Neither the Wiccans nor the Gentlemen communicate with those of a different perspective. The fact that the women (all these Wiccans are women)[8] are a source of humor and the Gentlemen a source of fear may reflect their relative power in this world.

The groups also relate to another subject repeatedly explored in *Buffy*, and that is the difference between formal groups and organic communities. In the Whedonverse (among other places) institutions are dangerous; communities can be life-giving. For me, one of the most enjoyable things about "Hush" is the domestic atmosphere created before the Gentlemen intrude. We see Willow and Buffy cozy in their dorm room, chatting; Buffy with her toothbrush, Willow in her cow jammies. Spike is being kept captive by Giles, but Spike pokes through the kitchen in search of Weetabix to crumble into his blood, while Giles comments, "Since the picture you just painted means I will never touch food of any kind again, you'll just have to pick it up yourself." "Sissy," Spike calls him. The flavor of the scene is of easy teasing. Anya and Xander are so at home that they enter without knocking. And when the scene moves to Xander and Spike at night (Xander taking Giles's duties), more teasing ensues. Xander and Spike, unlike Riley, are linguistically playful when it comes to sex and gender. Xander insists that he is "very biteable ... moist and delicious." When Spike does his high-pitched Anya imitation ("Xander, don't you care about me?"), he makes the latent content a little too open for Xander, whose response is "Shut up!" (which of course they will both very shortly do). The language play is part of the homey informality of atmosphere and adds to the drastic contrast with the silent formality of the Gentlemen or the ineffectual stiffness of Riley, who, as he says in the preceding episode, sometimes "do[es] a little prep work before [his] conversations" with Buffy.

So the organic, domestic, linguistically playful group is posed against the formality of those who wish to replicate an unspoken agenda or "power thingy." People like this can kill you, in one way or another. And it is noteworthy that "Hush" has, of all the Buffy episodes, perhaps the most diverse representation of a threatened population. Whedon notes that they went to some effort and expense to show, even if briefly, a variety of townsfolk affected by the silence. The first victim we see is a young white male; the newspaper headline says also that a fifteen-year-old girl had her heart ripped out; we see Tara chased; we see a sleeping old man unvoiced; and, again, one of the most frightening moments occurs when Giles's girlfriend Olivia, a black woman, comes face to face with a Gentleman. The monsters roam the college campus, it is true, but we come to see that the whole town is endangered—all ages, genders, races, classes—even other monsters (Spike stays indoors with the rest of the Scoobies). Everyone is threatened, everyone is silenced, by the Gentlemen.

Of course one of the most frightening things about "Hush" is the fact that the voices of the characters are stolen. As Buffy shows time and again, those in power can choose not to hear, not to know. The news broadcast in "Hush," in which the LA TV station reports that the town is merely suffering from a mass outbreak of laryngitis, is emblematic of the failure of those in power to hear the truth. Whether they're going to "rationalize what they can" or they're just "deeply stupid," the problem is still frightening ("The Harvest," 1.2; "Becoming," Part 2, 3.22). But just as frightening is the fact that this enemy does not speak. The Gentlemen are monstrously silent in the face of the horrors they create. And how many times will we see those in power maintain such a silence while evil proceeds? It is not surprising that their attendants wear straitjackets; their garb suggests the insanity of such behavior—the pretense of civilized politeness while killing is accepted as a matter of course.

And the straitjackets might also suggest the insanity that can result from failing to communicate our feelings and thoughts. Consider the closing scene. This episode presents patriarchy as horror in the form of the Gentlemen, and patriarchy with its best face on as the kindly, brave Riley. Riley can help Buffy defeat that worst side of patriarchy, but is he, its best incarnation, enough for Buffy? They can kiss and kill together, but they cannot dance and talk together. The episode closes with a series of parallel scenes about relationships in the aftermath of the experience. Willow and Tara delightedly talk, glowing at each other in a brightly lit scene; Giles and Olivia speak in the dark, physically touching but not looking in each other's eyes as she acknowledges that it may have been "too scary"; and Riley comes to Buffy's room. As she did for the picnic scene in the preceding episode ("Something Blue"), Cynthia Bergstrom has Buffy and Riley dressed in stereotypical girl-pink/boy-blue. They sit on opposite sides of the screen from each other as Riley says, "Well, I guess we have to talk" and Buffy answers "I guess we do." But they simply sit, wordless, their separate positions signs of their separate attitudes. Whedon has said that a theme of "Hush" is that "when we stop talking, we start communicating"— hence the transcendent moments: the shared look of Willow and Tara, the kiss between Buffy and Riley, the passion of Xander and Anya. But this is not such a moment. Buffy and Riley are not communicating; they are searching for words. To quote *Hamlet* from a scene describing the events of the *Aeneid*, they are "as hush as death" (2.2.447). Exactly a year later ("Into the Woods," 5.10), Riley is the gentleman who has "ripped the heart" out of Buffy. The whole episode is a prophetic dream of their relationship.[9]

One of the things Whedon says in his commentary is "As soon as you say something, you've eliminated every other possibility of what you might be talking about"—and I have certainly felt the truth of that in trying to write about "Hush." In every scene there are other elements I'd like to chatter on about. Sex, death, and politics—these are the topics I've hovered over and taken a stab at. "Hush" lets us speak about all these and more, and, young or old, it shows us what we're scared of. Whether we're talking about politics and information or personal relations, in the end, what we most fear is the silence.

Chapter 10

Poetry:

T. S. Eliot Comes to Television

"Restless"[1]

What are the roots that clutch, what branches grow
Out of this stony rubbish? Son of Man,
You cannot say, or guess, for you know only
A heap of broken images, where the sun beats,
And the dead tree gives no shelter, the cricket no relief,
And the dry stone no sound of water.

T. S. Eliot, *The Waste Land*, lines 19–24

In 1945, Joseph Frank said of T. S. Eliot's *The Waste Land* that it "cannot be read; it can only be reread" (Brooker and Bentley 24). The same might be said of the *Buffy the Vampire Slayer* episode "Restless" (4.22) which aired on 23 May 2000, as the last episode of the fourth season. Don Keller notes a third-season dream sequence that draws on imagery used in the section of *The Waste Land* called "What the Thunder Said" (175–6). I would like to propose an even more thoroughgoing correlation of technique between *The Waste Land* and the "Restless" episode.

Like David Lynch and Mark Frost's *Twin Peaks*, *Buffy the Vampire Slayer* is generally seen as *auteur* television, with the *auteur* in question being creator, writer, and director Joss Whedon (Lavery 251–2). The "Restless" episode is rich enough to support a book-length study on its own, and I hope someday to see it (or perhaps even write it). When I first drafted this chapter, I had just taught *The Waste Land*, and I am well aware that what I offer here is not an explication of the poem; it already has book-length discussions devoted to it. But in order to keep this discussion chapter-sized, I will concentrate on a few of the parallels between Eliot and Whedon in this particular episode.[2] I should also emphasize at the outset that although I will cover some specific similarities of content, my main focus is on similarities of technique.[3] In fact, Joss Whedon has himself compared the technique of "Restless" to poetry:

> The most important thing when I first started it was that the dreams be dream-like ... It's about combining the totally surreal with the totally mundane ... It then became a question of basically writing poetry. Um, basically free-associating. Obviously, things had to get worse at the end of each act—people had to be in peril because this thing was trying to kill them in their dreams. But beyond that, there really was no structure. So I was basically sitting down to write a forty-minute tone poem.
>
>   "Season Four Overview"

Both Whedon's and Eliot's works are fragmented into major sections; both depend on dream logic and non-linear segues ("a heap of broken images"). Both also depend heavily on allusion and symbolic resonance. Finally, both overcome the fragmentation by thematic unity and the power of myth.

At its first appearance, *The Waste Land* received both praise and disparagement, in part because of its fragmentary, nonlinear organization. In 1939, Cleanth Brooks declared, "There has been little or no attempt to deal with it as a unified whole" (59); though he and others like him soon addressed that critical challenge. The five sections of *The Waste Land*—"The Burial of the Dead," "A Game of Chess," "The Fire Sermon," "Death by Water," and "What the Thunder Said"—are now generally seen as depicting the sterility of modern life in light of the ancient myth of the Fisher King (as described by Jessie Weston), a king who needs to be reborn and redeem the land (and indeed, Eliot said as much in his notes). Each section can be seen as thematically focused (for instance, "A Game of Chess" explores sexual relationships). The dead desert land (the waste land of modern life), like the Fisher King, needs the baptismal, refreshing water of rebirth. One dream-like sequence floats to the next, as we move from children at the archduke's to the Son of Man to the Hyacinth Girl to Madame Sosostris to Stetson's friend, and from the Cleopatra-like beauty at her dressing table to Philomela to Dido to Lil's friend in the pub, and so on and on.

In television land, the dreamlike is justified by being presented as literal dream. The "Restless" episode comprises four dreams of the four main characters, enveloped by brief opening and closing segments in which we see that they have gathered for a late-night video-viewing, only to fall asleep. The four characters—to describe them at this stage of the seven-year story—are the hero, nineteen-year-old Buffy Summers, the Chosen One who battles vampires, demons, and the forces of darkness; her mentor, the British scholar Rupert Giles; and her best friends, the brainy young budding witch Willow Rosenberg, and the loyal, funny Xander Harris, brave but apparently incapable of worldly success. A typical *Buffy* season ends with the grand fight against the year's major villain, whether it be an ancient vampire, demonic ex-lover, town mayor turned gigantic snake, or bitch-goddess from another dimension. In "Primeval" (4.21), Season Four's penultimate episode, Buffy and company fight the Big Bad of the year, a California version of the Frankenstein monster made up of not only people parts but silicon, steel, and various demon bits. When the seemingly hapless but often helpful Xander points out that they'd need a "combo-Buffy" with the group's various skills to defeat their monster, Giles prepares them and Willow guides them in performing a magical joining of which the creature's mechanistic patchwork is mere parody. Together, they call on the spirit of Sineya, the very first Slayer in the long unbroken line of female fighters against evil and, together, they defeat the monster, the technological product of the science labs of the Initiative, a government-run military-industrial complex which represents, of course, the military-industrial complex.

"Restless," as I have noted elsewhere, expresses the psychic cost of that joining of the four friends ("Who Died," 9); most clearly, the emotional effort necessary for the magical bonding in the one episode "Primeval," but also, the difficulty of rejoining at the end of Buffy's freshman year of college, during which time the four friends have drifted apart (as episodes such as "The Yoko Factor," 4.20, make clear); even further, it might be said to represent the cost of the effort necessary throughout the entire series for the group to work together. And as many of us note again and again, relationship in community versus solo heroism is a highly important theme in *Buffy* (Wilcox, "Who Died"; Playdon; Rose).

In *The Waste Land*, Tarot cards are used by Madame Sosostris on one level simply for cheap fortune-telling; however, her words also genuinely foretell the need for rebirth; she tells the truth in spite of herself: "I do not find the Hanged Man [the savior]. Fear death by water"—Fear it, but it is what is needed (54–5). In "Primeval," Willow uses Tarot-like, large, named picture cards to identify each of the four main friends: Spiritus, spirit, for Willow, or Will, as she is called; Animus, Heart, for Xander; Sophus, Mind, for Giles; and Manus, the Hand, for Buffy. This segment is re-shown in the "Previously on *Buffy*" set of brief clips before the airing of "Restless" proper; and the dream sequences are then presented in the same order. The card choices represent qualities of each of the characters: Willow, who as a witch acts in the spirit-world and whose very strong will-power is spiritual, not physical; the non-magical Xander, who often has nothing but heart to keep him going; Mind, for the erudition provided by the well-educated ex-librarian Giles; and Buffy the warrior as the hands in battle. It might also be argued, though, that Spirit, Heart, Mind, and Body can be seen as aspects of one person; the first three all being non-physical qualities, and the fourth representing incarnation in the form of the hero. Thus, too, the four dreams in "Restless," the four acts in the teleplay, can each be seen as representations of the psychic difficulties of the four characters, and can also be seen as aspects of character necessary to be explored and joined in order to achieve a heroic wholeness. It is only when we reach Buffy's dream that the foe is conquered.

It should also be noted that the seemingly external threat battled in "Restless" is actually something from within (paralleling the idea that the whole dream-set represents aspects within a person, not just separate personalities). The characters only gradually catch glimpses of the threat: in Willow's first brief view it is not possible to tell if what she sees is human (it seems it might be a giant spider; it turns out to be a head of hair); and the same thing can be said in the second segment, Xander's. In Giles's view it can be identified as a person (one whom Whedon referred to as the Primitive), and the attentive reader may know by the end of Giles's section that the being who "never had a Watcher" is the very first prehistoric Slayer, Sineya (the beginning of an unbroken line of female champions), whom they called on in "Primeval." By the end of Buffy's segment, we are clearly seeing a young woman who, though she is dressed in ritual face paint, has a merely bemused expression on her face as she tips her head to listen to Buffy offering rather acerbic fashion correction. (There is humor strung throughout "Restless," despite the paucity of that commodity in this chapter; there is, after all, less of humor in Eliot than in Whedon, and we are focusing here on the similarities.) Though Buffy refuses to be controlled by the first Slayer (she tells her, "You're not the source of me"), still she recognizes that Sineya has shown her something within herself (the "roots that clutch"); and by the first episode of the following season, Buffy is asking Giles to help her explore that wilder side within. Thus the battle being fought in "Restless" can be seen as a struggle with the self. The unity of these friends is parallel and equivalent to unity within the self, unity of spirit, mind, and heart embodied in the hands that, in the larger myth of Buffy, hold the fate of existence (whether that existence is personal or universal). And the actions and interrelationships of these characters show some of the major themes of Buffy—communal connection vs. the solitary fight; growth and the search for self; and the importance of the ordinary in making meaning of life.

A thoroughgoing analysis of "Restless" would probably need to proceed act by act with exegesis. But for this brief chapter, I will, act by act, abstract some examples. In addition to the fragmentary but unified structure, a notable commonality of The Waste Land and "Restless" is the use of allusion to a degree atypical for their respective formats. T. S. Eliot, of course, provided extensive notes to explicate his allusions. Joss Whedon, on the other hand, does not use footnotes on network television (though I will nostalgically note that Northern Exposure once included a bibliographic entry in the closing credits); however, the information is accessible to TV readers through the many active internet discussions of Buffy. I mentioned exegesis a moment ago; Kip Manley has a website devoted to "Exegesis and Eisegesis" of "Restless." Often information comes out bit by bit in various online discussion groups; but it is a testament to this unusually rich text that "Restless" has its own site. It is worth noting that many readers of Whedon engage actively with the text in order to gain their equivalent of footnotes. More recently, Whedon has also offered voiceover commentary on the Season Four DVD. "Restless" uses both intertextual and intratextual allusions. The intratextual—references to other elements of the large text of Buffy itself—are perhaps the most important; but for this chapter, I will focus mainly on the intertextual, which are actually simpler, and which more directly follow Eliot's methods.

Willow's dream begins with one of the most attention-getting intertextual allusions in "Restless." Like Eliot, Whedon opens his poem with a quotation in Greek. During Season Four, Willow has entered into a lesbian relationship with Tara, a fellow UC Sunnydale student and witch, who makes her first appearance earlier in the season in the well-known episode "Hush" (see Chapter 9). Willow's dream begins in Tara's red-curtained, womb-like room, where Willow is using a brush to write black

Greek letters on Tara's back. It could hardly be more appropriate that she is spelling out a Sapphic ode, probably the most famous: the "Prayer to Aphrodite" ("Throned in Splendor, Deathless, O Aphrodite").[4] It is even more appropriate that in the second line, in the Richard Lattimore translation, Aphrodite is referred to as a "charm-fashioner"; the modern witch Willow is asking for a magic charm to gain love. Though in the source poem the love object is reluctant, Tara is not reluctant at this point (though she is later). However, Willow already has many self-doubts about her love relationships, which include years of unrequited love for Xander and a failed relationship with the werewolf musician Oz. Thus the allusion is multiply appropriate for Will because the poem touches on the ideas of Sapphic love, magic for love, and difficulty in love. Willow tells Tara, "I don't want to leave here"; she would prefer to stay in the womb-like space. But she needs to grow and uncover her true self.

Outside the window is a glaring desert brightness which Willow contemplates but does not directly enter. As Joseph Campbell notes, the desert is among the places of the unknown used "for the projections of unconscious content" (79), which represent that other world in which a hero must quest (58). It can also remind us of that dry land in need of redeeming by the sacrificial death of the Fisher King. The shriveled, aged Cumaean Sybil whose Greek words open *The Waste Land* reminds us that there are worse things than death: "I want to die," she says. Willow does not want to enter that desert, but she will be forced to explore herself nonetheless. Having told Tara she may be late for drama class (cf. Alice in Wonderland), Willow finds herself at school in that class thrust into a performance of a cowboy musical version of *Death of a Salesman*, with stage curtains of the same dark red as Tara's womb-like, protecting room—and for that matter as the red-room dream space in *Twin Peaks*. (Whedon says that he did not intend to allude to Lynch, but also acknowledges that viewers have made the connection.) Willow's fellow actor Buffy tells her, "Your costume's perfect. Nobody's going to know the truth—you know, about you." Tara, who is not in the play, serves now as a commentator to Willow (and later, even more like Eliot's Tiresias, to Buffy).[5] When Willow asks Tara if something is following her and Tara says yes, Willow follows up by asking, "What should I do? The play's gonna start soon and I don't even know my lines." Tara answers, "The play's already started—that's not the point ... Everyone's starting to find out about you—the real you. If they find out, they'll punish you—I can't help you with that."

In the sixth-season musical episode "Once More, with Feeling," one of the Whedon-written songs opens with the line, "Life's a show, and we all play our parts," and in "Restless," as in many other places in Buffy, the drama metaphor is very consciously explored. The play within Willow's dream has already started; the TV series Buffy the Vampire Slayer is at that moment under way; and of course, Willow's life (not to mention all of our lives) is already ongoing. She will have to step out of that womb of safety whether she wants to or not. Willow's fear of revealing her real self is something with which many people can identify, and is certainly applicable to other Buffy characters. In this context the opening scene with the Sapphic ode may suggest that Willow fears others' judging her lesbian sexuality, which has only recently been revealed to her closest friends. But the fear for her (and some of us) has other elements; for Willow, her intellectualism has made her different. In the last scene of her dream, Willow has regressed to a young girl standing in front of a class giving a report on The Lion, The Witch, and The Wardrobe, being dressed in a childish jumper that looks just like the one she wore in the series' first episode (the clothing that lay underneath her college outfit when dream-Buffy ripped it off). She is being mocked by her current and former lovers and all the rest of her closest friends. "This book has many themes," offers the child-version of the young intellectual who grows up to write in Greek and who is very well aware that there should not be a cowboy in Death of a Salesman. As the Jewish Willow Rosenberg, always the good/obedient schoolgirl, begins to explicate a book often assigned in school and well known for its Christian symbolism, her breath, spiritus, is sucked out of her. This is the first of three allusion-illuminated deaths which reflect the victim's role as indicated by the Tarot-like cards.

Eliot took his original epigraph for The Waste Land from Joseph Conrad's Heart of Darkness (Brooker and Bentley 34), and Heart of Darkness in the form of Apocalypse Now is the guiding allusion for Xander's dream. In the opening envelope section, Xander asks the friends at this vid-fest to choose to view the "feel-good romp" of Apocalypse Now, though Will asks for something "less Heart-of-Darkness-y." Both Eliot and Whedon chose Heart of Darkness in part, of course, because it is a story of a soul's descent into the underworld of darkness. Though the kindly Xander, the "heart" of the group, does not seem a candidate for darkness, and indeed his dream (like the entire series) has touches of revealing humor, it is still true that he grapples here with his own hidden problems. While Buffy and Willow have gone off to college, the academic underachiever Xander has not, and in the fourth season he searches fruitlessly for good work and is forced to live in the basement of his parents' home, a dark place from which he is unable to emerge. Metaphorically, he is unable to emerge from his parents' kind of life and from the darker sides of their natures. As the repeated line for Willow's dream is "they're going to find out about you," the repeated line for Xander (said by both Buffy and Willow) is "I'm way ahead of you." Near the beginning of Xander's segment, as they watch a purposefully bad dream representation of *Apocalypse Now*, Giles says, "I'm beginning to understand. It's all about the journey," and on the journey of life Xander feels his friends are ahead of him. He is still in the dark place, as a seriocomic interlude with Sunnydale Principal Snyder in the role of Conrad's Mr. Kurtz makes clear (in a shot-for-shot filmic allusion to the Martin Sheen/ Marlon Brando scene of Coppola's film).

David Lavery points out that in this dream sequence the character/actor, in moving from one dream moment to another, is literally moving via steady-cam from one connected series set to another (253–4). In effect, the dark space we need to explore is not only the parental basement but also the backstage of the series (a continuation of the stage metaphor in Willow's segment)—and the subconscious of our minds. Xander tells Snyder, "I'm just trying to get away"; he tells Buffy, "You gotta be always moving forward." He addresses her as she plays in a sandbox which is film-cut to be revealed as a desert—the desert Willow saw out her window. When he warns Buffy that "it's a pretty big sandbox," she answers, "I'm way ahead of you, big brother." But every time he tries to move forward, he finds himself back in the basement. Time and again he looks up the stairs towards the place his parents live—parents that Buffy-readers know to be drunken, argumentative, and neglectful—and Xander says, "That's not the way out." (It is no wonder that two years later, the sight of his arguing parents decides him against going through with his own wedding ceremony.) In the last scene of his segment, he confronts the dream version of his father, who berates him for not coming upstairs, saying Xander cannot change things: "You haven't got the heart." Then we see a blurry image of the face of Sineya as she rips his heart from his chest. Xander may be trying to acknowledge his dark side, as represented by his failed familial relationships, his sexual desires, the qualities in himself he sees as like his parents, and his own self-doubts—but he is not yet truly ready to move forward.

While Xander carries forth the desert motif, Giles moves forward more overtly with the dramatic motif. In his segment he takes a childlike Buffy and his overseas girlfriend Olivia, pushing an empty baby stroller, to a carnival in a cemetery, where Spike has hired himself out as a sideshow attraction, his scenes shot in black and white to suggest "an old thirties movie villain [because] he's such a showman," as Whedon says. Like Willow, Giles is faced with performing in this segment, though he—the most mature member of the group—is not troubled by being on the stage of life, and sings quite comfortably at the Bronze (where Anya also tells jokes in Giles's dreams). But like the others, he feels something is missing in life; both Buffy, as they enter the carnival, and Spike, as Giles turns from Spike's crypt, tell the Watcher, "You're gonna miss all the good stuff" (Spike says "miss everything"). Olivia reappears, weeping by the overturned baby stroller, clearly suggesting some unfulfilled elements of Giles's life (and, in fact, of Buffy's life: a normal marriage with children seems unlikely for either). And Spike, as he vamps for tourists' photographs, admonishes Giles: "You gotta make up your mind, Rupes. What are you wasting time for? Haven't you figured it all out yet with your enormous squishy frontal lobes?" The power of the mind is not adequate to solve all problems, as the id-character Spike well knows.

The source of Giles's problem is indicated by an intertextual allusion. When Olivia tells him to "go easy on [Buffy] the girl," he answers, "This is my business—blood of the Lamb and all that." The blood of the Lamb, of course, is the sacrifice of the innocent, specifically Jesus; and, as more than one Buffy reader has noted, especially since her fifth-season sacrificial death and sixth-season rebirth, Buffy is often a Christ-figure. Giles's life is absorbed by guiding the savior of the world—to the point that he has perhaps lost perspective on life. In the opening and closing scenes of his dream, he refers directly to his job as Watcher. In the latter, he recognizes the first Slayer and declares, "I can defeat you with my intellect"; but we next see thick blood pouring down as Sineya, the Primitive, slices his head: sophus. No matter how noble your purpose, enormous squishy frontal lobes are not enough.

In the last dream, the longest and farthest sojourn in the desert is made—by Buffy. There she sees a spirit guide in the form of Tara, who, like Eliot's Tiresias, is a character who has crossed sexual boundaries and now acts as a wise observer in strange places.[6] On her way there, Buffy confronts Riley in his role as an officer and a gentleman in the Initiative, and she meets the never-before-seen human version of the Initiative's Frankensteinian creature, who is himself an intertextual allusion, and not just to Mary Shelley. The creature is called Adam. Riley tells her, "Buffy, we've got important work to do. Lot of filing, giving things names." Buffy then asks of Adam, "What was yours?" And he answers, "Before Adam? Not a man among us can remember." After he says the name Adam, blue emergency lights come on and an intercom voice says, "The demons have escaped—run for your lives." When Adam says no one can remember the name he owned before he became changed by the military-industrial complex, he is referring to his loss of human identity (see Chapter 3). Also, though, given that he has worn the name of the Biblical first man, the namer of all creatures, it can be suggested that he refers to a prehistoric, pre-patriarchal age; and Zoe-Jane Playdon argues that *Buffy* references a pre-biblical, female-centered mythology. Adam and Riley, who see *Buffy* simply as a "Killer" and can think of nothing better to save the world than to make a pillow fort, display the failure of the patriarchal system as Buffy sees it in her dream. Whedon cites the pillow fort line and adds, "These guys are playing with their weapons."

Now in her dream Buffy herself goes forth to the place of testing in the desert (as did Jesus) and meets the primitive first Slayer, whom she is able to resist. She holds a stack of the Tarot-sized picture cards, and we see for the first time on the cards not a single still, drawn image, but the moving picture of the four friends, seated in Buffy's living room. With this talisman, visually representing the communal spirit of the four friends, Buffy is able to survive; and when told, "The Slayer does not walk in this world," she answers with an assertion combining the love of the simple and everyday with the voice of heroism and the saved Fisher King's prediction of the flood of redemption and growth: "I walk. I talk. I shop. I sneeze. I'm going to be a fireman when the floods roll back. There's trees in the desert since you moved out. And I don't sleep on a bed of bones. Now give me back my friends!"

The poetry of this speech is the climax of the episode—"the point of the thing," Whedon calls it. The words are dream language full of meaning. There are many possibilities of interpretation from such evocative phrases, but here are a few thoughts. "I walk. I talk. I shop. I sneeze."—These words remind us that Buffy has, as Spike later puts it and as most of us already realize, "ties to the world" that keep her going, keep her human— something many of us need to be reminded of sometimes. Whedon says, "The side of her that is Buffy is as important as the side of her that is Slayer. That is what in fact makes her the greatest Slayer that's ever been." She also says, "I'm going to be a fireman ..." Perhaps Buffy wishes to see herself as a more humble hero, tied to the workaday world; the fire and water images balance. (And of course fire imagery in various places in both Eliot and Whedon refers to sexuality as well—how different are their views of it?—a subject for another day.) "[W]hen the floods roll back": The Fisher King must sacrifice self for the renewal of the world that will happen as a result of the floods, and after the floods roll back. To save the world, Buffy has already sacrificed herself by drowning in "Prophecy Girl" (1.12). And she will sacrifice herself again a year from this episode (of that, more later). "There's trees in the desert": the Fisher King's sacrifice will result in growth, in trees; we may think of the Tree of Life. Of course, traditional Christian symbolism also uses the word Tree to refer to the Cross, on which the savior—the second Adam—is sacrificed before the world's redemption can occur. Reborn, we no longer "sleep on a bed of bones." Buffy chooses to awaken and to stay with humanity: "Give me back my friends!"

In the penultimate scene, the follow-up to the poetry of this speech, her desire to take a shower is a simple human wish for physical comfort; it also continues the imagery of the waters of renewal after the release from the desert. The sterile life of Eliot's "typist home at teatime," or Lil in the bar, needs the redemption of the Fisher King, of the sacrificial leader; in *Buffy* that sacrifice will be given, and that everyday life will be given value; her words here suggest what will come. It takes great struggle to achieve an ordinary life. Eliot's poem ends ambiguously, with a call for the "Peace that passeth understanding" ("Shantih"): are we to expect renewal or death? Whedon's episode ends mysteriously, with the words of the sybilline Tara, and the closing shot of an empty room.

Considering the depth of "Restless," I cannot finish here, but I will briefly conclude. ("Hurry up, please, it's time.") It is not possible to fully understand "Restless" without having viewed the other 143 episodes of the *Buffy* series: it both reflects the past and predicts the future of the series. To give one example: in Buffy's dream in the third-season episode "Graduation Day," Part 2 (3.22), Faith refers prophetically to "Little Miss Muffet counting down from seven-three-o," and thus adumbrates both the arrival of Buffy's heretofore nonexistent sister Dawn (later referred to as Miss Muffet) and Buffy's death exactly two years later, with 730 equalling two times 365 days, or two years (cf. Keller, 167; Kaveney 2004, 27). Now, in "Restless," Buffy says, "Faith and I just made that bed," explicitly recalling the third-season dream (through the intermediate reminder of a dream in the fourth season's "This Year's Girl," 4.15). Then we hear from another prophetic voice, Tara's. Buffy says that her friends need her to find them, and notes, "It's so late" (Xander and Willow have said the same). She looks at a clock which says 7:30 am—showing the numeral seven-three-o, again;

but now spirit guide Tara says, "That clock's completely wrong," because, in fact, the death is no longer 730 days away; time is counting down. And as Buffy leaves, Tara quietly tells her, "Be back before dawn," referring to a time of day and naming a character not yet in existence, but prepared for long ago. Dawn will finally appear in the next episode; Buffy will once more sacrifice herself to save the world at the end of the next season. In the depth of his intratextual references to years of material, Whedon explores untraveled territory. In this respect more than any other, perhaps, "Restless" needs to be re-read, not just read.

But for now it is worth noting that in his intertextual allusions, dream logic, mythic explorations, and unity beyond fragmentation, Whedon follows the path of T. S. Eliot. This chapter has only touched the deep waters of the desert dreams of "Restless." I'll close with the last words of the episode, spoken in the prophetic voice of Tara: they apply most directly to the nineteen-year-old Buffy, but also, as the episode's structure shows us, to the whole series (Lavery 254), to its authors, and to us the readers: "You think you know what's to come—what you are. You haven't even begun."

Chapter 11

Death:

They're Going to Find a Body

Quality Television and the Supernatural in "The Body"[1]

There is the house whose people sit in darkness; dust is their food and clay their meat … They see no light, they sit in darkness. I entered the house of dust.

> Gilgamesh mourns Enkidu in the epic of *Gilgamesh* (34)

I really made that episode to capture something very small. The black ashes in your mouth numbness of death.

> Joss Whedon[2]

You can shut off all the emotions you want, but eventually, they're going to find a body.

> Buffy to Faith in "Bad Girls" (3.14)

The popular vision of Quality Television has certainly been slanted toward Realism, with its supposed transparent verisimilitude. In *Television's Second Golden Age*, Robert Thompson, giving his list of defining characteristics for Quality TV, notes that Quality TV series "are usually enthusiastically showered with awards" (15). Yet the Emmy Awards, bastion of conservative popular taste, regularly disregard writers, directors, and actors from science fiction/fantasy series (with rare exceptions, such as Gillian Anderson's award in acting for The X-Files—but she played, of course, the character who did not believe in the paranormal). In the 2003 Academy Awards sweep of eleven Oscars for Lord of the Rings, director Peter Jackson noted that fantasy has been "the F word," the equivalent of obscenity among the tasteful—or, rather, those popularly presumed to be of mature taste.

In distinction from the popular view, scholars such as Fiske and Hartley have long recognized the constructed nature of the "realistic" view. None-theless, many scholars and professional critics have also equated Quality Television with realism. "Quality TV aspires toward 'realism'," declares Robert Thompson (15); and though one should acknowledge his use of quotation marks around the term, one might also note his disparagement of Twin Peaks in the same volume. More recently, scholars Piers D. Britton and Simon J. Barker have asserted, "The aspiration toward naturalism has become ever greater in television as the medium has sought to ape film" (18–19, emphasis added), seeming to imply that television is not yet evolved enough for true realism.[3] Science fiction or fantasy television is more likely to be described as Cult TV than Quality TV. And the term "cult" is typi-cally pejorative, with the suggestion that admirers of such series are few and fannish. The Buffy and Philosophy collection, edited by my friend James South, includes a last chapter titled "Feeling for Buffy," wherein Michael P. Levine and Steven Jay Schneider identify the series as Cult TV (295) and castigate by name several critics (myself and David Lavery among them) for liking it. Despite Matt Hills and his discussion of scholar-fans and fan-scholars, many in academe share the view of Levine and Schneider. We like it too much, so how can we know if it's good? It must be cult, not quality. O Apollonian fathers of art, watch out—the critical Maenads are coming.

Yes, "realism" can be identified with received taste (and thus the established power structure). Nevertheless, more and more scholars (as, for example, several collections edited by David Lavery show) have come to be fascinated by television which is unquestionably not realistic in the generally accepted sense of the term: Twin Peaks, The X-Files, Buffy the Vampire Slayer. The fifth-season Buffy episode "The Body" (5.16), in which characters react to the death of Buffy's mother, has often been cited as one of the series' best (see, for instance, Jonathan V. Last's 20 May 2003 Weekly Standard article). Written and directed by series creator Joss Whedon, it generated widespread critical praise and, indeed, much Emmy "buzz" (see, e.g., Joyce Millman on Salon.com, 12 March 2001). It never received an Emmy nomination. The praise right after its broadcast often focused on the episode's "raw, mournful realism" (Nussbaum, "Must-See Metaphysics" 58); and David Bianculli proclaimed it "super yet natural ... a gem of realism" in the *New York Daily News* of 27 February 2001. Critics often remarked on the instance of a vampire's appearance in the closing act as the single flaw in an otherwise uninterrupted realistic surface (the complaint was often implied rather than directly voiced; see, e.g., Bianculli; Phil Kloer in the *Atlanta Journal Constitution*). This non-realistic element of the otherwise highly realistic and highly admired episode offers a special opportunity for examining the confrontation of the realistic and the non-realistic in Quality TV. I contend that, far from being the single flaw in an hour of "quality," Buffy's encounter with the vampire in "The Body" is one of the episode's great strengths, a key moment of fractal resonance. Both its immediate emotional violence and its connection to the pervasive themes of the series are significant. Furthermore, it is the necessary prelude to and catalyst for the episode's exquisite, visually allusive closing scene.

I would like to take much of the chapter to examine certain elements of the episode's realism and to turn later to the fourth act's intrusion of the supernatural in action and symbol. While Fiske's *Television Culture* in particular analyzes choices that construct television realism as reinforcing certain class views, I will instead examine Whedon's choices to aesthetic effect. Among realistic elements I will focus on: first, the special use of seriality; second, the physical presentation of the characters; third, the use of sound; and fourth, "emotional realism," to use Joss Whedon's term.[4]

Critics such as Jane Feuer, Robert Thompson, and Horace Newcomb have long cited the peculiar advantage television as a medium can have through its serial nature. As early as 1974, Newcomb pointed out as an important "factor in the television aesthetic, the idea of continuity ... the possibility for a much stronger sense of audience involvement, a sense of becoming a part of the lives and actions of the characters they see" (253). He also pointed out the problem that in the 1970s characters had "no memory ... Each episode is self-contained. ... With the exception of soap operas, television has not realized that the regular and repeated appearance of a continuing group of characters is one of its strongest techniques for the development of rich and textured dramatic presentations" (253–54). But in 1984 Feuer used *The Mary Tyler Moore Show* to point out "Mary's evolution as a character," noting that "critics whose conception of dramatic change can accommodate only earth-shattering moments of reversal are likely to overlook it entirely" (40) because the change accrues gradually, through the serial form; and in 1995 she also noted the "potentially progressive narrative form" of serial television (128). In 1996, Thompson may have made the fullest argument for this realistic element of seriality (linked most notably with the 1980s Hill *Street Blues*); in contrast to Newcomb's plaint, Thompson could now say, "Quality TV has a memory" (14) and, noting Newcomb's parallel of television with novels, Thompson argues that "In soap operas and long-running series, we can see characters age and develop both physically and narratively in a way that even Wagner's longest operas or Dickens's most extended novels didn't allow" (32).

Of course, many series fail to take full advantage of the medium's serial opportunities; those of us who were fans of *The X-Files*, for instance, watched with dismay as that series began to trip over the cords of its own story. But in the introduction to *Fighting the Forces*, David Lavery and I argued for *Buffy* as a series with memory—in its seven years, perhaps the most successful series ever in that regard. And in October 2002 at the University of East Anglia's "Blood, Text, and Fears" conference (Chapter 2 of this volume), I made the case for a seven-year narrative arc based on Joseph Campbell's monomyth. The *Buffy* characters have grown and developed and become intimately known to faithful viewers.

This possibility for character familiarity means that television can portray death in a fashion available to no other medium. Neither paintings nor symphonies nor plays nor films can provide years of connection with a character and then withdraw that person as suddenly as a death in a real family. Television exists through time in a way no other fiction does. M*A*S*H, one of the shows often identified as Quality TV, shocked viewers in 1975 when it allowed the Korean War to kill Colonel Henry Blake (McLean Stevenson) after the audience had known him for three years. Viewers of *Buffy* had known Buffy's mother for five years when she died in 2001.

The series added to the realism by having had Joyce Summers fall ill as early as the fourth episode of the season ("Out of My Mind," 5.4); it is gradually discovered that she has a brain tumor. The sequence of events is played out bit by bit through the course of the next half dozen episodes, with an operation that apparently saves her in the tenth episode of the season. The audience is allowed to believe that Joyce is a successful cancer survivor until the end of the fifteenth episode, when Buffy discovers her mother's dead body. "Was it sudden?" Buffy later asks about the death of Tara's mother; "No—and yes," says Tara; and the same could be said by viewers of Joyce's death. It is an extraordinarily effective use of seriality to represent the realistic shock of loss.

The establishment of character over years which Newcomb, Feuer, and Thompson recommend is applied to noteworthy effect in the sequence of episodes directly relating to Joyce's death. As I have mentioned, Buffy discovers the dead body at the end of the fifteenth episode, whereas "The Body" is episode sixteen. And in episode fifteen, "I Was Made to Love You," Buffy reaches a notably mature realization when she says, near the end of the episode, "I don't need a guy right now. I need me. I need to get comfortable being alone with Buffy." The immediate cause for her statement, the person she has chosen not to pursue, is the combinant character Ben/Glory. The audience knows they share one body, though Buffy does not. Glory, the self-centered, clothes-obsessed blonde goddess, is a parody of the kind of character the unobservant sometimes believe Buffy to be; and the handsome but ultimately self-centered young doctor Ben seems the incarnation of the traditional male "good catch." Buffy has turned away from a two-sided, double-gendered, superficial version of the old-fashioned American Girl's Dream. It is an act of significant maturity. Thus it is all the more poignant that, when she confronts her mother's body a few moments later, Buffy's last words in the episode are "Mom? Mom? Mommy?" Her emotional regression highlights the fact that this is yet another test she must pass on her way to adulthood.

The preceding episode, therefore, specifically aims the serial story at the theme of maturation. The use of serial development of characterization is clear. Even further, I would note, Buffy makes another use of the temporal nature of serial television in presenting the death of Buffy's mother. The last scene of episode fifteen is replayed as the first scene of the next episode. David Lavery, in his "Apocalyptic Apocalypses: The Narrative Eschatology of Buffy the Vampire Slayer" (Slayage 9, 2003), categorizes the ending of "I Was Made to Love Her" as, in Buffyspeak, "set-uppy"; preparing the way for a narrative pay-off. He notes that as many as thirty Buffy episodes fit into this category. None of these, however, had ever before reiterated an entire scene (as Joss Whedon notes in his commentary on "The Body"). Joyce's wide-eyed corpse clearly displays her death to the audience, if not to her desperate daughter; this is not a simple cliffhanger. But the fact that the content of the event reaches outside the confines of the single episode gives the effect of a reality that extends beyond the conventional limitations of the episode, even in its contemporaneous serialized form. There is life between the episodes.[5]

The use of seriality, then, clearly plants "The Body" in a field of relative realism. Just as important, however, is the immediate visual presentation of the episode, most notably the physical presentation of the characters. Buffy has long been interrogated—particularly in terms of its feminism—because of the glamourous image of its stars, above all, Sarah Michelle Gellar, aka the Maybelline Makeup representative. Patricia Pender has nicely summarized (before challenging) complaints in this regard; as she says, Buffy "might justifiably be accused of subscribing to, and therefore reinscribing, commercial and patriarchal standards of feminine beauty: she is young, blond, slim, and vigilantly fashion-conscious" (36). Sheryl Vint has argued for the importance of distinguishing between the representations of Gellar (in ads and interviews, for instance) and the representations of Buffy herself. Though I will not interrupt this discussion to illustrate at length, I would argue that there have been, throughout the series, instances of normalizing the physical presentation of the character. In any case, for anyone willing to watch with open eyes, it can be seen that "The Body" realistically presents the character as far from glamorous. Joss Whedon has spoken more than once of his wish to engage viewers, and particularly young men, to the point that they might feel comfortable with a strong female character. In the early seasons, Buffy's appearance is almost always conventionally attractive. By the time of the fifth season, he could risk showing a young woman as she might really appear in the stress of waiting at the hospital to hear the verdict on the nature of her mother's death. Instead of seeing her dancing through a choreographed fight sequence punctuated by quips, we see her sitting, slumped, almost unable to speak. Her tied-back hair looks flat and a bit greasy; her skin is pale; there are shadows under her eyes. The v-neckline of her red sweater is slightly askew, not showing cleavage but bony collarbone. Under the harsh hospital lights she is seated next to the blue-clad Tara, a character whose more or less average body size has always presented resistance to Hollywood standards. I defy anyone to find glamour in that scene.

In fact, while Buffy's physical presentation is notably realistic, perhaps in part by contrast with her normal appearance, still all of the characters in "The Body" are presented in a physically realistic fashion. In particular, the dead body of Joyce is not a traditional Hollywood corpse. Her eyes are not closed as if in sleep; her limbs are not charmingly disposed. She is open-eyed, stiff, and pale. A close-up of her dead body, focusing on the face and upper torso, is the opening shot in each of the three acts after the first, in which Buffy discovers her, open-eyed and splayed stiff-limbed on their couch. The reiterated physical presentations of the characters combine to suggest physical vulnerability, mortality, just as glamour (consider the magical connotation of the word) futilely attempts to suggest immortal, invulnerable beauty. "Now get you to my lady's chamber, and tell her, let her paint an inch thick, to this favour she must come" (*Hamlet*, 5.1—the gravediggers' scene).[6]

The third element of realism in "The Body" has often been briefly noted: its use of sound. The entire series makes a careful, conscious use of sound, but this episode is particularly noteworthy. Other than the theme song, this episode has no non-diegetic music. A number of critics have commented on the lack of background music as a reinforcement of the episode's realism. But, just as the realistic presentation of Joyce's dead body is artfully selected to frame the opening of each act, so too the use of sound is both "realistic" and artfully structured.

I've commented at length in Chapter 2 on the use of sound in the first act, so I'll limit myself here. We hear and see wind chimes moving in an open window, suggesting the sensation of a breeze and the beauty of the outdoor world at the same time that we hear Buffy vomit in reaction to the realization that her mother is indeed dead. The wind of the world is still there, and she faces it for a moment, rising to open the back door and stand listening to the sound of children, the sound of distant music, of more distant ocean waves. This selection of sounds is on the surface realistic for a California neighborhood, but they are clearly selected for their symbolic value as well—the ocean of life continuing beyond her door. Never before or after do we hear the ocean from Buffy's home.

The next act begins with the single sound of the zipper of the body bag in which we see Joyce being enclosed. The zipper sound bleeds over into the next visual, in which we see Dawn standing in her school restroom, her friend Lisa about to emerge from a toilet stall. In this act, Buffy tells Dawn of their mother's death. She leads Dawn from her art class, a room enclosed in large glass windows, and the point of view shifts from the hallway in which they speak to the students and teacher (who looks very like Joyce—a live counterpoint to their dead mother) standing, watching in frozen sympathy from within the class. Thus, we hear Buffy and Dawn's conversation until just before the moment in which Buffy speaks the news of her death, when the point of view changes; realistically, we cannot hear the announcement of death; we, the students, the teacher, see through the glass, not darkly, but unable to touch them through the separation, the screen between us (whether it is the classroom window or the TV screen). Our hearing of Dawn's "no" is muted. Again, every sound is realistic, but the choice of the moment to shift the point of view and to shift the presentation of sound is made to emphasize the emotion and convey the theme of the emotional isolation of the survivors.

Similarly, in the third act, when we first see Anya and Xander, the use of sound is both realistic and constructed to effect. Just as we have seen Buffy and Dawn through glass, so now we see Anya, quiet and physically withdrawn, through the glass of an automobile windshield. When the camera shows Xander, we hear the sound of the car, no speech from the characters. But in the moments before, during the shot of Anya from outside the car through the glass, we do not hear the sound of the car; the scene starts, in fact, with no sound, diegetic or otherwise. Both the separation of the glass and the soundlessness seem to suggest the character's withdrawal. In fact, the now-silent Anya will soon verbally express her emotional difficulty in an outpouring which viewers found memorable because, in language both realistic and profound, she voices a question for many:

> I don't understand how all this happens. How we go through this. I mean, I knew her, and then she's, there's just a body, and I don't understand why she just can't get back in it and not be dead any more. It's stupid. It's mortal and stupid. And, and, Xander's crying and not talking, and, and I was having fruit punch, and I thought, well, Joyce will never have any more fruit punch ever, and she'll never have eggs or yawn, or brush her hair, and no one will explain to me why.

The rise in pitch of Anya-actress Emma Caulfield's voice on that word is part of the meaning, a realistic sound of loss of control—an echo of the greater loss of control of death, which the whole speech questions. (Some time after noting this, I viewed Whedon's commentary, in which he points out that he specifically requested that change in pitch to give a childlike effect; cf. Buffy's regression to "Mommy" in the teaser.) The loss of control is also implicit in Whedon's structuring of the speech, with its realistic stops and starts, fragments, and repetitions. Thus, once again, sound—this time in the shape of words—is selected to be both realistic and thematically significant.

It may be apparent by now that the fourth element I wish to consider, "emotional realism," in some ways inheres in all the others. But I will focus on certain instances which represent the psychology of the characters, again through methods which are at once realistic and artfully constructed. I should perhaps first reiterate that the phrase "emotional realism" is one that Joss Whedon used repeatedly to indicate one of his major intentions for the series (Wilcox and Lavery xxiv). His DVD commentary clearly indicates his aesthetic purposefulness in construction. For example, he comments on the framing of a scene in which the Emergency Medical Technicians give Buffy the news of her mother's death. Most of the frame is taken up with the black-jacketed back of an EMT, with the result that Buffy appears "trapped," as Whedon puts it, in her small slice of the frame. He notes his pride specifically in conveying the emotion through the framing. There are many more such effects, and I will here concentrate on just a few.

Willow, for instance, rather than moving with action-adventure purposefulness to console Buffy, spends almost the entirety of Act 3 trying to choose the right clothing to wear. Joss Whedon has reported that he experienced this obsessiveness himself in similar circumstances; and it certainly seems a realistic example of psychological displacement, obsessiveness in response to the lack of control. Not only the characters' actions but the camerawork also represents this psychological distortion. In one of Willow's speeches about her clothing, the camera cuts repeatedly, continuing to focus on her each time and from the same angle, but at slightly different distances. Thus the interrupting cuts represent Willow's emotionally uncontrolled distress and match her interrupted speech: "I-I-I-I should wear the purple [cut]—the purple I think [cut] the purple."

Similarly, in Act I, while the EMT is telling Buffy the terrible news, the camera focuses on his mouth, placing the top of his head out of frame. The framing choice can be seen as reflecting the psychological response of the character, focusing not on the whole person, but on the lips making the announcement. When Buffy telephones Giles to incoherently tell him the news, her point of view on the telephone shows the numbers enlarged, looming in extreme close-up as a reflection of the disorientation of the emotion she feels. (Whedon says that he saw this as the moment she realized her mother's death.)

The extremity of Buffy's emotion is also shown with sound later in the episode: in Act 4, as the doctor reports on his examination of her mother's body and tries to reassure Buffy that Joyce would have felt little pain, she hears his voice say, "I have to lie to make you feel better," while she and the camera focus on his lips clearly mouthing other words. (Similar effects appear in the 2001 pilot of Six Feet Under.)[7] The moment remains realistic because it can be accounted for by the character's psychological reaction to the events.

The audience is also drawn into the psychology of the experience through instances of flashback and fantasizing in the episode. After the teaser (in which Buffy discovers the body) and the theme song and opening credits, a commercial break is followed by a Christmas dinner scene in the Summers home with all the Scooby Gang—Giles, Xander, Willow, Tara, Dawn, Anya—and Joyce, very much alive. Signifiers of life—food, wine, and sex—come together in a kitchen scene in which Giles asks if he should open another bottle of wine, and Buffy makes an oblique, teasing reference to the episode in which Giles and her mother had sex ("Band Candy," 3.6). The whole communal scene is a happy family ritual of the sort regular viewers know Buffy longed for (cf. "Pangs," 4.8). The small imperfections of life are represented as pleasurable, as the mother and daughter consult over a slightly burnt pumpkin pie (part of the dinner ritual). When Buffy accidentally knocks the pie to the floor, we cut from this small domestic destruction immediately to ultimate destruction—an extreme close-up of Joyce's dead, open-eyed face.

It would seem at this point that we have just seen a memory of Buffy's which concentrated the essence of loving family life in the sharing of the meal and its accidental interruption. Because Whedon chose to place this scene immediately after the first commercial break, there is not what Feuer terms the "fantasy transition" (*Seeing*, 86)—there are no wavy lines or music of the harp to suggest a flashback. Some viewers may briefly wonder whether this is a subsequent, rather than an earlier, Christmas (although "spoiled" viewers would know otherwise, and the title of "The Body" would work against that interpretation, too). To one degree or another, viewers will share in Buffy's wrenching return when the episode cuts back to the dead body; we share in the emotional shock of the moment: real emotion in the audience, realistic emotion in the character.

Similarly, a few minutes further into the episode, Buffy imagines that the EMTs are able to revive her mother. To strengthen her fantasizing, Buffy imagines the EMTs saying that they've never seen someone brought back after so long and calling it a "miracle." Again, there is no visible "fantasy transition"—no marker for the beginning of the fantasizing, even though this time the vision in Buffy's mind begins within the scene—so viewers may be shocked when the episode returns from a shot of Buffy, Dawn, Joyce, and the doctor rejoicing in the hospital to the sight of Joyce's body still dead on the floor of the living room. (The brevity of the scenes which constitute the fantasizing may cue attentive readers to doubt—because of the lack of development.) Nonetheless, this experience can be conceived as contained within psychological realism, the "emotional realism" of the flow of Buffy's thoughts.

Many other instances could be cited, but I hope that these illustrations suffice to show that—through the special use of seriality, the physical presentation of the characters, the use of sound, and the "emotional realism" conveyed through multiple techniques—this episode is both highly realistic and artfully constructed scene by scene. Yet the entire episode is imagaically and thematically unified as well. I'd like to focus on two unifying patterns: thresholds and bodies. As I noted in Chapter 2, the episode is saturated with threshold images. The whole episode is, of course, about a threshold event—death. Several of the threshold images I have already mentioned in the course of this analysis, and some I have yet to touch on. The episode begins with Buffy's crossing a threshold: she enters the house of dust, the house of death, when she opens her front door. In spite of the flowers sent by her mother's recent date, Brian—a sign of the life she could have had—here Buffy has to confront death. The camera moves with her to emphasize her desperate emotion as she walks rapidly back and forward through doorway after doorway inside the house, calling for and failing to find help from outside. Repeatedly as she stares at her mother on the couch, we see her head in close-up in the left of the frame and behind her, the stairwell. The stairwell in Buffy's house is symbolically significant, often the site of emotional passages: for instance, Spike looks up it and Buffy looks down to him when he tells Buffy, just before her death, that she treats him like a man; and their positions recur when they see each other for the first time after her return from death (see Chapters 2 and 7). On this stairwell are placed several pictures of thresholds. In "The Body," we repeatedly see, along with the stairwell, one of the threshold images in the right of the frame as Buffy's face is shown in close-up contemplating her mother's corpse.

As she waits for the ambulance and the EMTs, she stands in the open doorway but does not cross outside; in the upper corner of the frame, a small, leafy green branch of a tree waves—life in the outer world still—but she no longer steps into it. When the EMTs leave, we see her again standing in the open door, but not stepping through it—wishing them good luck as they move on to help someone who does have a chance at life. After she falls to the floor and vomits, she once more raises herself and opens the back door to look out upon the living world—but once again, though she looks out, she does not step across that threshold, as if acknowledging the depth of separation. Just so, Act 2's school room scene behind the glass and Act 3's automobile windshield scene reiterate the uncrossed threshold.

But Buffy's friends do cross an emotional threshold, do go out into the world to connect with her; and, near the beginning of their act, Act 3, the camera moves in through the window of Willow's room and, at the end of the act, the camera moves back out through the window as they leave to go help Buffy. ("It's what we do," says Xander; though "How will we help?" asks Anya.) In the Act 4 scenes in the hospital, the door to the morgue is focused on—and the long dark corridor through which the doctor walks, steps echoing, emphasizes the passage to the other state of existence. The camera also dwells on Dawn moving through the same dark corridor (to face the morgue door) and later on Buffy as she follows Dawn. To save Dawn, whom she can hear being attacked, Buffy breaks through the locked double doors to the morgue, breaks through the physical threshold to prevent Dawn's crossing the threshold of death. The uncrossed threshold images in the first part of the episode, emphasizing the helplessness of the characters, are in some degree balanced in the last part of the episode by images of thresholds crossed by choice.

Another set of images also unifies the episode thematically—images, not surprisingly, of the body. In Act 2, which focuses on Dawn, we see in her art class three body images which parallel her mother. First, director Whedon chose for the teacher a woman who looks quite like Joyce Summers—blonde, attractive, adult but not aged: the teacher and mother as live/dead counterparts. Second, the students are drawing a white marble, Greek-style statue of a female—the colorless stone and classic form a counterpoint for a live body—and the dead body just a bit closer to the stone. Finally, the camera also focuses on the students' charcoal drawing of the artificial body—one step farther removed from reality. As Buffy approaches Dawn, and Dawn recognizes that some dreadful news is coming, we see her hand, in extreme close-up, drop across the paper, charcoal dragging down with her emotions. The teacher has instructed, "We're not drawing the object—we're drawing the negative space around the object." Just so, the episode deals with the reaction around Joyce—or rather, around the body. "Negative space—what's that about?" Dawn asks just before Buffy enters; it is, of course, about loss, about absence.

Earlier in the same act, we have heard mention of Dawn's "cut[ting her]self"; the episode itself mentions family trauma and a rumor that Dawn was adopted, and faithful viewers know that the cutting was at least in part in reaction to Dawn's questioning her own identity, her own reality—her incarnation in a human body. At the beginning of Act 3, the shot of Joyce's body shows that it is about to be cut open, this being intimated by the sight of her slip being cut by scissors in bodiless hands; and at the beginning of Act 4, the marks on her now naked body suggest that it has been cut open. Dawn's self-inflicted wound and the opening of Joyce's body find an echo in Act 3 when Xander vents what he calls "some pent-up ..." by smashing his fist through the wall as he stands just inside the doorway (one more threshold) of Willow's room. We see a shot of his bloodied hand, and Xander and Tara exchange small smiles as she says, "It hurts." It is a curious and, to me, inexpressibly touching response: perhaps it refers to his having created a physical copy of the emotional pain; it does recognize the fact that he feels the pain because he is alive—as Whedon comments, "physically, as a living thing, not just a dead thing." It is in any case a combination of images of the body and the threshold. Like Dawn, he has broken into his own body; but his attempt to smash through the wall is as fruitless as an attempt to cross the larger threshold they face.

The combination of images of threshold-crossing and body-wounding should not be surprising in a text that, as a whole, focuses on vampires. Buffy's vampire mythology does follow the tradition of the importance of the threshold to vampires. The threshold can, of course, be seen as a sexual threshold—vampires penetrate the body, and vampires can only cross the threshold to the home (representing the body) when invited. There is a notable exception: if the person is dead, the vampire needs no invitation: the threshold has already been crossed, the home/body already entered. And with this context we can move to contemplate the entry of the vampire into the text of "The Body." (Yes, the episode; but I'll accept wider applications of those words.)

With the entry of the supernatural—the vampire—the episode crosses a genre-threshold from realism to fantasy. "The Body" leads viewers to experience death in consciously physical terms. Buffy turns from thinking of the possibility of romance for her mother, *smelling* flowers sent by her mother's date, to *seeing* Joyce splayed stiffly, blank-eyed, on the couch. As she tries to administer CPR, she and we *hear* her mother's bones crack, with "almost obscene physicality," as Whedon says. "She's *cold*" [emphasis added], she tells the emergency worker on the 911 telephone line. Sense after sense is engaged in the horror. When Buffy vomits, it is "as if her very body rejected what had happened," as Carolyn Korsmeyer notes (167). Buffy pulls her mother's skirt down over her slip, and Willow later searches for the sweater she feels she should wear—but nothing can clothe this misery. In the autopsy, the doctor cuts into Joyce's slip and then her body. Buffy, waiting in the hospital with her friends and sister, inhabits her body in a fashion devoid of glamour, as she and Tara sit hunched together, talking of their mothers. Sartre writes of the body as the signifier of one's reality (see Badley, *Film*, 28); and Nancy Chodorow collates Freudian views, noting "the reality principle is in the first instance this separateness [from the mother]" (69). Thus in representing the death of the mother, Whedon has chosen the ultimate confrontation of self with reality. Why, then, the intrusion of unreality in the shape of a vampire?

Buffy engages in another major realistic confrontation with death in Season Three, in the arc in which Faith, the second Slayer, accidentally kills a human being (Wilcox, "Who"). When Faith attempts to deny the significance of the event, Buffy tells her, "You can shut off all the emotions you want, but eventually, they're going to find a body." The authorities will find a corpse—or (as I confess I first understood the line): emotions will take shape, be embodied, made real in you. In either reading, it is necessary to confront both the physical and emotional reality of death. The third-season arc deals with the death of the Other, while Season Five deals with the death of the mother and thus, metonymically, the self. At the same time, it is separation from the mother that indicates facing reality; thus facing her death means facing reality and moving towards maturity. And as I hope I have shown, this episode gives an extraordinarily realistic depiction of the characters confronting death.

But, as Cynthia Fuchs has pointed out, this series has been "seven seasons of death." In episode after episode, Buffy "dusts" vampires—she holds off the fear of death for us again and again. For a while in "The Body," it seems she is to be allowed a time of quiet grieving with family and friends. But death is always there; the vampire is always there. A number of commentators have noted that, since it is Buffy's day-to-day job to kill vampires, the presence of the vampire reminds viewers of the unwelcome presence of mundane responsibilities even in times of mortal misery—and Whedon's commentary confirms that that is part of the meaning. But because of the preceding verisimilitude of the episode, the vampire's attack in the morgue—its intrusion into the realism—is as violent as death itself. It is death within death. This vamp does not have to cross Buffy's threshold; Buffy and Dawn have entered the house of dust, the morgue. The formal generic intrusion is constituted of the series' reiterated metaphor for death (the vampire attack) entering into the realistic portrayal of the death of the mother/self: metaphor attacking the real. It is the culmination of the unifying motif of threshold-crossing. In the context of years of instruction by the series, it is possible for a viewer simultaneously to contain the metaphor, the realism, and the meta-metaphor of the genre transgression.

Consider, furthermore, the construction of the vampire attack. Dawn, feeling the need to see her mother's body, has sneaked into the morgue alone. She is attacked by another body in the morgue, which has just arisen as a vampire. Buffy breaks down the locked doors and fights the vampire to save Dawn. Other than the vampire, then, the three people involved are Buffy, her mother, and her sister—who is often seen as a symbolic daughter for Buffy. Mother, daughter, self: in a sense, then, we see three aspects of the same being, placed against death. The larger patterns live within the realistic presentation. And in spite of the vampire's supernatural nature, the presentation otherwise does continue to be realistic. Instead of the usual genre convention of heroic score music, we hear only the grunts of the struggle between Buffy and her enemy: this scene, like all the others in the episode, is as scoreless as most of life, denied the usual emotional cues of music. The hero's opponent is not dashing: this vampire lives in mottled, dead flesh. Another series anomaly, the vampire's nakedness (continuing the motif of the failure to clothe death) reasserts the physicality of death. (Whedon says, "Here's young Dawn confronted by not only a vampire but a naked man—it's an intrusion, it's offensive, it's completely physical.") In the body shot at the beginning of Act 4, we have seen from her bare shoulders that Joyce, too, is naked under the sheet, before the doctor covers her entirely. In the confrontation with the vampire, the covering sheet is drawn from the top of Joyce's body. Stephen King says, "All our fears add up to one great fear ... of the body under the sheet. It's our body" (Badley, Film, 25). Joyce's body under the sheet is now as frightening, in its own way, as that vampire: mother, daughter, sister, death live in the same space: generation and dissolution coexist. The battle against the vampire Death results in pulling that sheet, that divider, aside. By the encounter with death incarnate as the anonymous vampire, the physical realism of the episode is made contiguous with the metaphysical. It is a metaphor as extreme, in its way, as that of a Metaphysical poet; John Donne's stiff twin compasses are no more strenuous in their extension.[8]

As Buffy pulls the vampire off her sister/daughter, she finally destroys it with one of the autopsy instruments. Struggling on the floor, she beheads the creature and, as the dust of its death dissipates into the air, she falls back, exhausted. Having dusted the vampire in the presence of her mother's corpse, she has saved Dawn, but we are keenly aware that she has not, ultimately, turned back death: it is in the room with them—flesh of their flesh, bone of their bone—inevitably, their dust as well. The camera shows Buffy, in her red sweater, lying face up on the floor of the morgue in the same position that Joyce's body had lain on the floor of their home. Dawn, also on the floor, looks up to see just the edge of her mother's head above her.

The episode closes with a shot which visually recalls images from Kubrick and Michelangelo, in which a human hand attempts to touch ultimate mystery. In Michelangelo's Sistine Chapel painting "The Creation of Adam," one of the best-known images of western culture depicts God reaching out his hand and Adam reaching to God in a clear connection of the divine to human, the spark of the spirit. In Stanley Kubrick's 2001: A Space Odyssey, the sequence titled "The Dawn of Man" shows the ape-like being reaching out to tentatively touch the black monolith as the sun rises behind it; and, as reviewer Tim Hunter noted at the time of the film's release, "the monolith ... represent[s] something of a deity" (154); and, he notes, by the end of the film, "Kubrick shows an ambiguous spiritual growth through physical death" (153). (During the writing of 2001, Kubrick recommended Joseph Campbell to Arthur C. Clarke.) As J. P. Telotte says in discussing 2001, "The genre questions its very fundament, hesitates in and even subverts its own efforts at explaining and schematizing human experience" so that "this world seems suspended between the mysterious and the real" (23, 22). These two well-known images by Michelangelo and Kubrick inform the final image of "The Body." Instead of the sun in alignment at the Dawn of Man or the Creation of Adam, we have Dawn aligned with our hero-woman. The camera moves to pull our vision to see Buffy, arms out towards Dawn, arms out towards their mother. (Whedon notes that he "desperately wanted" this "three-shot [...] to go from Buffy to Dawn to the three.") Dawn rises over their mother as the sun rose over the monolith. The last words of the episode are Dawn's question, in effect the same question Anya asked: "Where'd she go?"

In the last moments of the episode, her fingers reach towards her mother, as the fingers reached in Michelangelo's and Kubrick's images; but the connection is never made. Just before the fingers can touch, the picture cuts to black; the episode is over. That unmitigated cut to black—sharp, sudden, silent—is itself a representation of death. We do not cross the threshold; the final blackness plunges us into mystery. At the end of this episode, we "see no light"; it is closer in spirit to Gilgamesh's mourning for Enkidu than the Christian work of Michelangelo or the superhumanism of Kubrick. We are left to consider the crossing from the natural to the supernatural: can it be made?

To put it simply: it all works together, realist and supernatural elements alike. The realistic elements are an extraordinary replication of the suffering of those who see death. This realism is constructed from a myriad of choices, some of which are in effect visual or aural metaphor, such as the cuts interrupting the distracted Willow's speech. The supernatural elements are another level of metaphor which introduces the contemplation of the metaphysical—a contemplation which spills out over the end of the episode, as we are plunged into mystery. If we accept the fact that all television is constructed, then we may see that the distance between the symbols capable of inhering in "realistic" texts are not so far from the symbology of fantasy after all. I once heard Ursula Le Guin say, with a cheerful sarcasm at the sociopolitical implications of the terms, "Women write fantasy. Men write 'magical realism'." If I may advert briefly to Zizek's work on Lacan, we might say that neither realism nor fantasy is Real; both are variant kinds of the Symbolic. Those who do not recognize or maintain consciousness of the constructedness of televison are less likely to accept the connection. I hope that we will work to expand the still generally accepted definition of Quality TV so that work such as "The Body" will be honored as it deserves.

Chapter 12

Song:

Singing and Dancing and Burning and Dying

Once More, with Textual Feeling[1]

True to his title in his last act, [he] has died the death of all Lord Chancellors in all courts ... where false pretences are made, and where injustice is done. Call the death by any name Your Highness will, attribute it to whom you will, or say it might have been prevented how you will, it is the same death eternally—inborn, inbred ...—Spontaneous Combustion, and none other of all the deaths that can be died.

> The omniscient narrator in *Bleak House* by Charles
> Dickens (346)

Xander: Somebody set people on fire? That's nuts! ...
Giles: Certainly emotions are running high, but as far as I could tell the victims burnt up from the inside. Spontaneously combusted. I just saw the one—I managed to examine the body while the police were taking witness arias.

> "Once More, with Feeling" (6.7) by Joss Whedon

> The musical [has a] heartfelt belief that musical movies are born of spontaneous combustion. The more sophisticated ones set out to destroy this illusion.
>
> Jane Feuer, *The Hollywood Musical* (45)

In the spring of 2002, I was invited to give a lecture about *Buffy the Vampire Slayer* to a general audience, not academics, at Atlanta's Eyedrum, a nonprofit arts and music organization. During the discussion afterwards, we turned to "Once More, with Feeling," and I asked the audience if anyone knew the other most famous fictional occurrence of Spontaneous Combustion. Almost immediately, someone piped up "Dickens" and then someone added "*Bleak House*."[2] In the fall of that year, I discussed the Dickens-Whedon connection further in a talk at the University of East Anglia's "Blood, Text, and Fears" conference, comparing Joss Whedon's Buffy Summers and Esther Summerson, the creation of Charles Dickens, whom Whedon has called one of his favorite writers. In *Bleak House*, the novel for which Esther serves as the narrator for half the chapters, Dickens uses Spontaneous Combustion as a metaphor for the self-destruction of either an individual or an institution involved in secrecy and pretense. Whedon's use of the metaphor in "Once More, with Feeling" is clearly parallel. One could also, however, suggest that he spontaneously combusts the standard relationships of traditional musical comedy, as well.

The Dickens literary connection is only one of a myriad of connections laid in place by this episode of *Buffy*. The simple fact that television calls on multiple media is often ignored by those who wish to criticize its art. Joss Whedon and Co. use multiple avenues of communication and enrich the text of every episode by references both to their own earlier and upcoming episodes, and to other texts from a wide variety of fields. The sixth-season episode "Once More, with Feeling" is one extraordinary example of this richness. Allusions (verbal, visual, musical) to the worlds of literature, film, television, and music play through the episode. From Dickens to Disney, from Simon and Garfunkel to Sondheim, "Once More, with Feeling" is a constant dance of reference.

At the same time as the episode has viewers mentally reaching out to other texts, it is drawing us in to the emotional core of the characters' lives, including their moral and philosophical quests. One of the major themes of *Buffy* has always been the importance of community. As major characters struggle into their adulthood, "Once More, with Feeling" depicts the difficulty of balance between the individual and the community—

"Understand we'll go hand in hand, but we'll walk alone in fear," they sing in the finale—just as it depicts the interplay between solo and harmony, duet or group. (Compare the double narration of Dickens's *Bleak House*—the story of the individual interwoven with the panorama of society.) The device of the episode—having the characters magically forced to sing their true feelings—works like a soliloquy, in that we can be assured we will hear interior truth for that character.[3] This magical assurance of emotional truth counterbalances the high consciousness of textuality in the episode.

In my title, I refer to textuality. I am here using the term to subsume extratextuality (reference to the "real" world outside the text), intertextuality (reference to other texts), and intratextuality (reference to other elements within a long text such as the *Buffy* series). The very fact that "Once More, with Feeling" was originally broadcast for 68 minutes—breaking from the series' normal 60–minute time slot in a fashion almost unprecedented for narrative television (as opposed, for example, to televised sporting events)—meant that the audience was unusually conscious of its straining at textual bounds (see Chapter 7). Pre-broadcast extratextual information meant that faithful viewers of the series in a sense cooperated in the break with the standard format, thus entering the viewing experience with a heightened consciousness of form. As Anahid Kassabian says, "The boundary between unconscious and conscious processes is permeable" (88).

As the characters balance the drive toward their individual searches with communal caring and purpose, the audience balances textual consciousness with emotional immersion. Just so, performers who practice a scene "once more, with feeling" must both attend to formal details of presentation and simultaneously invoke emotion. This balance can be found within the episode, and one can hear Hollywood harmony at the end. Analysis of the episode as a standalone production, however, provides an incomplete picture of the re-visioning of the musical genre offered by the episode when it is viewed as a part of the larger *Buffy* text.

The balance between textual immersion and distance is key to Jane Feuer's discussion of *The Hollywood Musical*. Feuer argues that "The Hollywood musical as a genre perceives the gap between producer and consumer, the breakdown of community designated by the very distinction between performer and audience, as a form of cinematic original sin" (3). She notes that the pretense of spontaneity is a standard technique to induce immersion and identification. Furthermore, many musicals—such as "backstage musicals"—include an internal audience to cue us emotionally (26–7) and to bridge that breakdown. We are offered a "doubled or split identification of both stars and internal audience" (29). For those films for which there is no diegetic performance, no play-within-a-play, Feuer argues that "proscenium or stage-like arenas are often created" (23) so that, for example, Judy Garland is framed in windows in Meet Me in St. Louis (23–4). In other words, the distance between performer and audience is created only to be collapsed, for the pleasure of being overcome. Along the way, Feuer notes that techniques of apparently distancing the viewer from the fiction—such as the use of direct address by a performer—can, in fact, be used to give quite the opposite effect depending on the context. "One may argue that direct address is inherently subversive or radical. It is not," she says (39) and instances the difference between the subversive effect of a Godard film, on the one hand, and the wink to the audience of Maurice Chevalier, who allows viewers to imagine a connection to the fictional world. Thus in even sophisticated Hollywood musicals, Feuer contends, there is a process of distancing or "demystification and remystification ... The narrative gets sutured back together again for the final bow" (43–4). I would like to offer her ideas as critical background in part to make clear the originality and effectiveness of what UPN called The Buffy Musical.

Buffy has always used sound, music and musical reference very consciously. Janet Halfyard has analyzed at length the theme song's play with traditional genre and gender tropes (as well as the interrelationship with the theme song of the Angel series). As with many other categories of knowledge, the Buffy writers assume of the audience a familiarity with and ability to reference Hollywood musicals. In Season Two's "The Dark Age," after Jenny Calendar has emotionally withdrawn from Rupert Giles because of an encounter with a demon from his Ripper past, she says that she is fine—"I mean I'm not running around, wind in my hair, the hills are alive with the sound of music fine, but I'm coping" (2.8). His later unhappy translation of this for Buffy is the brief, sad, but humorously inexplicit report that "The hills are not alive." The characters in the Buffyverse do not live in the emotional world of The Sound of Music; its Nazis are eminently more escapable than the vampires and demons which incarnate the evil that imbues Buffy's world.

Not only allusion to the world of music but music itself, and sound, are delicately employed in the series. In "The Body" (5.16), there is no non-diegetic music. At a particularly poignant moment, when Buffy, coming to terms with her mother's death, stands with her face in the sun looking out over the threshold of her back door, she hears the sounds of life proceeding—children's voices, the distant rush of the ocean, and a horn playing scales. The rise and fall of the notes is faintly irregular and inexpert; it suggests someone making an effort, someone learning, and—as the scales continue—the idea of life persisting. As Kassabian says, there is an "attention continuum" (52) with some music, particularly vocalized music, more consciously notable; but the sounds in this scene in "The Body" cooperate to create a finely tuned emotional and thematic effect.

The emotional effect of the diegetic use of "Tales of Great Ulysses" in "Forever" (5.17) depends on, among other things, its being doubly allusive. When Giles and Joyce listen to the Cream song in "Band Candy" (3.6), in which they magically lose their inhibitions and return to an exaggeratedly emotional state, the song served to signify, through its connection to the sixties, Giles's Ripper attitude. We also see that for this encounter, Joyce is going to be sharing his music and following his attitude, rather than the reverse. Thus the first level of the allusion. In the episode "Forever," Giles plays the music again after Joyce's funeral, and it serves as an emotional connection to the past and a reward to faithful viewers, the recognition of the musical reference allowing a consciousness of involvement with the series' fictional world. This particular musical instance of continuity is widely cited by scholars and fans alike; Viv Burr, in The Refractory, for instance, cites it as an example of intertextuality (or what I would here call intratextuality) creating connection for fans.

A very different effect is created by Giles's own song in his dream sequence of the fourth-season finale "Restless" (4.22). Giles repeats Willow's focus on performance in dream—hers dealing with acting, his with singing—as he performs a song in the Bronze with Xander, Willow, and other Bronze patrons listening. But the song is at the same time a declaration of information—operatic in function, though not in style—as Giles ponders aloud the mystery of their dream danger. As Halfyard says in her essay "Singing Their Hearts Out," "Effectively, this song manages to be both diegetic and non-diegetic simultaneously. Although Giles clearly knows he is singing, he and everyone else fail to perceive what we the audience do, namely that the song itself is abnormal, the usual rules of musical diegesis having been suspended by the dream-state" (14). While Giles's playing "Tales of Brave Ulysses" serves to bind viewers to the characters' world, awareness of the nature of Giles's "Restless" dream song, in contrast, separates viewers from characters (though this may serve to indicate a failure in perception on the part of the character, and does not necessarily indicate a separation of viewer from identification with the text).

Throughout the series, then, there is a precisely effective use of music and sound. By the time of the sixth season—their "baroque period," as Marti Noxon called it—Whedon and Co. could draw on considerable expertise in these techniques as well as in the use of narrative, language, and visuals. Michael Dunne argues in the forthcoming *Hollywood Musicals: Singing and Dancing, Fear and Loathing, and Big Production Numbers* that "Once More, with Feeling'"s "self-conscious separation of 'natural' diegesis and 'unnatural' musical production numbers would seem to fulfill Bertolt Brecht's program for denaturalizing art" (14). Of the standard "fused" production Brecht complains, with imagaic prescience, that "Witchcraft of this sort must of course be fought against" (38). And in "Once More, with Feeling" we share in fighting the spell.

Even before the episode aired, as Halfyard notes, the trailers "combined clips from the forthcoming show with footage of the actors both rehearsing in a dance studio and singing in the recording studio" (15) and, as I've mentioned, Joss Whedon let it be known through the Internet and the popular press that the episode would run long—both of these pre-episode tactics leading to demystification.

Consciousness of the textual form is interwoven with reminders of the story in which we are to lose ourselves ("It's wonderful to get lost in a story, isn't it?" Andrew asks in "Storyteller," 7.16). The "Previously on *Buffy*" segment locates us in the narrative. It appears on screen immediately after UPN informs us that we are about to see a "television event": "The Buffy Musical"—in itself an extratextual direction towards heightened textual awareness. The first words we hear in the "Previously" are Spike's declaration of love to Buffy, and we see her rejection. The images show us Buffy physically reincarnating as she returns from the dead, brought back by Willow, Tara, Anya, and Xander. Buffy has told only Spike, however, that she feels that she has been torn out of heaven by the return; while insisting that they cannot tell the others, she has become conversationally close with him in spite of rejecting his advances. Xander and Anya, in contrast, have finally openly declared their intention to get married. The troubled Dawn, we are shown, has been stealing. The "Previously" images do not make clear (though seasoned viewers know) that her thefts are unrecognized, but the images do make clear that Buffy has attempted to pass off to Giles the parental burden of dealing with whatever is troubling Dawn. We are also shown that Willow, who led the group in returning Buffy to this life, has been accused by Tara of "using too much magic" and has in response—in one of the most chilling moments of the series—magically wiped her lover's memory. With the "Previously on *Buffy*" segment, we are reminded that this episode is part of a longer narrative, a narrative which some viewers will know well, others in part, and some very little or not at all—except that they will have garnered information from the "Previously" segment, if they attend to it.[4]

The episode proper begins with distancing, demystification, through various avenues, many of them allusive. The *Buffy* theme song, as Halfyard has noted, normally starts with instrumentation recalling horror movies and shifts to rock instruments, thus indicating the series' genre-bending take on horror, with the rock music associated with the feminist hero Buffy ("Love, Death"). For "Once More, with Feeling," instead of a rock arrangement, there is an orchestral arrangement of the theme song with instrumentation and rhythm recalling 1950s and 1960s television. The visuals add to the effect: the names—series title, characters, actors, and creator—are presented in cartoon red lettering, and the faces (not including Whedon's) are presented in cartoon outline, in sepia colors. I thought of the *Bewitched* series and was confirmed in my impression by Keith Topping's having made the same connection (75)—though the *Bewitched* opening uses even more cartoon elements and a different tempo and instrumentation.

After the commercial break, the screen again shows cartoon red lettering with the episode title. Incidentally, for Keith Topping the episode title is an allusion to Joan Armatrading's "Love and Affection" (71), while for Michael Dunne (11), it is a reference to the title of a "1960 Stanley Donen film starring Yul Brynner and Kay Kendall and the Broadway play on which it was based, with all the aura of musical show business common to both." For the first several moments of the action on screen, we hear an orchestral overture and are given glimpses of the characters without, however, hearing any dialogue; furthermore, their motions are correlated with the rhythm of the music. All of this goes towards creating distance—the conscious realization that we are watching a special episode, which is balanced for many of us against an emotional investment of many years' standing. And this pull of distancing vs. emotional identification can be seen in the group dynamics of the characters as well.

Other credits run as the overture proceeds; the penultimate credit acknowledges Joss Whedon for the music and lyrics of the songs, and last we see that the episode was written and directed by Whedon; these letters disappear from the screen just before the first notes of the first song number. The *Buffy* series has been noteworthy to many of us for its emphasis on communal values and group cooperation which directly undercut the declared solo heroics of the standard opening voiceover claim that "she *alone* will fight the vampires, the demons, and the forces of darkness." In this episode's so-called "I Want" song for the protagonist, however, Buffy makes clear that she feels cut off from that sense of connection; in fact, she feels cut off from life—and to reconnect is what she wants. Buffy's anomie (as Dunne terms it) is hardly a standard old-time musical complication (though one could reference more modern works such as Fosse's *All That Jazz*). The adult nature of her emotional problem is emphasized by contrast with the fact that this number is what Whedon calls the "anti-Disney." (It might be seen as having some elements in common with the opening number of *Beauty and the Beast*—in itself a variant on the usual Disney because of the heroine Belle's unhappiness with small-town anti-intellectuals. But Buffy's number is certainly anti-the-usual-Disney.) Instead of dancing with cute little mice, or tea cups, or sea creatures, she dances with monsters. Instead of closing her song in a Little Mermaid's spray of hair and foam, she is framed in a spray of vampire dust (76)—ashes of the dead cheerfully crossing musical comedy with horror. (Someone should contrast the camp of *Rocky Horror* and *Little Shop of Horrors*.) And the capital H Handsome Young Man she rescues—with his Disney-like flowing white shirt and shining blond hair—who by all appearances should be playing the role of romantic hero—is so far from interesting her that he does not even merit formal rejection, merely the one word "Whatever" before she turns away from him. It is appropriate that the alienated Buffy is singing solo, only heard by the monsters—though they are occasionally harmonious.

The next number, "I've Got a Theory," purports to celebrate the sense of community. Giles, Xander, Anya, Tara, Willow and Buffy try to decide how to deal with the curious situation in which people all over town (including a large dancing chorus of customers expressing the ecstasy of successful dry cleaning) tell their feelings in song. The "Theory" number is structured with various solo vocals as different characters express different theories—from Giles's spot-on but self-dismissed "dancing demon" to Anya's bunnies—culminating in Buffy's solo question "What can't we face if we're together?" which is then reiterated in choral unison by the Scoobies. The singers look into each other's eyes as they sing, then conclude by turning to face in the same direction—as if towards the edge of a stage—though not directly into the camera. The superficial vocal and visual togetherness, however, is undercut lyrically by Buffy's theory that "it doesn't matter"; and though she then seems to say we don't need to care because we can be confident of success, she also adds that, since these are "the same old trips, why should we care?"—a question which Giles hears clearly, if the others do not.

As noted, the device of the episode is that the characters are involuntarily expressing their hidden feelings; as Dickens long ago suggested, "false pretences" can lead metaphorically to spontaneous combustion; as the Lord of this dance, the demon Sweet, says, "*Some* characters just die combusting"—apparently those who were holding in so much that the final release is overpowering. But there needs to be someone to listen to the vocal expression. In "I've Got a Theory," the Scoobies chant the same old message to each other. When Giles tries to tell Buffy that he is "standing in the way," however, she does not look him in the eye; instead she moves right into that training montage from a 1980s movie which she had declared she wished to avoid, dancing by him as he sings, and concludes his solo by asking him, "Did you say something?" When Spike sings "Rest in Peace," she rolls her eyes, but at least she listens.

Towards the end of the episode, "Walk Through the Fire" operates like the "Tonight" number in Sondheim and Bernstein's *West Side Story*, cutting from character to character in different locations as they sing first separately, then in interwoven parts, just as they move together physically as well.[5] But "Walk Through the Fire," in the Christophe Beck/Jesse Tobias arrangement, begins with the same guitar notes that open Simon and Garfunkel's "Sounds of Silence," that ultimate ode to the failure to communicate. And for that matter, the "Tonight" number in *West Side Story* propels us towards tragedy.[6] Michael Dunne praises "I've Got a Theory," saying, "The song sets all of the characters in motion and even predicts the ultimate resolution because Buffy does need the help of others to stand up to Sweet in the end." But as Buffy and her friends seem to move towards each other in "Walk Through the Fire," they are not simply singing of the traditional idea of going through difficulty for each other, walking through fire for each other; they end the song by singing that they will "let it burn." And, in fact, in the succeeding number, "Something to Sing About," they do almost let Buffy burn: they are so shocked by her announcement that they have pulled her out of heaven, that they do nothing as she begins to spontaneously combust, to dance herself to death. It is the late-arriving Spike (presumably the most flammable among them) who stops her, not the group acting together (although Giles has earlier asked Tara and Anya to act as her "back-up"). It should also be noted that when Buffy uses direct address to the audience in "Something to Sing About"—looking at the camera and singing "and you can sing along"—she is inviting the audience to share not the traditional musical wish-fulfillment, but her sense of lonely despair. No Maurice Chevalier here.[7]

The closing production number, "Where Do We Go from Here?" does bring the group together physically on the floor of the Bronze, which has become the stage of the small screen; but the number undercuts that togetherness in a variety of ways. While in "I've Got a Theory," the Scoobies sing directly to each other, in "Where Do We Go," they start the song scattered about the stage, facing different directions; only Buffy and Spike are facing each other, and they seem hardly to dare to glance at each other; similarly, Xander and Anya look at each other only briefly, and the others do not make eye contact. In fact, their placement echoes the positioning of the mourners in Edvard Munch's 1893 painting *Death in the Sickroom*.[8] Not only composition but color is significant. Costumer Cynthia Bergstrom notes, "Throughout the episode there was a very subtle color coding going on. I had picked various colors for each character" (74). In this scene at one point, the eight characters—an octave—stand in a line literally displaying all the colors of the rainbow. The rainbow could suggest joining in variety, or simply difference. But the interrelationships are even more specific: Willow and Tara are in complementary colors, violet and yellow; Xander and Anya are in similarly complementary orangey-brown and grayish blue; Spike and Buffy are dressed in the same colors of black and red. The separation of colors could, of course, indicate the separation of the characters—or, in Buffy and Spike's case, the joining that would soon come. "The color coding," as Bergstrom terms it, is perhaps most clearly apparent at the part of the production number which displays the tension between individual and group: all the characters stand in a diagonal line, clasping hands in a heavy-handed, mechanical fashion in time to the music, one after another, and then at once flinging apart from each other. The accompanying lyrics for this visual in the dance are "Understand we'll go hand in hand, but we'll walk alone in fear"—Not "We'll walk alone in fear, but understand we'll go hand in hand"—and it hardly takes a rhetorical expert to note the difference in the emphasis.

I could, and will, say more about this. But for now I hope that the main point of this section of the chapter is clear: "Once More, with Feeling" demonstrates that working in community is not a simple or easy thing. Its narrative, visual, musical, and dance structures challenge, without finally rejecting, this important Buffyverse value (though one should recognize that the nature of community in the Buffyverse is a debated issue). The effect is all the more significant because the *Buffy* musical concomitantly questions the traditional Hollywood musical value of the concluding reintegration into the community. And this questioning finds repeated support in the episode's various methods of demystification.

Jane Feuer, as I have mentioned before, demonstrates that many Hollywood musicals provide both demystification and remystification. In particular, she emphasizes that "Heterogeneous levels of reality are created so that they may be homogenized in the end through the union of the romantic couple" (68). Certainly one of the most memorable images from "Once More, with Feeling" is the concluding Buffy-Spike kiss, given the seal of closure with the "rising music" (Spike's descriptive term from the next episode, "Tabula Rasa," 6.8) and the big red "The End" shining over the couple (with just enough space between the words so that we can still see them kissing). There is much more to be perceived, however, in this conclusion. Furthermore, Feuer's very useful discussion does not take cognizance of the kind of structure provided by the "Once More, with Feeling" episode as part of the *Buffy* series (though she does elsewhere acknowledge the difference in film and serial television's long-term structure, *Seeing Through the Eighties*, 122). As Jamie Clarke says, "Music as utopian and therefore demonic interferes [with] and distracts from the day-to-day experience of living, suffering, and living as struggle. Indeed the significance of the episode within the series is to drag Buffy back from heaven/utopia and into the real world of struggle and slaying." In the last section of this chapter, I would like to examine the two elements of closure linked by Feuer—the romantic union and the narrative structure. Do these romances make for, in Buffy's words, "Something to sing about"?

In "Once More, with Feeling" there are three major romantic couplings: Xander/Anya, Willow/Tara, and Buffy/Spike. The ironically titled Xander/Anya number "I'll Never Tell" is perhaps most clearly modeled on a traditional Hollywood couples dance; Anya calls it a "retro pastiche," and not only the setting of their apartment, as Whedon points out (77), but also the clothing they wear evokes the 1930s—as costume designer Bergstrom confirms it was intended to do (74). They use direct address in a way that could be interpreted as bringing the audience into their humorous complaints (to receive Xander's mugging unhappiness over Anya's cheese, we must locate ourselves in the back of their refrigerator), and they invite identification by longterm viewers with intratextual references such as Anya's complaint (referring to "Pangs," 4.8) that "his penis got diseases from the Chumash tribe." And they exhibit a seemingly chipper reflexivity, such as Xander's irritation at Anya's vocal interruption: "This is my verse, hello!" At the end of the number, they fall together laughing in a typical musical comedy closing suggestive of the supposed spontaneity of their performance (cf. *Singing in the Rain*).

This, however, is not where we are allowed to rest. We cut immediately to Xander and Anya complaining vociferously to Giles about the experiences, and their unhappiness with each other, while still humorous, seems worrisome. Xander—who we later learn has set the whole business in motion—asks "And we're sure it's all connected—the singing and dancing and burning and dying?" His wording suggests to me the Siva dance of creation and destruction which we see so many times in life and in this series. (This is the scene in which we hear Giles speak of spontaneous combustion.) Anya also undermines the jolly audience connection by complaining, "I felt like we were being watched, like a wall was missing from our apartment, like there were only three walls, *no fourth wall*." Instead of the joy of barrier-breaking for the characters and those who identify with them, we are given a sense of loss of control. At the end of the musical we find that Xander, the least magical of the Scoobies, has invoked the demon of the dance—because, as he says, addressing Anya, "I wanted to be sure we'd work out. Get a happy ending." Even by the end of this episode, with Anya and Xander barely looking at each other, the musical comedy ending is in doubt; and before the end of the series we have seen Xander leave Anya at the altar and Anya return to being a vengeance demon—"There's wedding and betrayal." This is, as Whedon calls them, the "comic couple" (77).

Willow and Tara, instead of comedy, have a beautifully romantic number with Amber Benson's performance of "I'm Under Your Spell." Like Xander and Anya, they wear distinctive costumes—not evocative of the 1930s, but rather of an imaginary medieval romance. They, like Xander and Anya, at first seem to express ludic pleasure in the power of breaking through dramatic walls; as they whirl in the dance, they magically move from the idyllic park scene directly into their bedroom in an identification of magic, music, and sexual intercourse. But, once again, we are not allowed to exult in the completion of the experience. As Tara sings "You make me complete," she is interrupted in her magically third and presumably last iteration after the first three words: "You make me." There is a smash cut to Xander and Buffy complaining of Willow and Tara's "get-a-roomy" behavior, and high romance shifts gears to sexual comedy. We are not allowed that completion. The gears shift even further, of course, when Tara later realizes that being under Willow's spell is not a metaphorical but a literal matter. And, in the subsequent "Tabula Rasa" episode, she charges Willow with "violating" her. It is worth noting that Willow sings very little in this episode; aside from the extratextual reason of Alyson Hannigan's request not to, in the context of the episode it means that we are not given too direct an indication of Willow's coming darkness. It also means that Willow does not sing to Tara. Once again the denial of the Hollywood happy ending is hinted at in the episode and demonstrated in the series as a whole. And of course series viewers, in re-watching "Once More, with Feeling," know that by the end of the season Tara will be dead. The interruption of the song corresponds to the interruption of the relationship.

This use of the interrupted song occurs again in what is perhaps the most startling break in structure for "Once More, with Feeling"—an extra musical number which occurs approximately a year later in a separate episode. No Hollywood musical ever managed such an effect as this. Whedon and Co. show us that television is capable of creating a structure which is temporally beyond the capacity of most other media. In the seventh-season episode "Selfless" (7.5), Anya flashes back to the time of "Once More," and we hear her sing another number about her relationship with Xander—one only she heard originally—in which she declares, in effect, her intention to give up her name and her self in order to become "Mrs. Xander Harris" (see Chapter 3). It closes with a smash cut from Anya singing of her joy in her wedding dress to Anya with a sword through her heart. Like the Willow/Tara relationship, the Xander/Anya relationship ultimately ends in death—again, after the episode is over, but within the series.

The central couple, Buffy and Spike, close the episode with a really smashing kiss (yes, it's a pun). The lyrics have just recited "the curtains close with a kiss, God knows"—and they kiss to the accompaniment of what Spike in a later episode describes as "rising music"—"all Gone with the Wind" ("Tabula Rasa"). Anyone who chooses to can focus on that wish-fulfilling image and sound; and Michael Dunne declares that Buffy "regains her lust for life ... That's what we would expect from series television." But, as Kassabian argues, all the elements of a musical scene should be taken into account. The visual and the orchestration are positive, but the lyrics of the group are calling attention to the fact that the scene is a closing cliché ("the curtains close with a kiss, God knows"). And the next lyrics, of course, are asking "Where Do We Go from Here?" The typical Hollywood musical ending is about having arrived. Furthermore, if we return to the earlier-mentioned pattern of expression and listening, individual and connection, it should be noted that Buffy and Spike break from the group, interrupting the communion of the finale; even further, it is not at all clear that Buffy and Spike hear each other in the words they sing to each other for their episode conclusion. While Spike's lines offer the typical romantic view that his love lives beyond death—no idle hyperbole for a vampire— Buffy is simultaneously singing "This isn't real, but I just want to feel." And again, the text continues beyond the episode. What lies in store for Buffy and Spike? Shattering sex, anguish, and ultimately death for Spike.

Clearly, the *Buffy* musical overtly refers to and then thoroughly undermines the Feuer pattern of the Hollywood musical both in its denial of the standard romantic union and its extraordinary disruption of structure at every level. It does this through intertextual references such as the anti-Disney number; it does this through extratextuality, such as viewers' awareness of the extra length of the broadcast; it does this through interruption of musical numbers; and it does this preeminently through intratextual connections such as the seventh-season song and the later romantic disposition of the characters. By the end of the series, every one of the core Scoobies has lost a significant other to death: the oldest, Giles, goes first, losing Jenny Calendar in Season Two; Season Six brings the death of Tara, and Anya and Spike die in the last episode of the series. In answer to the song's question, this is where they have gone.

This is not, however, the complete story. Consider further the concluding relationships of the couples. Xander and Anya become once again what Anya would call "orgasm friends." There is no indication that they expect to marry, but they clearly forgive each other and make their peace. They both fight evil in the last battle of Sunnydale. Willow and Tara reconcile; they are torn apart by external forces rather than spontaneously combusting. And in the end, Willow achieves the self-acceptance and power that Tara would have wished for her. Buffy uses then renounces Spike—and then comes his attempted rape, his self-recognition, and his quest for a soul. At the point of his self-sacrificial death, Buffy is able to tell him that she loves him; for his part, he has been able to provide her with the self-confidence that allows her to share her power. In this world, the only certain source of happiness is not romance but virtue. Though *Buffy* thoroughly combusts the institution of the Hollywood happy ending, it shows a way to make a good end. It is part of the fascination of "Once More, with Feeling" that we can, if we wish, choose to select our relationship with the text and dwell on a happy ending—or we can share the struggle of the characters. Through various avenues (Internet discussion, scholarly conference, fanfiction, fan conventions, repeated viewings, etc.) we are offered the opportunity to participate in an involvement with the text which surpasses such opportunities for the Hollywood musical film in terms of immediacy,[9] continuity, and length; yet the text itself does not recommend wish-fulfillment, but right relationship with the world.

And in the end, we feel with the song. There is a joy in the realization of the music itself—of our ability to sing—that balances the pain of our suffering, that can give solace for human misery. Like the pleasure of the dance of language we have seen from Season One, the music in "Once More, with Feeling" holds off the tide of night. This musical was not "born of spontaneous combustion," but of the triumphal, hard-won effort of scores of artists working in concert with a man of genius. The very existence of a work like Buffy shows us the power of our humanity. Where do we go from here? Like all great literature, Buffy returns us to reality. As Spike says, "Life's not a song"; and as Buffy later teaches us, "It's real. It's the only lesson ... It's always real" ("Lessons," 7.1). By the end of the episode we see that "The curtains close with a kiss, God knows." But by the end of the series we can see that it is "all connected—the singing, and dancing, and burning, and dying."

Episode Guide

2.13/Surprise (Part 1 of 2)/Marti Noxon/Michael Lange

2.14/Innocence (Part 2 of 2)/Joss Whedon/Joss Whedon

2.15/Phases/Rob Des Hotel and Dean Batali/Bruce Seth Green

2.16/Bewitched, Bothered, and Bewildered/Marti Noxon/James A. Contner

2.17/Passion/Ty King/Michael E. Gershman

2.18/Killed by Death/Rob Des Hotel and Dean Batali/Deran Serafian

2.19/I Only Have Eyes for You/Marti Noxon/James Whitmore, Jr.

2.20/Go Fish/David Fury and Elin Hampton/David Semel

2.21/Becoming (Part 1)/Joss Whedon/Joss Whedon

2.22/Becoming (Part 2)/Joss Whedon /Joss Whedon

Season Three

3.1/Anne/Joss Whedon/Joss Whedon

3.2/Dead Man's Party/Marti Noxon/James Whitmore, Jr.

3.3/Faith, Hope, and Trick/David Greenwalt/James A. Contner

3.4/Beauty and the Beasts/Marti Noxon/James Whitmore, Jr.

3.5/Homecoming/David Greenwalt/David Greenwalt

3.6/Band Candy/Jane Espenson/Michael Lange

3.7/Revelations/Douglas Petrie/James A. Contner

3.8/Lovers Walk/Dan Vebber/David Semel

3.9/The Wish/Marti Noxon/David Greenwalt

3.10/Amends/Joss Whedon/Joss Whedon

3.11/Gingerbread/Jane Espenson and Thania St. John/James Whitmore, Jr.

3.12/Helpless/David Fury/James A. Contner

3.13/ The Zeppo/Dan Vebber/James Whitmore, Jr.

3.14/Bad Girls/Douglas Petrie/Michael Lange

3.15/Consequences/Marti Noxon/Michael Gershman

3.16/Doppelgängland/Joss Whedon/Joss Whedon

3.17/Enemies/Douglas Petrie/David Grossman

3.18/Earshot/Jane Espenson/Regis Kimble

3.19/Choices/David Fury/James A. Contner

3.20/The Prom/Marti Noxon/David Solomon

3.21/Graduation Day (Part 1)/Joss Whedon/Joss Whedon

3.22/Graduation Day (Part 2)/Joss Whedon/Joss Whedon

Season Four

4.1/The Freshman/Joss Whedon/Joss Whedon

4.2/Living Conditions/Marti Noxon/David Grossman

4.3/The Harsh Light of Day/Jane Espenson/James A. Contner

4.4/Fear, Itself/David Fury/Tucker Gates

4.5/Beer Bad/Tracey Forbes/David Solomon

4.6/Wild at Heart/Marti Noxon/David Grossman

4.7/The Initiative/Douglas Petrie/James A. Contner

4.8/Pangs/Jane Espenson/Michael Lange

4.9/Something Blue/Tracey Forbes/Nick Marck

4.10/Hush/Joss Whedon/Joss Whedon

4.11/Doomed/Marti Noxon, David Fury, Jane Espenson/James A. Contner

4.12/A New Man/Jane Espenson/Michael Gershman

4.13/The I in Team/David Fury/James A. Contner

4.14/Goodbye Iowa/Marti Noxon/David Solomon

4.15/This Year's Girl (Part 1 of 2)/Douglas Petrie/Michael Gershman

4.16/Who Are You? (Part 2 of 2)/Joss Whedon/Joss Whedon

4.17/Superstar/Jane Espenson/David Grossman

4.18/Where the Wild Things Are/Tracey Forbes/David Solomon

4.19/New Moon Rising/Marti Noxon/James A. Contner

4.20/The Yoko Factor/Douglas Petrie/David Grossman

4.21/Primeval/David Fury/James A. Contner

4.22/Restless/Joss Whedon/Joss Whedon

Season Five

5.1/Buffy vs. Dracula/Marti Noxon/David Solomon

5.2/Real Me/David Fury/David Grossman

5.3/The Replacement/Jane Espenson/James A. Contner

5.4/Out of My Mind/Rebecca Rand Kirshner/David Grossman

5.5/No Place Like Home/Doug Petrie/David Solomon

5.6/Family/Joss Whedon/Joss Whedon

5.7/Fool for Love/Doug Petrie/Nick Marck

5.8/Shadow/David Fury/Daniel Attias

5.9/Listening to Fear/Rebecca Rand Kirshner/David Solomon

5.10/Into the Woods/Marti Noxon/Marti Noxon

5.11/Triangle/Jane Espenson/Christopher Hibler

5.12/Checkpoint/Jane Espenson and Douglas Petrie/Nick Marck

5.13/Blood Ties/Steven DeKnight/Michael Gershman

5.14/Crush/David Fury/Daniel Attias

5.15/I Was Made to Love You/Jane Espenson/James A. Contner

5.16/The Body/Joss Whedon/Joss Whedon

5.17/Forever/Marti Noxon/Marti Noxon

5.18/Intervention/Jane Espenson/Michael Gershman

5.19/Tough Love/Rebecca Rand Kirshner/David Grossman

5.20/Spiral/Steven DeKnight/James A. Contner

5.21/The Weight of the World/Douglas Petrie/David Solomon

5.22/The Gift/Joss Whedon/Joss Whedon

Season Six

6.1/Bargaining (Part 1)/Marti Noxon/David Grossman

6.2/Bargaining (Part 2)/David Fury/David Grossman
6.3/After Life/Jane Espenson/David Solomon
6.4/Flooded/Douglas Petrie and Jane Espenson/Douglas Petrie
6.5/Life Serial/David Fury and Jane Espenson/Nick Marck
6.6/All the Way/Steven S. DeKnight/David Solomon
6.7/Once More, with Feeling/Joss Whedon/Joss Whedon
6.8/Tabula Rasa/Rebecca Rand Kirshner/David Grossman
6.9/Smashed/Drew Z. Greenberg/Turi Meyer
6.10/Wrecked/Marti Noxon/David Solomon
6.11/Gone/David Fury/David Fury
6.12/Doublemeat Palace/Jane Espenson/Nick Marck
6.13/Dead Things/Steven S. DeKnight/James A. Contner
6.14/Older and Far Away/Drew Z. Greenberg/Michael Gershman
6.15/As You Were/Douglas Petrie/Douglas Petrie
6.16/Hell's Bells/Rebecca Rand Kirshner/David Solomon
6.17/Normal Again/Diego Gutierrez/Rick Rosenthal
6.18/Entropy/Drew Z. Greenberg/James A. Contner
6.19/Seeing Red/Steven S. DeKnight/Michael Gershman
6.20/Villains/Marti Noxon/David Solomon
6.21/Two to Go/Douglas Petrie/Bill Norton
6.22/Grave/David Fury/James A. Contner

Season Seven

7.1/Lessons/Joss Whedon/David Solomon
7.2/Beneath You/Douglas Petrie/Nick Marck
7.3/Same Time, Same Place/Jane Espenson/James A. Contner
7.4/Help/Rebecca Rand Kirshner/Rick Rosenthal
7.5/Selfless/Drew Goddard/David Solomon
7.6/Him/Drew Z. Greenberg/Michael Gershman
7.7/Conversations with Dead People/Jane Espenson and Drew Goddard/Nick Marck
7.8/Sleeper/David Fury and Jane Espenson/Alan J. Levi
7.9/Never Leave Me/Drew Goddard/David Solomon
7.10/Bring on the Night/Marti Noxon and Douglas Petrie/David Grossman
7.11/Showtime/David Fury/Michael Grossman
7.12/Potential/Rebecca Rand Kirshner/James A. Contner
7.13/The Killer in Me/Drew Z. Greenberg/David Solomon
7.14/First Date/Jane Espenson/David Grossman
7.15/Get It Done/Douglas Petrie/Douglas Petrie
7.16/Storyteller/Jane Espenson/Marita Grabiak
7.17/Lies My Parents Told Me/David Fury and Drew Goddard/David Fury
7.18/Dirty Girls/Drew Goddard/Michael Gershman

7.19/Empty Places/Drew Z. Greenberg/James A. Contner
7.20/Touched/Rebecca Rand Kirshner/David Solomon
7.21/End of Days/Douglas Petrie and Jane Espenson/Marita Grabiak
7.22/Chosen/Joss Whedon/Joss Whedon

Notes

Introduction

1. *Buffy* has an impressive dragon in its hundredth episode, "The Gift" (5.22).
2. The Critical Heritage comment on Dickens is attributed to Abraham Hayward (62); that on Wordsworth to Frances Jeffrey (382).
3. My article used *Moonlighting* and *Remington Steele* as test cases.
4. More enlightened attitudes towards acknowledging the participation of all contributors account for part, but certainly not all, of this increase.
5. She is speaking particularly of Andrew, and I will share the comparison—though I hope I too know when to turn off the camera.

Chapter 1

1. Chapter 1 was first presented as a lecture titled "'There Will Never Be a "Very Special" *Buffy*': *Buffy* and the Monsters of Teen Life" at the Popular Culture in the South Conference in Augusta, GA: 8–10 October 1998. It was published in the *Journal of Popular Film and Television* 27.2 (Summer 1999): 16–23, and appears here (in revised form) courtesy of the journal and Heldref Publications. It was also republished in *Slayage: The Online International Journal of Buffy Studies* 2 (2001).
2. Quoted in Rochlin, 19.
3. Auerbach comments on the multiplicity of vampire types through the ages and places: "There is no such creature as 'the Vampire'; there are only vampires" (5).
4. Cordelia's truthfulness actually does fit the Shakespearean character; see Chapter 3. However, Whedon's Cordelia is significantly more selfish than Shakespeare's—at least in the beginning.
5. Note, e.g., Philip Martin's "The Vampire in the Looking Glass: Reflection and Projection on Bram Stoker's *Dracula*," 84, 90.

6. The interrelationship of the supportive outsider friends in *Buffy* is quite different from the group interaction of those who hunt Stoker's Dracula with, as Auerbach describes it, a "corporate ethos" and the guidance of the "overbearing patriarch" Van Helsing (78).

7. Writer David Greenwalt calls the demon "the giant phallic symbol of the show" in the DVD episode commentary, and notes that "There's a little feeling of ... we sacrifice women so we can control and keep and have our male power."

8. This linguistic trait is less applicable to Spike's mad, beloved Drusilla, but even she uses the occasional "okay."

9. While I was working on this discussion of language in 1998, Michael Adams was working on a much more expert exploration into the linguistics of *Buffy*. Our original articles came out in the same summer, his being "Slayer Slang (Parts I and II)," in *Verbatim: The Language Quarterly* 24.3–4 (Summer/Autumn 1999): 1–4, 1–7. He later developed this work as *Slayer Slang: A Buffy the Vampire Slayer Lexicon* (Oxford: Oxford University Press, 2003).

Chapter 2

1. Chapter 2 was first presented as a lecture titled "'Pain as Bright as Steel': The Monomyth and Light as Pain in *Buffy the Vampire Slayer*." It was the opening keynote lecture at the University of East Anglia's Blood, Text, and Fears: Reading Around *Buffy the Vampire Slayer* conference in Norwich, England, 19–20 October 2002.

2. Among published discussions referring to *Buffy* and Campbell's monomyth are Wilcox, "Who", 6–7; Edwards, 96; and Playdon, 144–5. See also Porter on Eliade, resurrection patterns, and Christian imagery. More recently, Nancy Holder added to the discussion her "Slayers of the Last Arc"; and Laurel Bowman's work is noted later in this chapter.

3. With their explanation of "reading," Fiske and Hartley emphasize perception specific to the medium of television; they also, however, emphasize the continuity of intellectual perception in their paralleling of television with Shakespearean drama (14), and it is this aspect of the term "reading" which I am here emphasizing. My discussions are also intended, nonetheless, to show many of the varieties of ways of making meaning which are available to television.

4. Cf. Braun's "*The X-Files* and *Buffy the Vampire Slayer*: The Ambiguity of Evil in Supernatural Representations."

5. Cf. Chapter 7 on "precaps."

6. It is one of the virtues of the series, in my view, that the story does not end with any marriage for the central character, since this might imply marriage (or

the equivalent) to be Buffy's and B*uffy*'s ultimate purpose. See Chapter 6 on leaving the story open.

7. Katy Stevens calls the music "an ethereal piece, complete with siren song" in part of a larger discussion of the significance of sound.

8. In a scene very shortly before Buffy's sacrificial death, Spike—standing (with moral appropriateness as he begins his climb) at the bottom of the stairwell— says to her on the steps above, "I may be a monster, but you treat me like a man."

9. When asked by Janet Weeks, the Academy of Television Arts and Sciences Panel Discussion moderator, "Wasn't Spike trying to get the chip out of his head?" Whedon answered, "Noo—but you were meant to believe that he was. This is a thing that I personally have devised called a 'plot twist.' I think it's going to catch on with the young people." The post-Season Six debate among fans does attest to the ambiguity of the presentation. And as late as 2004, the third volume *Watcher's Guide* asserts that the soul is "not the [reward] he had expected" (Ruditis 152).

10. Again, compare to Chapter 7's discussion of "precaps."

11. The point in this sentence was of course added after the end of the series. Given that Spike had to die, I must say that I was delighted to see the light-as-pain motif carried out. The scene referred to is naturally Spike's last, but not the last scene of the series overall; again, see Chapter 6.

12. The seventh season suggests that *palingenesia* may be necessary for Spike (and others) as well—as does the *Angel* series.

13. After Buffy's momentary death at the end of the first season, the audience is given to understand that she has been emotionally affected over the summer months, and the proportionately smaller cost of her reaction to this brief death is depicted in the first episode of the second season, "When She Was Bad." By the fifth season, the audience has grown to be able to contemplate a greater cost.

14. Kip Manley notes that a fan pointed out these stairwell pictures as appearing in "Restless"; however, as I note, they appear two seasons earlier. It is also worth noting that in "Inca Mummy Girl" (2.4) different pictures can be seen on the stairwell; it seems that a decision was made to substitute the threshold images. They seem to be present in a very blurry view in the grim "Ted," (2.11) and are distinctly shown for the first time in the pivotal "Innocence," which was written and directed by Whedon; see Chapter 7.

15. See Wilcox, "Who," on Mayor Wilkins as a representative of patriarchy.

16. Faith's words allude to the Robert Frost poem "Stopping by Woods on a Snowy Evening." These words, repeated in the poem's ending, are taken by

many critics to suggest a longing for death which must be postponed in favor of duties—appropriately enough for Slayers, especially considering Spike's declaration that "Every Slayer has a death wish" ("Fool for Love," 5.7).

17. Kaveney 2001 notes, "Their dreams [in "Restless"], like those Buffy shares with Faith, foreshadow bits of the future" (24).

Chapter 3

1. Chapter 3 was first presented as a lecture titled "'I Think I'll Name Me Joan': Onomastics and Identity in *Buffy the Vampire Slayer*" at Spectacle, Rhythm and Eschatology: A Symposium, University of Melbourne, Melbourne, Australia, 24 July 2003.

2. See Chapter 12 on inter-, intra-, and extratextual references.

3. In fact, Jane Espenson later said that his moral nature was decided in progress.

4. Consider also campus Catholic Newman clubs, named for John, Cardinal Newman.

5. Billy Fordham was played by Jason Behr, who went on to star in *Roswell*. His on-screen work with Sarah Michelle Gellar was successful enough that he co-starred as her love interest in the 2004 film *The Grudge*.

6. Jane Espenson notes that "we would not consciously have given them [Angel and Spike] the same name" (107). However, I refer here to effect, not intention; and note that she qualifies her remark with the word "consciously."

7. See Chapter 8 on "stitched segués."

8. "I'm an attainathon!" Buffy declares in "Touched" (7.20).

Chapter 4

1. Chapter 4 was first presented in an earlier form as a lecture at the Popular Culture Association Conference, Philadelphia, PA, 11–14 April 2001. See also Andrew Blake's 2002 book *The Irresistible Rise of Harry Potter* for Buffy/Harry parallels including synchronicity and social symbolism. I am indebted to Stevie Simkin for this reference.

2. See, for example, Keller; Kaveney 2001 and 2004.

3. Mere coincidence, but fun to note.

4. And in fact James South has provided such an exploration ("All Torment"). South's is an interesting combination of Shakespearean and Marxist analysis, with the vampires as blood-sucking exploiters and an emphasis on the importance of solidarity for those fighting evil. See also my comments in this chapter on the relationship of institutions of power to the magical world. Of course, magic has multiple symbolic referents in the Buffyverse.

5. On Buffy's dreams, see Keller; for examples of Harry's dreams, see *Prisoner of Azkaban*, 265, 353 and *Goblet of Fire*, 16–17.

6. Farah Mendelsohn argues that the Harry Potter books generally reinforce conservative social patterns, asserting, for example, that Harry's strength comes from inheritance, and that "at no time does Harry act with anything which can be called his own or the result of hard work and application" (289–90). But see my discussion of work earlier in this chapter. Like Blake (93), she cites the model of relationship to adults to be found in the Enid Blyton books.

7. The worlds of both Harry and Buffy realistically reflect male inhabitation of the institutions of power; and the worlds of both show those institutions to be flawed. See, e.g., Wilcox, "Who"; Clark and Miller.

8. Those in power will also choose not to deal with problems which they find reinforce the status quo; see, e.g., Mayor Wilkins' secret use of vampires as a tool.

9. It should be acknowledged that Angel helps Xander find Buffy. See Chapter 5, especially note 2.

10. The use of Christian imagery (such as Xander the carpenter saving the world [and Jewish Will] through extending love and forgiveness in "The Grave" (6.22) or Buffy's rebirth) is complicated; it is part of an overall pattern of images (as described by Campbell) rather than itself a governing symbology. See Erickson, Riess; see Chapter 2.

Chapter 5

1. Chapter 5 was first presented as a lecture titled "'Every Night I Save You': Vampire Versions and Redemption in *Buffy*" at the Popular Culture Association Conference, Toronto, Canada, 13–16 March 2002. It was subsequently published in *Slayage: The Online International Journal of Buffy Studies* 5 (2002).

2. In "Prophecy Girl" (1.12), Angel and Xander work together to first find (Angel) and then breathe life (Xander) into Buffy. In "Angel" (1.7), Angel stakes Darla; in "Fool for Love" (5.7), Riley intervenes when Buffy has been stabbed; but in these and similar cases, Buffy is certainly in on the fight and might have succeeded in the end without help. Cf. Spike in "Intervention" (5.18), as he allows himself to sink down in the elevator only after he knows Buffy has arrived to fight Glory's minions; he had previously prepared himself to go on fighting alone.

3. See Chapter 8 on stitched segués.

4. Thanks to Dawn Heinecken and Susan Wright for pointing out to me the fact that Spike was flinching from the sun.

5. In "Dead Things" (6.13), Buffy asks Tara to find out if Buffy has "come back wrong" from her resurrection. The idea that she is "wrong," changed to be closer to evil, may have made it easier for Buffy and Spike to come together sexually. However, Tara says that while Buffy has undergone a slight physical change which apparently fools Spike's chip, she is still the same person. Thus Buffy must confront the fact that her reaction to Spike is something within her "normal" self.

6. As Chaucer says of the five-times-married Wife of Bath, "wel she coude that olde daunse."

7. Or, as Buffy said seven months after I first published this sentence, "You don't know me. You don't even know you" ("Never Leave Me," 7.9).

Chapter 6

1. Chapter 6 was first presented as a lecture at Staking a Claim: Exploring the Global Reach of *Buffy the Vampire Slayer*: An International Symposium, at the University of South Australia, Adelaide, Australia, 22 July 2003.

2. One could also, of course, discuss Spike's difficult return in the *Angel* series.

3. He mockingly refers to her as a "lost lamb" in "Halloween" (2.6) but it is a description rather than a form of address, a nickname.

4. Jinna Lee and I discussed the idea of the disappearing shadow by email in 2003.

5. See my PopPolitics roundtable (round 3) with David Lavery, James South, and Stephanie Zacharek.

6. Whether or not the writers planned any specific reference, the *Buffy* series so resonates with the zeitgeist that viewers often irresistibly apply it to current events.

7. I refer here not to the psychotic Buffy, but to the normal Buffy who, in "Normal Again" (6.17), reports having been briefly hospitalized by her parents upon trying to confide in them about vampires when she first became the Slayer.

8. In "Tabula Rasa" (6.8), Spike refers to the "rising music" of the preceding episode ("Once More, with Feeling") to justify his belief in the emotional meaning of the kiss he shared with Buffy; i.e., the significance of the music is acknowledged in this text.

9. See Zacharek on the "Will to Power."

Chapter 7

1. Chapter 7 was first presented as a lecture titled "Time, Love, and Loss in *Buffy the Vampire Slayer*'s 'Surprise'/'Innocence'" at the Popular Culture in the South Conference, New Orleans, LA, 23–25 September 2004.

2. See also Chapter 8 and Rogers and Scheidel.

3. Some of Dickens's novels were serialized weekly; some, monthly.

4. I am certainly not the only person who teaches *Faust* in World Literature by reference to *Angel*. And at the Slayage Conference on *Buffy the Vampire Slayer*, the subject was discussed in a paper by Erma Petrova.

5. Stevie Simkin thoroughly discusses the varying sexual symbolism (though not the Pandora myth) in regard to the various boxes in "'You Hold Your Gun Like a Sissy Girl': Anxious Masculinity in *Buffy the Vampire Slayer*," pars. 14–19, and relates it to Buffy's "anxiety over her burgeoning sexuality," par. 15.

6. I am not here trying to identify the precise meaning this myth had in Greco-Roman culture (*pace* Foucault, *requiescat in pace*), but noting its existence as it lives in our culture today. For Foucault's exploration of historicized theoretical contexts for this subject, see, for example, *The Use of Pleasure*, volume 2 of *The History of Sexuality*.

7. After being discovered, Angel temporarily stops him by dropping a heavy object on him from its ceiling mounts. The object is the giant television in which Spike has viewed videotapes of Buffy in "Halloween" (2.6). Angel and Buffy thus use television to fight evil.

8. Similarly, Buffy's fifth-season death and rebirth were correlated to the series' move to another network and the summer hiatus.

9. Christophe Beck, in scoring the series, sometimes used real instruments and sometimes electronic sound.

10. In the DVD episode commentary, Whedon explains that D. P. Gershman put a light on an arm and moved it continuously during the scene.

11. David Lavery highlights Whedon's wordplay in "'Emotional Resonance and Rocket Launchers': Joss Whedon's Audio Commentaries on the *Buffy the Vampire Slayer* DVDs."

12. The Peckinpah comparison is made by Whedon in the commentary. This episode begins the alignment in position of Spike with Buffy, being wronged by Angelus and Drusilla, respectively.

13. The preceding episode, "Bad Eggs" (2.12), in fact has the Scoobies being taught sex education and the "unwanted consequences of teen sex"—another way in which Mutant Enemy presented the material conscientiously for its teen audience; and Joyce, when she later finds out that Buffy had sex, asks if she used protection ("Passion," 2.17). Since Angel had explained in "Bad Eggs" that he, as a vampire, could not have children, viewers are not left wondering if Buffy will become pregnant (nor is Buffy).

14. Whedon notes in the commentary that his "post-production guys" brought him this clip; but of course he chose to use it; the artistic effect was collaborative.

Chapter 8

1. Chapter 8 was first presented as a lecture at the Word in Praxis series of the arts nonprofit organization Eyedrum in Atlanta, GA, 7 December 2004.

2. Quoted in Roeckelein, 63.

3. Whedon notes that from childhood he used humor to get the attention of a sophisticated audience, his mother being a teacher and his father and grandfather having been professional television comedy writers (Havens 5).

4. Steven DeKnight, among others, also describes the writing process as collaborative ("Writing," 126–7).

5. Comics-conscious Xander, creation of comics-conscious Whedon, might recognize in the Xand-man nickname an allusion to the famous Neil Gaiman Sandman, who navigates a dangerous fantasy world.

6. Cf. Steve Wilson, who says, "The show's writers are fond of making punchlines out of editing techniques, as when Buffy asks Tucker why he's trained Hellhounds to descend on the prom and he replies mysteriously, 'I have my reasons.' Cut to a three-second scene of Tucker asking a girl to the dance and getting rejected" (89).

7. Michael Adams, Slayer, 177, analyzes this term in his lexicon of Slayer slang; it is one of what Jane Espenson, in the introduction to his book, calls "creative compounds," vii.

8. An homage to Magnolia, as Joss Whedon notes in the commentary.

9. In the discussion following the reading of this chapter at Eyedrum, Brian Matson noted the similarity of this episode to American Graffiti—in terms of the blonde, the cars, the loss of innocence, and the point of view.

10. Cf. Buffy in "I Was Made to Love You" (5.15) when she no longer feels she has to have a man in her life.

11. Contrast the cruelty of the use of this social cliché in "Innocence" (2.14).

12. Stevie Simkin refers to the zombies as "stereotypical jocks on a male bonding night," and speaks of the blonde (named Lysette in the closing credits) as "turned on specifically by the phallic symbol itself (the car) and not by the man behind the wheel," par. 14.

13. Laura Mulvey's "Visual Pleasure and Narrative Cinema," on the significance of the male gaze in film, is both luminously useful and grossly overused. See my Teleparody contribution, "Visual Pleasure and Nasal Elevation."

14. See, e.g., "Primeval" (4.21) and "Restless" (4.22).

15. Lewis is defining the nature of virtue by means of the device of a series of letters from the upper echelon demon Uncle Screwtape to his nephew, a junior tempter—a device not so far, after all, from the technique of Buffy. Fans of Spike/Joyce scenes might note with pleasure that among the potentially

soul-saving humble pleasures, Lewis includes "drinking cocoa" (60). Spike's speech in "Becoming" praising the physical pleasures that make this world worth saving (even "humans ... Happy Meals with legs") is part of his long journey towards real change, as he makes the important step of temporarily allying himself with Buffy.

16. "My mouth saved the world!" he adds to Buffy and Dawn in "Same Time, Same Place" (7.3).

Chapter 9

1. Chapter 9 was first presented as a lecture at the Slayage Conference on *Buffy the Vampire Slayer*, Nashville TN, 28–30 May 2004; the main institutional sponsor of the conference was Middle Tennessee State University.

2. See "'Emotional Resonance and Rocket Launchers.'"

3. Mary Hammond discusses *Buffy*'s monsters' connections with the old world. Regarding the "suits," cf. Whedon's commentary on Riley and Adam in "Restless" (4.22), and my discussion of them in Chapter 6.

4. For commentary on Athena and Buffy, see my foreword and Frances Early and Kathleen Kennedy's introduction to *Athena's Daughters*.

5. The script specifies that Riley should be shown in front of the fire.

6. In her "After the Revolution" lecture at the Slayage Conference, Nancy Holder noted that there was normally a conscious effort to subdue the sounds of death for humans (as opposed to monsters) in the series. Natasja Worsley, also at the Slayage Conference, discussed the idea of the silence confronting abuse victims as symbolized by this episode.

7. Whedon notes this in his episode commentary.

8. The only acknowledged Wiccans I have ever met have been young men.

9. See Chapter 7 on precaps.

Chapter 10

1. Chapter 10 was first presented as a lecture at the Popular Culture in the South conference, Charlotte, NC, 3–5 October 2002. It was subsequently published in *Slayage: The Online International Journal of Buffy Studies* 7 (2002), www.slayage.tv.

2. Stephanie Zacharek has repeatedly used epigraphs from Eliot to open her articles on *Buffy*. See, e.g., "A Hole in Our Hearts" and "Willow, Destroyer of Worlds."

3. I will not, for example, discuss Eliot's use of vampiric images ("A woman drew her long black hair out tight/ ... /And bats with baby faces in the violet light/ ... /crawled head downward down a blackened wall ...", 381–5).

4. Having studied Greek a bit myself, I used the pause button (repeatedly) to verify that it is, indeed (as various internet lists noted) Sappho's Aphrodite Ode written on Tara's back. The presentation is a bit confusing because the words are not separated; hence, on Tara's back, the second line begins "tAphrodite" (to use our alphabet). In the DVD commentary Whedon confirms the source, and notes that makeup artist Todd McIntosh researched the source and copied it in Greek onto Amber Benson's (Tara's) back.

5. See Chapter 8 on Xander as Tiresias; a fuller discussion of Tiresias figures in *Buffy* would be a pleasure to see.

6. In Greek myth, the gods changed Tiresias from male to female and back again; he famously reported that females enjoyed sex more than males. Tara crosses boundaries of sexuality in a different fashion, of course.

Chapter 11

1. Chapter 11 was first presented as a lecture at the American Quality Television conference at Trinity College, Dublin, Ireland, 1–3 April 2004. I am deeply grateful to Mary Alice Money for reading the paper for me after I had been in a serious car accident.

2. Quoted in Havens, 71.

3. Piers Britton, in an email, has stated that the authors' intention was to suggest that TV should take advantage of its own qualities rather than try to copy film. The phrasing, however, has unfortunate connotations.

4. See Heinecken on Ien Ang's earlier use of the term (95).

5. Compare the scheduling of the two-part "Surprise"/"Innocence," as discussed in Chapter 7.

6. Whedon has noted more than once that he sometimes held weekend Shakespeare readings with members of the cast in his home.

7. In the "Restless" commentary, Whedon cites as an influence Steven Soderbergh's *The Limey*, which also uses the technique of speech displacement.

8. In "A Valediction: Forbidding Mourning," he writes of the souls of two who love comparing them to the two legs of the compass: "Thy soul the fixt foot, makes no show/To move, but doth, if th'other doe."

Chapter 12

1. Chapter 12 was first presented as a lecture titled "A Complex of Echoes: Once More, with Textual Feeling" at the Sonics Synergies: Creative Cultures conference at the University of South Australia, Adelaide, Australia, 17–20 July 2003.

2. *This Is Spinal Tap* was also cited.

3. The day before I presented my lecture at Sonics Synergies, Diana Sandars presented a lecture on the same topic, including the comparison of the songs in this episode to soliloquies. She and I subsequently collaborated on an essay for the forthcoming collection *Sounds of the Slayer*, edited by Vanessa Knights and Paul Attinello.

4. See Philip Mikosz and Dana Och, "Previously on *Buffy the Vampire Slayer* ..."

5. Ostow cites David Fury as saying "Obviously it was patterned after a sort of 'Tonight' number from *West Side Story*" (79).

6. I thank Tommy DeFrantz for reminding me to think of the darker elements in some of the older musicals.

7. See the opening epigraph for Chapter 2.

8. I thank Professor Masoud Nourizadeh for calling this painting and the composition of the figures to my attention. I do not, incidentally, suggest it as a source, but wish to emphasize the parallel use of figure composition to indicate emotional alienation.

9. Film scholars often note the difference in viewing circumstances between film and television. It is worth noting that there have been viewings of *Buffy* episodes by large groups in darkened auditoriums.

Bibliography
of Works Cited

Acocella, Joan. "Under the Spell: Harry Potter Explained." *The New Yorker* 31 July 2000: 74–8.

Adams, Michael. "Slayer Slang, I–II." *Verbatim: The Language Quarterly* 24.3 (1999): 1–4; 24.4 (1999):1–7.

---. *Slayer Slang: A Buffy the Vampire Slayer Lexicon*. Oxford: Oxford University Press, 2003.

Aldiss, Brian. Foreword. *Blood Read: The Vampire as Metaphor in Contemporary Culture*. Ed. Joan Gordon and Veronica Hollinger. Philadelphia: University of Pennsylvania Press, 1997.

Algeo, John. "Magic Names: Onomastics in the Fantasies of Ursula Le Guin." *American Name Society* 30.2 (1982): 59–67.

Alley, Robert, and Horace Newcomb. *The Producer's Medium: Conversations with the Creators of American TV*. New York: Oxford University Press, 1983.

Alterman, Eric. *Altercation*, weblog. Available from <http://www.msnbc.com/news/eric_alterman.asp>.

American Academy of Television Arts and Sciences Discussion Panel. Moderator Janet Weeks. *Buffy the Vampire Slayer Season Six DVD Collection*. Twentieth Century Fox, 2003.

Appelo, Tim. "Interview with the Vampires." *TV Guide* 25 July 1998: 24–6.

Auerbach, Nina. *Our Vampires, Ourselves*. Chicago: University of Chicago Press, 1995.

Bacon-Smith, Camille. "The Color of the Dark in *Buffy the Vampire Slayer*." Foreword. Wilcox and Lavery.

Badley, Linda. "Bad Taste: Zombie Splatter Comedy." Paper presented at the Popular Culture Association in the South Conference. New Orleans, LA, 23–25 September 2004.

---. *Film, Horror, and the Body Fantastic*. Westport, CT: Greenwood, 1996.

Badman, Derik. The Academic *Buffy* Bibliography. <http://madinkbeard.com/buffy>. Also linked through <www.slayage.tv>.

Bakhtin, Mikhail. "Discourse in the Novel." *The Dialogic Imagination: Four Essays by M. M. Bakhtin.* Trans. Caryl Emerson and Michael Holquist. Austin: University of Texas Press, 1981. 259–422.

---. *Rabelais and His World.* Trans. Helene Iswolsky. Cambridge: Massachusetts Institute of Technology Press, 1968.

Battis, Jes. "'She's Not All Grown Yet': Willow as Hybrid/Hero in *Buffy the Vampire Slayer.*" *Slayage: The Online International Journal of Buffy Studies* 8 (2003). <www.slayage.tv>.

Bell, Barbara. "'Holden Caulfield in Doc Martens': *The Catcher in the Rye* and *My So-Called Life.*" *Studies in Popular Culture* 19.1 (1996): 47–57.

Berenstein, Rhona J. *Attack of the Leading Ladies: Gender, Sexuality, and Spectatorship in Classic Horror Cinema.* New York: Columbia University Press, 1996.

Bergson, Henri. *Laughter, An Essay on the Meaning of the Comic.* Trans. Cloudesley Brereton and Fred Rothwell. New York: Macmillan, 1911.

Bettelheim, Bruno. *The Uses of Enchantment: The Meaning and Importance of Fairy Tales.* New York: Vintage/Random, 1989.

Bianculli, David. "Super Yet Natural: Tonight's 'Buffy' Is a Gem of Realism." *New York Daily News* Online Edition. 27 February 2001. <www.nydailynews.com>.

---. *Teleliteracy: Taking Television Seriously.* New York: Continuum, 1992.

Bible, The. King James.

Blake, Andrew. *The Irresistible Rise of Harry Potter.* London and New York: Verso, 2002.

Bloustien, Geraldine. "Fans with a Lot at Stake: Serious Play and Mimetic Excess in *Buffy the Vampire Slayer.*" *European Journal of Cultural Studies* 5.4 (2002): 427–49.

---. "Carpe Diem or 'Fish of the Day'? Time as Leitmotif in *Buffy the Vampire Slayer.*" Paper presented at the Slayage Conference on *Buffy the Vampire Slayer.* Nashville, TN: 28–30 May, 2004.

Blumenthal, Ralph. "A Fear of Vampires Can Mask a Fear of Something Much Worse." *New York Times Online,* accessed 4 January 2003; available from <http://www.nytimes.com/2002/12/29/weekinreview/29BLUM.html>.

Bolton, Cynthia J. "Proper Names, Taxonomic Names and Necessity." *The Philosophical Quarterly* 46 (April 1996): 145–57.

Bowers, Cynthia. "Generation Lapse: The Problematic Parenting of Joyce Summers and Rupert Giles." *Slayage: The Online International Journal of Buffy Studies* 2 (2001). 30 March 2001. <www.slayage.tv>.

Bowman, Laurel. "Buffy the Vampire Slayer: The Greek Hero Revisited." Homepage (2002). 12 October 2002. <http://web.uvic.ca/~lbowman/buffy/buffythehero.html>.

Boyette, Michele. "The Comic Anti-Hero in *Buffy the Vampire Slayer*, or Silly Villain: Spike is for Kicks." *Slayage: The Online International Journal of Buffy Studies* 4 (2001). 15 June 2002. <www.slayage.tv>.

Braun, Beth. "The X-Files and *Buffy the Vampire Slayer*: The Ambiguity of Evil in Supernatural Representations." *Journal of Popular Film and Television* 28.2 (2000): 88–94.

Brooker, Jewel Spears, and Joseph Bentley. *Reading The Waste Land: Modernism and the Limits of Interpretation.* Amherst: University of Massachusetts Press, 1990.

Brooks, Cleanth. "The Waste Land: Critique of the Myth." *Modern Poetry and the Tradition.* Chapel Hill: University of North Carolina Press, 1939. 136–72. Rpt. in *A Collection of Critical Essays on "The Waste Land."* Ed. Jay Martin. Twentieth Century Interpretations. Englewood Cliffs, N.J.: Prentice-Hall, 1968. 59–86.

Brooks, Mel. Interview with Susan Stanberg. *Morning Edition.* National Public Radio. 8 August 2004.

Brown, Dan. *The Da Vinci Code: A Novel.* New York: Doubleday, 2003.

Buffyverse Onomasticon, The. 20 April 2003. <www.geocities.com/geekexmachina/onomasticon.html>.

Buffy the Vampire Slayer. Biography. A & E. 14 May 2003.

Burr, Vivien. "'It All Seems So Real': Intertextuality in the Buffyverse." *Refractory: A Journal of Entertainment Media* 2 (March 2003). <www.ahcca.unimelb.edu.au/refractory/journalissues/vol2/vivienburr.htm>.

Busse, Kristina. "Crossing the Final Taboo: Family, Sexuality, and Incest in Buffyverse Fan Fiction." Wilcox and Lavery, 207–17.

Campbell, Joseph. *The Hero with a Thousand Faces.* 2nd ed. Princeton: Princeton University Press, 1968.

Cashdan, Sheldon. *The Witch Must Die: The Hidden Meaning of Fairy Tales.* New York: Basic Books, 1999.

Chin, Vivian. Discussion following "Blade Meets Buffy: Saving the World and What Else?" Popular Culture Association Conference, New Orleans, LA, 16–19 April 2003.

Chodorow, Nancy. *The Reproduction of Mothering: Psychoanalysis and the Sociology of Gender.* Berkeley: University of California Press, 1978.

Clark, Daniel A., and P. Andrew Miller. "Buffy, the Scooby Gang, and Monstrous Authority: BtVS and the Subversion of Authority." *Slayage: The Online International Journal of Buffy Studies* 3 (2001). 9 December 2001. <www.slayage.tv>.

Clarke, Jamie. "Affective Entertainment in 'Once More, with Feeling': A Manifesto for Fandom." *Refractory: A Journal of Entertainment Media* 2 (March 2003). <www.ahcca.unimelb.edu.au/refractory/journalissues/vol2/jamieclarke.htm>.

Cummings, Barb. *Necessary Evils,* fan fiction. Accessed 30 May 2003; <http://www.

towermountain.net/barb/neintro.htm>.

Dale, Alan. *Comedy Is a Man in Trouble: Slapstick in American Movies.* Minneapolis: University of Minneapolis Press, 2000.

Dancing Lessons. [Fanfiction, multiple authors]. <http://randomthoughts.addr.com/redemptionista/>.

Dante Alighieri. *The Inferno.* Trans. John Ciardi. New York: The New American Library, 1954.

de Lauretis, Teresa. *Alice Doesn't: Feminism, Semiotics, Cinema.* Bloomington: Indiana University Press, 1984.

DeCandido, Graceanne A. "Bibliographic Good vs. Evil in *Buffy the Vampire Slayer.*" *American Libraries* 30.8 (1999): 44–7.

Dekelb-Rittenhouse, Diane. "Sex and the Single Vampire: The Evolution of the Vampire Lothario and Its Representation in *Buffy.*" Wilcox and Lavery, 143–52.

DeKnight, Steven. "Writing the Vampire Slayer: 2." Interview with Roz Kaveney. In Kaveney, 2004, 117–31.

Dickens, Charles. *Bleak House.* 1853. Intro. and ed. Morton Dauwen Zabel. Cambridge, Mass.: Riverside, 1956.

---. *Great Expectations.* 1861. Harmondsworth: Penguin, 1965.

Dickens: The Critical Heritage. Ed. Philip Collins. London: Routledge and Kegan Paul, 1971.

Dickinson, Emily. "Because I Could Not Stop for Death—." *The Norton Anthology of World Masterpieces: The Western Tradition.* Vol. 2: *Literature of Western Culture Since the Renaissance.* 6th ed. Ed. Maynard Mack et al. New York: Norton, 1992. 871–2.

Donne, John. "The Canonization." *The Complete Poetry and Selected Prose of John Donne & the Complete Poetry of William Blake.* New York: The Modern Library, 1941. 8–9.

---. "A Valediction: Forbidding Mourning." *The Complete Poetry and Selected Prose of John Donne & the Complete Poetry of William Blake.* New York: The Modern Library, 1941. 33–4.

Dunne, Michael. *Hollywood Musicals: Singing and Dancing, Fear and Loathing, and Big Production Numbers.* Forthcoming.

Early, Frances, and Kathleen Kennedy. Introduction. *Athena's Daughters: Television's New Women Warriors.* Ed. Frances Early and Kathleen Kennedy. Syracuse: Syracuse University Press, 2003.

Edwards, Lynne. "Slaying in Black and White: Kendra as Tragic Mulatta in *Buffy.*" Wilcox and Lavery, 85–97.

Eliot, T. S. "The Waste Land." *The Norton Anthology of English Literature.* Vol. 2. 6th ed. Ed. M. H. Abrams. New York: Norton, 1993. 2147–60.

Erickson, Gregory. "'Sometimes You Need a Story': American Christianity, Vampires, and Buffy." Wilcox and Lavery, 108–19.

Espenson, Jane. "Writing the Vampire Slayer: 1." Interview with Roz Kaveney. In Kaveney, 2004, 100–17.

Espenson, Jane. Introduction. Adams, Slayer Slang.

Feuer, Jane. "The MTM Style." MTM 'Quality' Television. Ed. Feuer, Paul Kerr, and Tise Vahimagi. London: BFI, 1984. 32–60.

---. Seeing Through the Eighties: Television and Reaganism. Durham: Duke University Press, 1995.

---. The Hollywood Musical. 2nd ed. British Film Institute Series. Basingtoke: Macmillan, 1993.

Fisher, Walter R. Human Communication as Narrative: Toward a Philosophy of Reason, Value, and Action. Columbia: University of South Carolina Press, 1987.

Fiske, John. Television Culture. New York: Routledge, 1987.

Fiske, John, and John Hartley. Reading Television. New Accents. London: Methuen, 1978.

Forster, E. M. "Art for Art's Sake." Two Cheers for Democracy. New York: Harcourt, Brace, 1951. 88–95.

Foucault, Michel. The Use of Pleasure. Volume 2 of The History of Sexuality. Trans. Robert Hurley. New York: Pantheon Books, 1985.

Freud, Sigmund. Jokes and Their Relation to the Unconscious. Trans. James Strachey. New York: Norton, 1960.

Friedman, Thomas L. The Lexus and the Olive Tree. New York: Farrar, Straus, Giroux, 1999.

Frye, Northrop. Anatomy of Criticism: Four Essays. Princeton: Princeton University Press, 1957.

Fuchs, Cynthia. "Life After Death." Poppolitics May 2003. <www.poppolitics.com>.

Gilgamesh. Trans. N. K. Sandars. The Norton Anthology of World Masterpieces: The Western Tradition. Vol. 1: Literature of Western Culture Through the Renaissance. 7th ed. Ed. Sarah Lawall and Maynard Mack. New York: Norton, 1999. 18–47.

Golden, Christopher, and Nancy Holder. Buffy the Vampire Slayer: The Watcher's Guide. Volume I. New York: Pocket, 1998.

Golden, Christopher, Stephen R. Bissette, and Thomas E. Sniegoski. Buffy the Vampire Slayer: The Monster Book. New York: Pocket, 2000.

Greenberg, Harvey R. "In Search of Spock: A Psychoanalytic Inquiry." Journal of Popular Film and Television 12.2 (1984): 52–65.

Greenwalt, David. "Reptile Boy" Commentary. Buffy the Vampire Slayer: The Complete Second Season on DVD. Twentieth Century Fox, 1997–98; DVD release 2002.

Halfyard, Janet. "Love, Death, Curses and Reverses (in F minor): Music, Gender, and Identity in *Buffy the Vampire Slayer* and *Angel*." *Slayage: The Online International Journal of Buffy Studies* 4 (2001). <www.slayage.tv/essays/slayage4/halfyard. htm>.

---. "Singing Their Hearts Out: Performance, Sincerity, and Musical Diegesis in *Buffy the Vampire Slayer* and *Angel*." *Blood, Text, and Fears: Reading Around Buffy the Vampire Slayer* Conference. University of East Anglia, Norwich, England: 19–20 October 2002.

Hamilton, Edith. *Mythology: Timeless Tales of Gods and Heroes*. New York: The New American Library, 1942.

Hammond, Mary. "Monsters and Metaphors: *Buffy the Vampire Slayer* and the Old World." *Cult Television*. Ed. Sara Gwinllian-Jones and Roberta Pearson. Minneapolis: University of Minneapolis Press, 2004. 147–64.

Hanks, Robert. "Deconstructing Buffy." *The Independent*. 1 July 2002. <news/ independent.co.uk/media/story.jsp?story=310937>.

Hardy, Barbara. "The Change of Heart in Dickens' Novels." *Victorian Studies* 5 (1961–62):49–67. Rpt. in *Dickens: A Collection of Critical Essays*. Ed. Martin Price. Twentieth Century Views. Englewood Cliffs, N.J.: Prentice-Hall, 1967. 39–57.

Havens, Candace. *Joss Whedon: The Genius Behind Buffy*. Dallas: Benbella Books, 2003.

Heinecken, Dawn. *The Warrior Women of Television*. New York: Peter Lang, 2003.

Held, Jacob M. "Justifying the Means: Punishment in the Buffyverse." South, 227–38.

Hills, Matt. *Fan Cultures*. London and New York: Routledge, 2002.

Hofacre, Alexandra James "A. J." [Raya Haddad]. *Out of My Head*, fan fiction. Accessed 20 May 2003; <www.angelfire.com/darkside/impisheyes/oomh1.html>.

Holder, Nancy. "After the Revolution: Greetings Sans Citations from a Cultural Worker in the Buffyverse." Paper presented at the Slayage Conference on *Buffy the Vampire Slayer*. Nashville, TN: 28–30 May 2004.

---. "Slayers of the Lost Arc." Yeffeth, 195–205.

---. *Buffy the Vampire Slayer: The Watcher's Guide*. Vol. 2. New York: Pocket, 2000.

Howard, Megan. "Slayer-Speak." *Entertainment Weekly* 31 October 1997: 84.

Hulbert, Dan. "The Hoopla over Harry." *The Atlanta Journal-Constitution* 2 July 2000: A1, A17.

Hunter, Tim. Review of *2001: A Space Odyssey*. *The Making of 2001: A Space Odyssey*. New York: The Modern Library, 2000. 151–8.

Jameson, Fredric. "Notes on Globalization as a Philosophical Issue." *The Cultures of Globalization*, ed. Fredric Jameson and Masao Miyoshi, 54–77. Durham and London: Duke University Press, 1998.

---. *The Political Unconscious: Narrative as a Socially Symbolic Act.* Ithaca: Cornell University Press, 1981.

Johnson, Samuel. "[The Praise of Variety.]" From *The Plays of William Shakespeare.* London, 1765. 8.311. Rpt. in *Hamlet: An Authoritative Text, Intellectual Backgrounds, Extracts from the Sources, Essays in Criticism.* 2nd ed. Ed. Cyrus Hoy. A Norton Critical Edition. New York: Norton, 1992. 148–9.

Jowett, Lorna. "Masculinity, Monstrosity, and Behaviour Modification in *Buffy the Vampire Slayer.*" *Foundation* 84 (Spring 2002): 59–73.

Jung, C. G. *The Portable Jung.* Trans. R. F. C. Hull. Ed., intro. Joseph Campbell. New York: Penguin, 1976.

Kassabian, Anahid. *Hearing Film: Tracking Identification in Contemporary Hollywood Film Music.* New York: Routledge, 2001.

Kaveney, Roz, ed. *Reading the Vampire Slayer: An Unofficial Critical Companion to Buffy and Angel.* London and New York: I.B.Tauris, 2001.

---, ed. *Reading the Vampire Slayer: An Unofficial Critical Companion to Buffy and Angel.* Rev. ed. London and New York: I.B.Tauris, 2004.

---. "'She Saved the World. A Lot': An Introduction to the Themes and Structures of *Buffy* and *Angel.*" Kaveney 2001, 1–36.

---. "'She Saved the World. A lot': An Introduction to the Themes and Structures of *Buffy* and *Angel.*" Kaveney, 2004, 1–82.

Keller, Donald. "Spirit Guides and Shadow Selves: From the Dream Life of Buffy (and Faith)." Wilcox and Lavery, 165–77.

Kloer, Phil. "With 'Buffy' Coming of Age, Comic Book Image Withers." *Atlanta Journal Constitution* 17 April 2001: D3.

Korsmeyer, Caroline. "Passion and Action: In and Out of Control." South, 160–72.

Krimmer, Elisabeth, and Shilpa Raval. "'Digging the Undead': Death and Desire in *Buffy.*" Wilcox and Lavery, 153–64.

Kripke, Saul A. *Naming and Necessity.* Oxford: Basil Blackwell, 1980.

Krzywinska, Tanya. "Hubble-Bubble, Herbs, and Grimoires: Magic, Manichaenism, and Witchcraft in *Buffy.*" Wilcox and Lavery, 178–94.

---. Email to the author. 30 June 2003.

Larbalestier, Justine. "*Buffy*'s Mary Sue Is Jonathan: *Buffy* Acknowledges the Fans." Wilcox and Lavery, 227–38.

Last, Jonathan V. "Where Do We Go From Here? A Farewell to 'Buffy the Vampire Slayer' and a Look Back at the Show's Ten Best Episodes." *The Weekly Standard* 20 May 2003.

Lavery, David. "Afterword: The Genius of Joss Whedon." Wilcox and Lavery, 251–6.

---. "Apocalyptic Apocalypses: The Narrative Eschatology of Buffy the Vampire

Slayer." *Slayage: The Online International Journal of Buffy Studies* 9 (2003). <www.slayage.tv>.

---. "A Religion in Narrative: Joss Whedon and Television Creativity." *Slayage: The Online International Journal of Buffy Studies* 7 (December 2002). <www.slayage.tv>.

---. "'Emotional Resonance and Rocket Launchers': Joss Whedon's Audio Commentaries on the *Buffy the Vampire Slayer* DVDs." *Slayage: The Online International Journal of Buffy Studies* 6 (September 2002). <www.slayage.tv>.

---, ed. *Full of Secrets: Critical Approaches to Twin Peaks.* Detroit: Wayne State University Press, 1995.

---, ed. *This Thing of Ours: Investigating The Sopranos.* Chichester, West Sussex; New York: Wallflower, Columbia University Press, 2002.

---, Angela Hague, and Marla Cartwright, eds. *Deny All Knowledge: Reading The X-Files.* Syracuse: Syracuse University Press, 1996.

---, James South, Rhonda V. Wilcox, and Stephanie Zacharek. "*Buffy the Vampire Slayer* Season Seven Discussion Forum: Round 3." *Poppolitics.com* 17 March 2003. <www.poppolitics.com/articles/printerfriendly/s003-03-13-buffyround3.shtml>.

Le Guin, Ursula K. "The Child and the Shadow." *The Language of the Night: Essays on Fantasy and Science Fiction.* Rev. ed. Ed. Ursula K. Le Guin. New York: Harpercollins, 1992. 54–67.

---. "Myth and Archetype in Science Fiction." *The Language of the Night: Essays on Fantasy and Science Fiction.* Rev. ed. Ed. Ursula K. Le Guin. New York: HarperCollins, 1992. 68–77.

---. "She Unnames Them." *The Norton Anthology of American Literature.* Vol. 2. 7th ed. Ed. Nina Baym, et al. New York: Norton, 1998. 2039–46.

---. Le Guin Symposium. Emory University, Atlanta, GA. November 1993.

---. *The Other Wind.* New York: Ace Books, 2003.

---. "Why Are Americans Afraid of Dragons?" *The Language of the Night: Essays on Fantasy and Science Fiction.* Rev. ed. Ed. Ursula K. Le Guin. New York: HarperCollins, 1992. 34–40.

Levine, Michael P., and Steven Jay Schneider. "Feeling for Buffy: The Girl Next Door." South, 294–308.

Lewis, C. S. *The Screwtape Letters: With Screwtape Proposes a Toast.* New York: Macmillan, 1961.

Makes Sense: The "Restless" Fanlisting. Accessed 1 July 2003. <www.dothewacky.com/~restless/index2.html>.

Manley, Kip. "Exegesis and Eisegesis: Restless." <www.lead-to-gold.com/kipmanley/exegesis/>.

---. Email to the author. 31 January 2003.

Marshall, C. W. "Aeneas the Vampire Slayer: A Roman Model for Why Giles Kills Ben." *Slayage: The Online International Journal of Buffy Studies* (August 2003). <www.slayage.tv>.

Martin, Philip. "The Vampire in the Looking Glass: Reflection and Projection in Bram Stoker's *Dracula*." *Nineteenth-Century Suspense: From Poe to Conan Doyle*. Ed. Clive Bloom et al. Basingstoke: Macmillan, 1988. 80–92.

McDonald, Stef. "Touched by an Angel." *TV Guide* 2 August 1997: 20–21.

Mendelsohn, Farah. "Crowning the King: Harry Potter and the Construction of Authority." *Journal of the Fantastic in the Arts* 12.3 (2001): 287–308.

Mikosz, Philip, and Dana Och. "Previously on *Buffy the Vampire Slayer* ...." *Slayage: The Online International Journal of Buffy Studies* 5 (2002). <www.slayage.tv>.

Millman, Joyce. "The Death of Buffy's Mom." *Salon* 12 March 2001. <www.salon.com>.

Money, Mary Alice. "The Undemonization of Supporting Characters in *Buffy*." Wilcox and Lavery, 98–107.

Moore, Steven. "Layers of Slayage: Buffy as Text [Review of *Reading the Vampire Slayer* and *Fighting the Forces*]." *Rain Taxi* (2002): 24–5.

Mulvey, Laura. "Visual Pleasure and Narrative Cinema." *Screen* 16.3 (1975): 6–18.

Munch, Edvard. *Death in the Sickroom*. 1893.

Newcomb, Horace, ed. *Encyclopedia of Television*. 3 vols. Chicago: Fitzroy Dearborn, 1997.

Newcomb, Horace. *TV: The Most Popular Art*. New York: Anchor, 1974.

Nixon, Nicola. "When Hollywood Sucks, or, Hungry Girls, Lost Boys, and Vampirism in the Age of Reagan." *Blood Read: The Vampire as Metaphor in Contemporary Culture*. Ed. Joan Gordon and Veronica Hollinger. Philadelphia: University of Pennsylvania Press, 1997. 115–28.

Noxon, Marti. Interview with Mary O'Connell for "Buffyworld," *Ideas*, CBC Radio One. Accessed 14 May 2003. <www.cbc.ca/ideas/features/buffy>.

Nurss, Delores J. "Spike as Shadow." *Fists and Fangs*. 2001. <http://hypnotized.waking-up-slowly.net/essays/shadow1.html>.

Nussbaum, Emily. "Must-See Metaphysics." *New York Times* 22 September 2002.

Ono, Kent. "To Be a Vampire on *Buffy the Vampire Slayer*: Race and ("Other") Socially Marginalizing Positions on Horror TV." *Fantasy Girls: Gender and the New Universe of Science Fiction and Fantasy Television*. Ed. Elyce Helford. Lanham: Rowman & Littlefield, 2000. 163–86.

Ostow, Micol, ed. *Buffy the Vampire Slayer: "Once More, with Feeling," The Script Book*. New York: Simon and Schuster, 2002.

Overbey, Karen Eileen, and Lahney Preston-Matto. "Staking in Tongues: Speech

Act as Weapon in *Buffy*." Wilcox and Lavery, 73–84.

Pasley, Jeffrey L. "Old Familiar Vampires: The Politics of the Buffyverse." South, 254–67.

Pender, Patricia. "'I'm Buffy and You're ... History': The Postmodern Politics of *Buffy*." Wilcox and Lavery, 18–34.

Petrova, Erma. "'You Cannot Run from Your Darkness.'/'Who Says I'm Running?': *Buffy* and the Ownership of Evil." *Refractory: A Journal of Entertainment Media* 2 (Mar. 2003): Special Issue on *Buffy the Vampire Slayer*. <www.sfca.unimelb.edu/au/refractory/journalissues/vol2/ermapetrova/htm>.

———. "The Faust Paradigm: Soul-Having in *Buffy the Vampire Slayer* and Marlowe's *Doctor Faustus*." Paper presented at the Slayage Conference on *Buffy the Vampire Slayer*. Nashville, TN: 28–30 May 2004.

Playdon, Zoe-Jane. "'What You Are, What's to Come': Feminisms, Citizenship, and the Divine." Kaveney, 2001, 120–47.

Porter, Jennifer. "Death and Resurrection in *Buffy the Vampire Slayer*." Paper presented at the Popular Culture Assocation conference. Toronto: 13–16 March 2002.

Potts, Donna. "Convents, Claddagh Rings, and Even the Book of Kells: Representing the Irish in *Buffy the Vampire Slayer*. *Simile: Studies in Media and Information Literacy Education* 3.2 (May 2003). <http://www.utpjournals.com>.

Propp, Vladimir. *Morphology of the Folk Tale*. Trans. Laurence Scott. 2nd ed. American Folklore Society Bibliographical and Special Series 9; Indiana University Research Center in Anthropology, Folklore, and Linguistics Publication 10. Austin: University of Texas Press, 1968.

Pullman, Philip. *The Golden Compass: His Dark Materials Book One*. New York: Knopf, 1995.

———. *The Subtle Knife: His Dark Materials Book Two*. New York: Ballantine, 1997.

Rieff, David. "Goodbye, New World Order." *Mother Jones* July/August 2003, 36–41.

Riess, Jana. *What Would Buffy Do? The Vampire Slayer as Spiritual Guide*. San Francisco: Jossey-Bass, 2004.

Rochlin, Margy. "Slay Belle." *TV Guide* 2 August 1997: 17–21.

Roeckelein, Jon. E. *The Psychology of Humor: A Reference Guide and Annotated Bibliography*. Westport, CN: Greenwood Press, 2002.

Rogers, Brett, and Walter Scheidel. "Driving States, Driving Cars: California Car Culture, Sex, and Identity in *Buffy the Vampire Slayer*." *Slayage: The Online International Journal of Buffy Studies* 13/14 (2004). <www.slayage.tv>.

Rose, Anita. "Of Creatures and Creators: *Buffy* Does *Frankenstein*." Wilcox and Lavery, 133–42.

Rowling, J. K. *Harry Potter and the Chamber of Secrets*. New York: Scholastic, 1999.

———. *Harry Potter and the Goblet of Fire*. New York: Scholastic, 2000.

---. *Harry Potter and the Prisoner of Azkaban*. New York: Scholastic, 1999.

---. *Harry Potter and the Sorcerer's Stone*. London: Bloomsbury, 1997; New York: Scholastic Press, 1998.

Sandars, Diana. "The Truth Will Be Heard and It Will All End in Tears." Paper presented at the Sonics Synergies: Creative Cultures Conference at the University of South Australia, Adelaide, Australia: 17–20 July 2003.

Sappho of Lesbos. "[Throned in Splendor, Deathless, O Aphrodite.]" Trans. Richard Lattimore. *The Norton Anthology of World Masterpieces: The Western Tradition*. Vol. 1: *Literature of Western Culture Through the Renaissance*. 7th ed. Ed. Sarah Lawall and Maynard Mack. New York: Norton, 1999. 515–16.

Sayer, Karen. "'It Wasn't Our World Any More. They Made It Theirs': Reading Space and Place." Kaveney, 2001, 98–119.

"Season Four Overview." *Buffy the Vampire Slayer Season Four DVD Collection*. Twentieth Century Fox, 2003

Shakespeare, William. *Hamlet: An Authoritative Text, Intellectual Backgrounds, Extracts from the Sources, Essays in Criticism*. 2nd ed. Ed. Cyrus Hoy. A Norton Critical Edition. New York: Norton, 1992.

Shelley, Mary. *Frankenstein: The 1818 Text, Contexts, Nineteenth-Century Responses, Modern Criticism*. Ed. J. Paul Hunter. A Norton Critical Edition. New York: Norton, 1996.

Shwayder, D. S. Review of *The Meaning of Proper Names*, by Holger Steen Sorenson. *Journal of Philosophy* 61 (1964): 450–7.

Siemann, Catherine. "Darkness Falls on the Endless Summer: Buffy as Gidget for the Fin de Siècle." Wilcox and Lavery, 120–9.

Simkin, Stevie. "'Who Died and Made You John Wayne?': Anxious Masculinity in *Buffy the Vampire Slayer*." *Slayage: The Online International Journal* 11/12 (2004). <www.slayage.tv>.

---. "'You Hold Your Gun Like a Sissy Girl': Anxious Masculinity in *Buffy the Vampire Slayer*." *Slayage: The Online International Journal of Buffy Studies* 11/12 (2004). <www.slayage.tv>.

Skwire, Sarah. "'Whose Side Are You on, Anyway?' Children, Adults, and the Use of Fairy Tales in Buffy." Wilcox and Lavery, 195–204.

Slotkin, Richard. Email to David Lavery. 4 June 2003.

South, James B. "'All Torment, Trouble, Wonder, and Amazement Inhabits Here': The Vicissitudes of Technology in *Buffy the Vampire Slayer*." *Journal of American and Comparative Cultures* 24.1/2 (2001): 93–102.

---, ed. *Buffy the Vampire Slayer and Philosophy: Fear and Trembling in Sunnydale*. Popular Culture and Philosophy 4. Chicago and La Salle, IL: Open Court, 2003.

Spicer, Arwen. "'Love's Bitch But Man Enough to Admit It': Spike's Hybridized Gender." *Slayage: The Online International Journal of Buffy Studies* 7 (December 2002). <www.slayage.tv>.

St. Romaine, Madeleine. Email to the author. 30 March 2002.

Stafford, Nikki. *Bite Me! An Unofficial Guide to the World of Buffy the Vampire Slayer.* Rev. ed. Toronto: ECW Press, 2002.

Stevens, Katy. "Moans, Thuds, and Power Chords: Sounding Sex in *Buffy*." *all slay* 3 (2004): [32–38].

Stevenson, Gregory. *Televised Morality: The Case of* Buffy the Vampire Slayer. Dallas: Hamilton Books, 2003.

Stoller, Debbie. "The 20 Most Fascinating Women in Politics: Fresh Blood." *George* September 1998: 110–13.

Telotte, J. P. *Science Fiction Film.* Genres in American Cinema. Cambridge: Cambridge University Press, 2001.

Thompson, Robert J. *Television's Second Golden Age: From Hill Street Blues to ER.* New York: Continuum, 1996.

Tracy, Kathleen. *The Girl's Got Bite: An Unofficial Guide to Buffy's World.* Los Angeles: Renaissance Books, 1998.

Turnbull, Sue. "'Not Just Another Buffy Paper': Towards an Aesthetics of Television." *Slayage: The Online International Journal of Buffy Studies* 13/14 (2004). <www.slayage.tv>.

Turner, Victor. "Liminality and the Performative Genres." *Rite, Drama, Festival, Spectacle: Rehearsals Toward a Theory of Cultural Performance.* Ed. John J. McAloon. Philadelphia: Institute for the Study of Human Issues, 1984. 18–24.

Vint, Sheryl. "'Killing Us Softly'? A Feminist Search for the 'Real' Buffy." *Slayage: The Online International Journal of Buffy Studies* 5 (April 2002). <www.slayage.tv>.

Virgil. *The Aeneid.* Trans. C. H. Sisson. Manchester: Carcanet and Mid Northumberland Arts Group, 1986.

Wall, Brian, and Michael Zryd. "Vampire Dialectics: Knowledge, Institutions and Labour." Kaveney, 2001, 53–77.

West, Dave. "'Concentrate on the Kicking Movie': Buffy and East Asian Cinema." Kaveney, 2001, 166–86.

Weston, Jessie L. *From Ritual to Romance.* Cambridge: Cambridge University Press, 1920.

Whedon, Joss. "The Body" Commentary. *Buffy the Vampire Slayer Season Five DVD Collection.* Twentieth Century Fox, 2003.

---. "Hush" Commentary. *Buffy the Vampire Slayer Season Four DVD Collection.* Twentieth Century Fox, 2003.

---. "Hush" Featurette. *Buffy the Vampire Slayer* Fourth Season DVD. Twentieth Century Fox, 2003.

---. "Hush" Script. *Buffy the Vampire Slayer* Fourth Season DVD. Twentieth Century Fox, 2003.

---. "Innocence" Commentary. *Buffy the Vampire Slayer: The Complete Second Season* on DVD. Twentieth Century Fox, 2002.

---. Interview with David Bianculli. *Fresh Air.* 9 May 2000. < http:whyy.org/cgi-bin/ Fashowretrieve.cgi?2876 >.

---. "The Last Sundown" Featurette. *Buffy the Vampire Slayer Season Seven DVD Collection.* Twentieth Century Fox, 2004.

---. "Once More, with Feeling" Commentary. *Buffy the Vampire Slayer Season Six DVD Collection.* Twentieth Century Fox, 2003.

---. "Restless" Commentary. *Buffy the Vampire Slayer: The Complete Fourth Season* on DVD. Twentieth Century Fox, 1999, 2000; DVD release 2003.

---. "Surprise" Interview. *Buffy the Vampire Slayer: The Complete Second Season* on DVD. Twentieth Century Fox, 2002.

---. "Welcome to the Hellmouth" Commentary. *Buffy the Vampire Slayer: The Complete First Season* on DVD. Twentieth Century Fox, 1997; DVD release 2001.

---. "Welcome to the Hellmouth" Interview. *Buffy the Vampire Slayer: The Complete First Season* on DVD. Twentieth Century Fox, 2001.

Wilcox, Rhonda V. "'Every Night I Save You': Buffy, Spike, Sex, and Redemption." *Slayage: The Online International Journal of Buffy Studies* 6 (April 2002). <www. slayage.tv>.

---. "'I Think I'll Name Me Joan': Onomastics and Identity in *Buffy the Vampire Slayer.*" Rhythm and Eschatology: A Symposium. University of Melbourne, Melbourne, Australia, 24 July 2003.

---. "Out Far or In Deep." Foreword. *Athena's Daughters: Television's New Women Warriors.* Ed. Frances Early and Kathleen Kennedy. Syracuse: Syracuse University Press, 2003.

---. "'Pain as Bright as Steel': The Monomyth and Light as Pain in *Buffy the Vampire Slayer.*" Blood, Text, and Fears: Reading Around *Buffy the Vampire Slayer* Conference. University of East Anglia, Norwich, England, 19–20 October 2002.

---. "Review of *Visual Pleasure and Nasal Elevation: A Television Teleology.*" *Teleparody: Predicting/Preventing the TV Discourse of Tomorrow.* Ed. Angela Hague and David Lavery. London, New York: Wallflower Press, 2002.

---. "T. S. Eliot Comes to Television: Buffy's 'Restless.'" *Slayage: The Online International Journal of Buffy Studies* 7 (December 2002). 30 December 2002. <www.slayage. tv>.

---. "Television." *The Greenwood Guide to American Popular Culture.* Ed. M. Thomas Inge and Dennis Hall. Westport, CT: Greenwood, 2002. 4: 1755–96.

---. "'There Will Never Be a "Very Special" *Buffy*': *Buffy* and the Monsters of Teen Life." *Journal of Popular Film and Television* 27.2 (1999): 16–23. Rpt. in *Slayage: The Online International Journal of Buffy Studies* 2 (2001). <www.slayage.tv>.

---. "TV and the Curriculum: Contemporary Television as Valid Undergraduate Course Material." *Humanities in the South* (Fall 1989): 6–8, 12.

---. "'Who Died and Made Her the Boss?': Patterns of Mortality in *Buffy*." Wilcox and Lavery, 3–17.

---, and David Lavery, eds. *Fighting the Forces: What's at Stake in Buffy the Vampire Slayer.* Lanham, Md.: Rowman & Littlefield, 2002.

William Wordsworth: The Critical Heritage. Ed. Robert Woof. London; New York: Routledge, 2001.

Williams, J. P. "Choosing Your Own Mother: Mother-Daughter Conflicts in *Buffy*." Wilcox and Lavery, 61–72.

Wilson, Steve. "Laugh, Spawn of Hell, Laugh." Kaveney, 2001, 78–97.

Wood, Robin. *Hollywood from Vietnam to Reagan.* New York: Columbia University Press, 1986.

Wordsworth, William. "Ode: Intimations of Immortality from Recollections of Early Childhood." *Selected Poems and Prefaces.* Ed. Jack Stillinger. Boston: Houghton-Mifflin, 1965. 186–91.

Worsley, Natasja. "Voicebox: Sex, Language, and Power in 'Hush.'" The Slayage Conference on *Buffy the Vampire Slayer.* Nashville: 28–30 May 2004.

Wyman, Mark. "Teen Kicks: *Buffy the Vampire Slayer.*" *XPosé* Special #5 (1998): 6–19.

Yeffeth, Glenn, ed. *Seven Seasons of Buffy: Science Fiction and Fantasy Writers Discuss Their Favorite Television Show.* Dallas: Benbella Books, 2003.

Zacharek, Stephanie. "Buffy's Will-to-Power." *Salon.com* 28 November 2001. <http://www.dir.salon.com/sex/feature/2001/11/28/buffy/index.html>.

---. "A Hole in Our Hearts." *Salon.com* 21 May 2003. <http://www.salon.com/ent/tv/review/2003/05/21/buffy_final/>.

---. "Willow, Destroyer of Worlds." *Salon.com* 22 May 2002. <http://archive.salon.com/ent/tv/feature/2002/05/22/buffy/>.

Zizek, Slavoj. *The Zizek Reader.* Ed. Elizabeth Wright and Edmond Wright. Oxford: Blackwell, 1999.

Index